D0084486

awkward in october

Bookish Romantics #1

teresa yea

ebook ISBN: 978-1-943087-19-8
Paperback ISBN: 978-1-943087-20-4

Visit me at teresayea.com
Sign up for my newsletter

also by teresa yea

Time Travelers (Chick Lit)

An Influencer in King Arthur's Court (#1)

Regency Influencer (#2)

Influencers Just Wanna Have Fun (#3)

Indigo Bay Series (Romantic Comedy)

Pixely Ever After (#1)

Once Upon a Photo Booth (#2)

Symphony in the Snow (#3)

Tea for Two (#4)

Golden Age of Monsters (Dark Fantasy Romance)

Love in a Time of Monsters (#1)

Empire of Sand (prequel)

Gothic Horror

Black Heart, Red Ruby (standalone)

chapter one

No little girl dreams of a career as a doormat.

Doctor? Yes.

Astronaut? Okay.

Female CEO of a Fortune 500 company? Yes, please!

Appeals & Grievance Specialist III in a health insurance company?

Um…

How do I *really* feel about my job?

I don't mind it, actually. I'm good at what I do. A less cheerful person would have broken down by now. I've been here since I was a starry-eyed twenty-two-year-old college grad with a mountain of student debt.

This was only supposed to be a temporary job until the recession blew over and I find something to do with my Art History degree. I specialize in early Colonial furniture making. That's got to be in high demand, right?

I turn thirty-two tomorrow, which officially means I've been here for ten years. *Yay?*

But seriously, this job has its perks. The health insurance is not great (see the irony there?) *but* there's stability and the pay is good (better than you'd think). I look forward to… to… lunch! *I look forward to lunch.*

And going home to work on my online sticker company, *Vincent Van Sproot*. Gotta have a side hustle these days.

Don't get me wrong.

I'm happy, debt free at last, and I try to paste a smile on my face when I enter my cubicle.

My cubicle is cozy and inviting as far as cubicles go.

I have an enviable collection of mini succulents in adorable froggy planters.

My chair is lushly cushioned and there's even talk amongst the higher ups of bringing in standing desks. I have a snack drawer filled with Hot Cheetos and a Kindle packed with spicy books. I've decorated my desk space with waterproof stickers I designed myself:

A bear with a sprout growing out of his head.

A milk carton with a sad face and puny little legs.

A potato in a cubicle, looking displeased by life. '9 to 5 Potato' is my best selling sticker, which tells me I'm not the only one living a *meh* life.

C'est la vie.

The company provides us with state-of-the-art hands-free headsets and stress balls of all shapes and sizes. My favorite is the eyeball—so I can pretend I'm squeezing the eyeball of the person on the other end of the line. I even have a pair of titanium stress balls which I roll around in my palm, mumbling 'Serenity Now' as the person on the other end screams bloody murder.

I've been yelled at seventeen times today and that's *before* lunch.

On a typical day, I average twenty disgruntled billers and patients alike. You'll be surprised by how irate people can get when their claims are denied and they're footing the bill for a $10K foot surgery. Health insurance is a savage business and I'm just a clog in the capitalist machine that profits off fear and human suffering.

Normally, I brush it off. Out of everyone in my department, I'm the best at shrugging off name calling, death threats, and the dreaded "Can I speak to your manager?"

I *am* the manager.

How did that happen?

I'll tell you how it happened!

Ten years of loyal service with a cheery disposition. Ten years of being a 9-to-5 Potato.

Now that I've climbed the career ladder to Grievance Specialist III, I get to deal with the *most* difficult customers. The real pieces of work. The *situations* immortalized in the company's Worst-Case Scenario training manual.

If Grievance Specialist I is reduced to tears and Grievance Specialist II chucks his stress ball across the room, the case gets escalated to me.

Yay?

As soon as I set my phone down, Line 2 buzzes. I eye the red light and take a deep breath. I offer up a prayer that this will be an easy call, except, in my position, there are no easy calls.

"Hello! Thank you for calling [Redacted] of California. My name is Theodora, your grievance specialist. How may I help you today?"

"How old are you?" The caller is raspy from yelling at the unfortunate Grievance Specialist II before me.

Oh boy.

I lean back in my chair, squeezing my foam eyeball. "How can I help you, ma'am?"

"HUH?"

"Ma'am?"

"Speak up!"

I repeat my greeting.

"You sound like you're thirteen-years-old. Where is your manager? I want to speak to someone older."

"How can I help you, ma'am?" I stay on track. That's one of the tactics I learned on my first day on the job. Never get personal. Never answer baiting questions. Keep to the script. *Never* deviate from the script.

The complaints are always the same:

Why isn't my insurance paying for my ultrasound?

3

You're telling me I have to pay a $300 deductible every month only to pay another $800 for knee surgery? What's the point of having health insurance?!!

Customers can get *real* angry *real* fast. I've witnessed tantrums and crying fits. I've even talked some customers out of suicide. This lady should be no different.

"... husband died of a heart attack," she says.

"I'm sorry to hear that, ma'am." My shoulders slump. I'm *truly* sorry to hear that, but it's nothing I haven't heard before. Ten years of grievances and there have been many heart attacks, strokes, and surgery complications. You name it. I've seen it.

"Why was his payment denied?" she asks.

"According to his chart," I say, pulling up her husband's claim on my dual monitor, "the trouble is procedure F2020. It's not covered under your plan. Let me see what I can do." I read the dense legal jargon. "If F2020 is billed in conjunction with V325A, the procedure is covered 80/20 under your deductible."

"What does that *even* mean?" she asks, oblivious to my cheerful tone. Doesn't she realize that I've saved her three thousand dollars?

"Your insurance takes care of 20% of your bill. You are responsible for the other 80%—"

"80% is fifty-thousand dollars!"

"That's right."

"But the cardiologist *had* to perform the procedure," she says.

"Yes, I know—"

"My husband died anyway."

"I'm sorry, ma'am." I count to three and dig my nails into my stress ball.

"Why didn't the doctor tell me how much it was going to cost beforehand?"

"That's not how it works, ma'am." I sigh. "Allow me to explain —"

"I can't pay it. This will bankrupt us..." A pause. "I mean me. There's no 'us' anymore. Forty-eight years... and he's gone over

4

night." Anger dissolves into heartbreak. Her voice breaks like a dam.

Have you ever heard a seventy-three-year-old woman cry?

I have.

Many times. Each time is no more easier than the next. Each time chips away another chunk of my soul.

"Why did we pay two hundred dollars in monthly premiums if this can't be covered?"

She has a good point, but I can't agree with her on a recorded call. It's not my place to make excuses for the failings of the U.S. health care system. As much as I want to offer condolences for her loss, this call is recorded. I'm being timed. I will get a write-up for inefficient grievance handling if I stray off script.

I can't even relate to her heartbreak. My longest relationship lasted only three months. I can't imagine being that much in love, let alone mourning a husband of forty-eight years.

"I'm sorry, ma'am. Allow me to transfer you to our finance department. We have a flexible payment plan for —"

"How could this happen?"

"Ma'am?"

"We were in the middle of dinner," she says. "Take out from his favorite pizza place. They mixed up the order and gave us Hawaiian. Larry's from Brooklyn. Pineapple on pizza? Can you imagine? He was complaining about the pineapples when… when…"

Oh no, ma'am. Please don't. Please don't cry.

I always know exactly what to do.

I'll apologize (always apologize, even though you don't know what you're apologizing for) and transfer her to the payment specialist. I'll take the next call, listen to the same story…

So many stories. Ten years' worth of stories.

Maybe it's something as minor as a sprained ankle dressing setting them back a few grand.

Or a stroke, leaving them in deep medical debt.

Or a breast cancer treatment they didn't know they couldn't

afford.

Because when you have insurance, it's supposed to cover you, *right?* Paying thousands after the death of a loved one isn't something you have to deal with. That's why you *have* insurance.

All this I've heard before. This time it's different.

I wipe my tear-streaked cheeks on the shoulder of my blouse and lift my head.

"Please stay on the line while I transfer you," I say over the sound of her sobs.

I click off.

Line 2 and 3 immediately start blinking.

I strip off my headset and stare absently at my cheerful arrangement of succulents.

I stare and I stare until my tears dry up. I can't continue with the script. I can't move.

Someone taps me on the shoulder.

"Theo?"

I touch the matte finish of my 9-to-5 Potato sticker. The sight of its derpy face always cheers me up. Not today. Today I just cut off a grieving widow. I'm officially going to hell.

"Theo?"

I swivel around. It's the Grievance Director. He's ventured from his glass office into my cubicle. This never happens.

He gestures to my blinking switchboard. "You want *me* to get that?" His smile is tight.

I blink. Oh my god. What am I doing? I shake my head to clear it and tuck my headset back on. "No, no... I'll get it."

"Good." Another fake smile. "Didn't know you were on break already."

Yeah. I'm totally getting a write up. Just because I've been doing this for ten years doesn't mean I get a free ride.

It doesn't mean anything. *I* don't mean anything. I'm just a soulless potato.

I press Line 1. "Hello. This is Theodora, your Appeals & Grievance Specialist. How may I assist you today?"

chapter two

I eat lunch in the parking garage. I'm not usually a loner. Today, I want to be alone.

The parking garage is dark, cool, and private—the perfect place to cry behind my steering wheel.

I'm sobbing and shoveling Greek salad into my mouth. I pause crying to chew (these cucumbers are crunchy) and resume sobbing after I swallow.

Cry, chew, swallow.

Cry, chew, swallow.

It's a pattern that works for me, which is saying something about where I am in life.

I wipe my eyes and drown my sorrows in a lukewarm can of lime *Le Croix*. With a burp, I reach into my purse and grab the one thing I know will make me feel better:

A book.

Not just any book.

My all-time favorite book: *The Witch of Blackbird Pond* by Elizabeth George Speare.

We all have our security blankets. Half of my co-workers stream re-runs of *The Office* while the other half re-watch *Friends*.

Me?

I like books about Puritans and colonial witch hunts, friendship amongst misfits, and a certain blond sailor with a bounce to his step and a saucy spark in his brilliant blue eyes.

Maybe my obsession with this book is a byproduct of my Early Colonial furniture making studies. Or maybe I'm fascinated by Early Colonial furniture *because* of this book.

Whatever the reason, every time I dive into the story of Kit Tyler, an orphan from Barbados who sails all the way to Connecticut colony in 1687 to live with her aunt and uncle, I'm instantaneously happy.

My paperback copy is the '70s edition. Kit Tyler stands in the tall grass of the meadows in a lush corseted dress, a defiant expression on her face as the wind whips back her flowing blonde hair (she's a brunette in the book, but '70's book covers were weirdly obsessed with blondes...you know how it goes). Her burgundy dress bleeds into the pink gradient of a New England sunset.

My copy is well worn and loved. The spine is cracked, the pages yellowed and dog-eared from so many readings.

Second to my hamsters Milk and Cereal, this book is my most prized possession.

The Witch of Blackbird Pond found me at a time in my life when I was young and impressionable, when the world still held a hint of magic and the future promised a happy ending. It's a memory, a hope, an old friend...

I've returned to books I've loved as a teen and the romance has fizzled, but *The Witch of Blackbird Pond* has always kept its promise of friends against loneliness and a bright future over the horizon.

More than any photo album, re-reading *The Witch of Blackbird Pond* is like opening up a time capsule.

I'm thirteen, basking in the sun with my friends at summer camp, snacking on a lime popsicle and falling in love with that cocky young sailor Nat Eaton.

I'm twenty, alone in the dark of my dorm room, feeling small and insignificant and in need of a friend.

I'm thirty-one going on thirty-two, crying in my car in a dank parking garage because Grievance Specialist III is not how I want to live my life.

There's a part when Kit runs to the Great Meadows in tears. She meets Hannah Tupper, the ostracized Quaker woman who lives on the edge of Blackbird Pond and makes a lifelong friend. Later, Kit returns to her home, stronger, better... a new Kit.

I sniffle, marking my spot in the book with my thumb.

For a long while, I simply stare at the parked Volvo ahead of me. I consider the mediocre trajectory of my life.

I live with my parents and drive a 2012 silver Prius.

I go on the occasional lackluster Bumble date and my job pays surprisingly well.

Vincent Van Sproot, my online sticker company, is thriving and keeps me busy during nights and weekends.

I made three true friends in summer camp '95 who share my love for reading and understand my obsession for *The Witch of Blackbird Pond*.

Everything is fine. Everything is okay.

Fine.

Okay.

Not bad, but nothing to write home about.

I shut the book, overcome with an unexpected bout of rage. I glance around the parking garage as if jolted awake from a deep sleep.

I don't want 'fine.'

I don't want 'okay.'

I, Theodora Dy, want more than this provincial life... er this provincial life in L.A. You get the picture. I've wasted *years* sleepwalking through my '20s when I could have been grabbing life by the balls and *living*.

I want adventure and mistakes, danger and excitement, balmy summer days and deep rooftop conversations with a snarky sailor with dreamy blue eyes. Okay, he doesn't have to be a sailor. I'll settle for a lobster fisherman so long as he, like Nat Eaton, is a smart and steadfast man of honor.

I want...

A beautiful romance.

"There's got to be more to life than being Grievance Specialist III. There's got to be…"

I glance down at *The Witch of Blackbird Pond*, the book that renews my faith in people every time someone yells at me over the phone. The book that encapsulates all my childhood hopes and dreams. It's given me an answer. I know it has.

Carefully, almost reverently, I slip the paperback into my purse and pack up my things.

In between hostile phone calls, I research everything there is to know about the town of Wethersfield, the book's real life setting. I surf Zillow and browse Connecticut real estate listings, apartments for rent, anything… but mostly, I check out the Cheap Old House Instagram account and an idea takes shape. My stomach roils in anticipation. I want to throw up. Is this what 'taking life by the balls' feels like?

"I'm doing this." I pinch myself. "I can't believe I'm really doing this."

I almost chicken out more times than I can count.

By 4:55 pm, I march into the HR office and hand in my two weeks' notice.

chapter three

Y*ou WHAT?*
    When? Today?!
Like 'quit' quit?

"Quiet! Quiet!" My cousin Camille, occupying the upper right-hand corner of my laptop screen, hushes Lena and Sadie, the other members of our bi-weekly ZOOM bookclub. "Let Theo talk."

Camille is my cousin and the bossiest member of Cabin 13.

Cabin 13 is the first cabin we roomed in during Tahoe summer camp '95 and does double duty as the official name of our long-distance book club.

Yes. We are aware that 'Cabin 13' sounds like teen slasher flick.

Yes. We've roomed in four different cabins since then, but I credit our friendship to that dusty pile of old paperbacks in Cabin 13. Out of that pile, we found our 'forever book', the book that defined our twelve-year-old hopes and dreams and shaped us into the women we are today.

You don't forget your first love or the first moment you picked up *the* book, and the world opens up for you.

In Cabin 13, I found *The Witch of Blackbird Pond*.

Camille discovered *The Vampire Lestat*. For the rest of that summer, all she could talk about was starting an '80's rock band, haunting a creepy old cemetery in New Orleans, and living forever. She currently lives in Austin and manages her family's chain of Pho restaurants.

Sadie fell in love with Jamie Fraser from *Outlander*. Now a marine biologist, she specializes in sea sponges, *Porifera* to be exact. She lives in sunny San Diego, as far away from Scotland and the standing stones as one can get. But there's always the hope that an international conference on sea sponges will take her to Inverness and into the arms of a real life Jamie Fraser.

And Lena, lover of plants, works in a hip nursery in downtown Seattle, the kind with expensive macrame plant holders and copper water canisters. Her favorite book is *Jane Eyre*. I don't recall Jane ever filling up her apartment with greenery, but I suppose, as much as I want to find my Nat Eaton, Lena is looking for her own Mr. Rochester too.

I tell them about the phone call, the old lady weeping over her dead husband, which led to me sobbing behind the wheel of my car during lunch time.

"And that's when I decided to re-read *The Witch of Blackbird Pond*..."

"Ah." Three heads nod in understanding.

See? That's why these girls are my best friends. Anyone else would have said "huh?" Not these girls. They understood.

Four summers together in the same cabin. Under the same oak tree. By the same lake bed.

Four summers stargazing and dreaming about the great things we'll become in the future.

Camille, Sadie, and Lena have read *The Witch of Blackbird Pond*, but I'm the only one who has read it twenty times. I'm the only one who has memorized the passages and who has written online fan fiction about Kit and Nat's adventures after the last chapter. Hint: there's piracy and spicy times in a cave. More on this later.

Camille rubs a hand over her face, smearing her cat-eye eyeliner. She looks especially tired tonight after a long shift at the restaurant. Her dark hair is gathered into a messy top knot and her thick-chopped bangs hangs over her eyebrows. Camille went full goth after freshman year of high school, but she has since toned it down and now she looks like an artist that just stepped out of a studio.

"So you quit," Camille began, "and *The Witch of Blackbird Pond* made you quit?"

"There were many factors, but yes…" My shoulders lift in a sheepish shrug. "The phone call was the trigger, the book was the spark, and in hindsight, I wish I'd quit sooner."

Not one to beat around the bush, Camille says, "Hope you're not making a big mistake. Maybe you should have slept on it?"

"I have slept on it! I've *been* sleeping for ten years."

On the bottom right-hand corner of my laptop, Sadie leans forward. Her vibrant red hair is wrapped up in a green bandana. She nods in approval as she rubs aloe vera on her sunburned nose and cheeks.

"What do you think, Sadie? Do you think I made a mistake?"

"How did your parents take it when you told them you quit?"

I gnaw on my bottom lip. "Not well," I shudder, recalling the 'real talk' that went down after dinner. My dad's apathetic silence. My mom shaming me about my 'alternate' career choices.

"Did you tell them about Vincent Van Sproot?" Sadie asks. "Did you tell them about the sponges?" She holds up her water bottle and points at the sticker of a sea sponge with an aloof expression. "These are bestsellers!"

"They think the stickers are a hobby and I'll come crawling back home in three months."

"Wow. *Three* months? That's specific."

"They're accountants."

"Well, I support you," Sadie says. "Do what you love! Screw what other people think."

I smile. "Thank you!"

Sadie is the poster child for following your dreams, especially when your dream is something as specific as marine sponges. To date, she's written a famous dissertation on Neptune's Cup, a rare marine sponge found off the coast of Cambodia, and is something of a superstar in the marine biology community.

"What about you, Lena?" I peer at the screen.

Lena cleans her glasses, which unfortunately always gets fogged up in the hothouse section of her plant shop. Her background is a jungle of hanging plants and her desk is crowded with propagated Pothos cuttings. She tucks her wireframes glasses back on her nose. Her thick lenses magnifies her eyes, giving her an owlish look.

"It's quite a bold move," Lena says, "but also exciting. I wish I can do the same."

"Why now?" Camille asks me.

"Remember that vow we made when we were twelve?" I conjure up the memory of Cabin 13. Of mosquito bitten knees and lime popsicles consumed under the canopy of our favorite sycamore tree. "Brides of Adventure?"

Sadie and Lena nod in remembrance. After we passed around a battered copy of *Anne of Green Gables*, the four of us swore to become 'brides of adventure.'

If, in our adulthood, one of us was not where she wants to be in life, she will make a bold move and the rest of us will help her out in any way necessary. One dream. Three fairy godmothers. It's a simple enough plan, but it requires…

"A big dramatic gesture," I say.

"I believe it's called the 'big stupid gesture,'" Camille reminds me.

"For a girl who wanted to live forever, you certainly play it safe," I say. "What happened to your restaurant in New Orleans and your haunted house by Lafayette Cemetery?"

"It died in a boiling pot of Pho." Code for juggling three family-owned *Pho 95*s in Austin. "What happened to you, Theo? You've read *The Witch of Blackbird Pond* a million times and you've never done something like this."

"I've had enough!" I slam a fist on my desk, shaking the hamster cage. Milk, my albino hamster runs in her wheel. Cereal

14

blinks at me with her beady eyes and scurries to the corner, twitching her whiskers in fright. "Sorry guys."

"I'm having the mother of all millennial life crises. Go big or go home, remember?" I gesture to my green-clay-mask-covered face. "I'm thirty-two and not even close to where I want to be. Do you understand?"

Sadie and Lena nod.

"I'm cashing in on my promise to my twelve-year-old self."

Camille throws her hands up in the air. "You used to pick your nose when you were twelve. Are you seriously taking advice from *that* Theo?"

"All I know is that I'm truly happy when I read *The Witch of Blackbird Pond*, so why not live it?"

"It's just a book," Camille mutters.

"How the book makes me *feel* is real. And Wethersfield *is* real *and* affordable."

Camille arches an eyebrow. "What are you going to do there?"

Good question. "I don't know. Concentrate on Vincent Van Sproot."

"Do you have enough savings?"

"I'm golden in the financial department. Guess there's a perk of living rent free with your parents until you're a thirty-two-year-old spinster with no active social life."

"I envy you there," Lena says. "I live in an apartment the size of a shoe box."

"I also have a diverse investment portfolio," I add, feeling like I have to show solid finances in order to get my friends' approval. "Did I tell you I bought Tesla stock before Tesla even became a thing? I'm good."

"So Wethersfield, huh?" Sadie types something and pauses, most likely doing a Google search on the town. "I can't believe this place is real."

"Remember the author's note in the back of the book?" Lena says. "Elizabeth George Speare actually lived there!"

"What's your living situation like?" Camille asks. "Have you found an apartment to rent? Are you staying at an Airbnb?"

"I'm staying," I say, prepping the calm before the storm, "in my *new* house."

I time the moment their heads explodes.

"You…" Lena begins. "Bought a house?!"

Chaos.

Congratulations.

A barrage of questions.

I raise my hands, signaling everyone to calm down. "It's nothing I can't afford."

"Jesus Christ!" Camille says. "How much are they paying you as a Grievance Specialist?"

"That's Grievance Specialist III," Sadie reminds her. "The 'III' means *cha-ching*."

"It's called The Witch House, and it's colonial-ish, but it also has '70s elements from a past renovation. And before you jump to conclusions, it's not that expensive. I saw it on the Cheap Old House Instagram and made a cash offer to the seller. Offer accepted same day."

"How much?" they ask.

"Six thousand and change," I say to a reception of shock and awe.

I grin, still amazed by how fast I've been able to move things along.

"Wow," Camille says, voicing my thoughts. "When you decide to make a move, you really go big."

"Much like Kit Tyler did when she left Barbados for Connecticut," I say. "Big Stupid Gesture for the win!"

Lena frowns. "But a house that old and cheap—"

"It's a fixer-upper," I say. "And you're all invited to come over for Thanksgiving."

It's currently late August. I *am* ambitious.

"How much fixing up are we talking about here?" Camille asks.

16

I send them the listing. After viewing the slideshow, their exuberance dries up.

Somber silence.

Sadie is the first to speak. "Um, Theo... I don't know how to tell you this. This renovation looks like a *ton* of work."

Lena polishes her glasses and squints at the photo. "Is that... a hole in the floor?"

"It's the main staircase," I say.

"The third and eighth step is a bit... caved in," Lena says.

"There's two sets of stairs, though. I don't really need to use the main one."

"The floral wallpaper..." Sadie shutters. "It's um..."

"I fully intend to do away with that wallpaper."

"What about the mold?" Lena asks.

"Is that mold?" I peer at the master bedroom photo. "Looks like dirt. Nothing a good power wash can't fix. So guys, what do you think?"

"It's great..."

"Great bones."

"It's a money pit," Camille says. "Are you sure you know what you're getting yourself into?"

I consider Camille's question.

Of course, the logistics of moving will have to be dealt with. Then there's the matter of breaking it to my parents. After telling them I quit my job, my mom became hysterical, so I figure I'll drop the bombshell of buying a derelict house in Connecticut when she's simmered down.

Relocating my online sticker company will be a cinch. And I'll have to move some investments around to cover the closing cost and the renovations...

The renovations! God, I hope they won't be *too* labor intensive. Finally, I'll be putting my colonial furniture making degree to good use. Not that I've ever made my own furniture, but I'm the queen of DIY. I'm sure I'll figure it out.

"I have no idea what I'm doing," I say at last, "but you know what they say?"

Camille narrows her eyes. "YOLO?"

"We're forgetting the elephant in the room," Sadie says, "Theo just bought a 'Witch House.' Why is it called the 'Witch House'?"

I scratch my nose. "The first owner was supposedly a witch."

"Did she die a horrible death?" Lena gasps. "*In* the house?"

"*No.*" I try to recall the historical records that came with my real estate purchase. The house was built in 1715 by a sea captain, much like Nat Eaton would have been after the book's end. The details are muddled after 1830. "She died in the backyard."

Camille's eyes light up. "Is the house haunted?"

"Nah."

"That's what all the people who buy haunted houses say," Camille grins. "If you survive by Thanksgiving, my Ouija board and I would *love* to visit."

chapter four

One month later…

    As the keys to my new house land into my palm, I clasp my realtor in a giant bear hug.

The startled realtor pats me on the back. "I'm more excited about this sale than you are."

"Not possible." I'm a newly lit firecracker, hopping with excitement. I try to restrain myself from jumping with joy as the realtor slaps a SOLD sticker on the weathered For Sale sign. By the looks of the sign, the house has been on the market for years. Decades, even. Thanks to the power of social media and a surprisingly speedy escrow, I was able to close faster than I anticipated.

Pro tip for first-time home buyers: look into abandoned homes on the outskirts of major cities. My buying experience was so easy and efficient. It's almost like the bank was giving the house away. Since I moved out of my childhood bedroom, I didn't have cumbersome furniture to move across country. No baggage. No hassle. A fresh start.

"The water's on, but you'll have to call the gas company to turn on hot water," the realtor says. "The electricity is also switched on, but some of the outlets are stripped."

"Really? Did that come up during the inspection?"

"Of course." Her eyes swung sideways. "Where are you staying during renovations?"

I beam and tap my foot on the weathered porch boards. "Here."

She arches an eyebrow. *"No."*

"Yes."

"No."

I point to my rental car. "I've got an air mattress, flashlight, cooler, and a portable phone charger. It'll be like camping."

"You're brave," she says, waving goodbye as she heads for her car. "Mind the floors!"

I give her a thumbs up and watch her pull away.

Once alone, I grab my hamster cage from the passenger seat and fan Milk and Cereal off. I left the window open, but my hamsters get overheated easily. Milk is a white fluff ball huddled in the corner of her cage. Across the plastic partition, Cereal weaves around listlessly, her beady eyes accusing me of bad hamster parenting.

I spritz them with my travel water bottle and hold up their cages so they can get a good look at their new home.

"This is it! Isn't she beautiful?"

Cereal licks her paw. Milk peers at me from the corner of her cage. I think they approve.

The colonial farmhouse is dingier in real life than in photos. Of course, it was sunnier when the photos were taken and today is cold and cloudy.

I suck in a breath of crisp New England air and gawk at the overhanging oaks and elms of my quaint little neighborhood. The leaves are still green in early September. I anticipate autumn colors in a month! An explosion of reds, oranges, and yellows around every corner. I can't wait to splash sidewalk puddles and crunch fallen leaves. Everything will be perfect once the world smells like pumpkin spice latte. I love Wethersfield already, and I haven't even explored the town.

The Witch House, as I discovered from my late-night sleuthing session, was built in 1715 by Admiral Thaddeus

Wolcott for his beloved wife, Eliza. Wikipedia says nothing about the sea captain being dashing or handsome, but I'm certain he is. I can see him leaning far out to grasp a billowing sail, his puffy white shirt flapping in the wind. He'll have a sword. No, wait! A cutlass! And tight pants that show off his tight assets.

Okay. Rein it in, Theo.

Thaddeus died at sea and Eliza lived in this house until her death at eighty-six. She slipped on a chestnut in her backyard. An old lady fall.

Because Eliza was a childless widow and aged into a cranky old woman who probably yelled at kids to get off her lawn, rumors of witchcraft swirled around her. One rumor after another lent a sinister air to the Wolcott residence until the townsfolk began calling it *The Witch House* and the name stuck. Fortunately, as the new owner of the Witch House, I don't believe in ghosts.

I whack my way through waist-high weeds.

Smothered in ivy, the Witch House is smaller up close and leans to the left. Crooked shutters. Weathered clapboard siding. A sagging back porch. A patchy roof. I can see how years of neglect may lend the Witch House a sinister air, but I think she's beautiful and brimming with a derelict romance. The abandoned house vibe screams cozy knit socks and stripped stockings. It's more *Hocus Pocus* than *The Conjuring*.

I can't wait until October! By then, The Witch House will be mostly restored and I'm going hog wild on Halloween decorations.

There's a giant tree (Oak? Elm? Birch? I'll have to send a photo to my plant expert Lena) in the front yard, perfect for cobwebs and dangling skeletons. I can see it now:

A giant spider in a web on the crumbling brick chimney. A small graveyard on the lawn. Witch legs poking out of the grass. Jack-o'-lanterns...

Omigod! Jack-o'-lanterns! I know *exactly* where these will go.

I race to the front window and tap the grimy glass.

Okay. False alarm. I thought these were original diamond-paned windows, much like the ones in—wait for it—*The Witch of Blackbird Pond*. Kit's suitor, William Ashby, had installed diamond-paned windows in his fancy new home and Nat (salty and jealous because he *totally had a crush* on Kit) placed jack-o'-lanterns on William's window sill and caused quite the scandal. Jack-o'-lanterns were a fire hazard and the 'work of the devil!" Nat ended up in the stocks and banished from Wethersfield on the threat of thirty lashes if he returned. It's the most romantic thing I've ever read. I run a hand across the window sill and my eyes fill with tears.

Calm down. I'm having a moment.

I hug my hamster cage to my chest, basking in blissful book nerdom. It takes me a while to register the sound of shoes pounding the pavement.

Someone's approaching.

I whirl around and my mouth drops open.

The jogger is tall and leanly built like a championship soccer player. His hair is the color of sun-kissed wheat. Did I mention that he's shirtless? That's the most important detail. He's got a golden tan and…

My gaze travels to his sweaty navel.

He's stacked. Forget the six-pack. We're talking about an eight-pack and change.

Is this his normal jogging route? *Please let this be his normal route.* Where is he headed? Maybe I'll take up running too. Blood rushes to my cheeks as I watch him come my way.

Be cool, Theo. Be cool.

But how can I be cool when the most gorgeous man alive is running toward me.

Omigod. He resembles…

This shirtless jogger *is* my version of Nat Eaton come to life, except older. How old is Nat Eaton supposed to be in the book, anyway? Nineteen? Okay, let's set the record straight: I stopped lusting after nineteen-year-olds when I was sixteen.

This shirtless marathon man is in the prime of his life (see age

22

appropriate for my purposes). I can easily picture him swaggering into a gas station in tight jeans or scoring a goal for England or swinging up the rigging of a 17th century merchant ship and chopping firewood. He's Brad Pitt, circa *Thelma and Louise*. He's David Beckham. He's Nat freaking Eaton.

Oh shit!

He's three houses away from my overgrown front lawn, his steely eyes fixed ahead, his ears plugged with AirPods.

What do I do? What do I do?

A normal person would wave. A braver woman would say hello and flash him a come-hither smile, hoping he'll notice her cute outfit...

My outfit! I glance down, wishing I could melt into the grass and crawl away.

I'm dressed in high waisted mom jeans, which I thrifted from my actual mom and a mustard yellow hoodie with a screen print of a giant potato (designed by me). I'm dressed to mop floors and dust cobwebs, not to meet the man of my dreams.

Oh no. He's closing in. I'm paralyzed to the spot. I want to run and hide, but I can't move. I can't look away. I can't stop staring at his chest. What if he notices?

Oh my god. He's noticing! He's slowing down. His naked chest is heaving, and he's tilting his head up.

He gives me the 'Hey' nod, but doesn't actually say 'Hey.'

Say hello. Say it. Do something.

I lift the hamster cage up to my face and hide.

Milk and Cereal scamper and squeak, angry at being jostled. If I can't see him, he can't see me. Only problem: I *can* see him through the cage.

Real life Nat Eaton halts in front of my house.

"You okay?" he asks, jogging in place. His voice is deep and buttery, precisely the type of voice that would make me tingle all over. "Do you need help?"

I can see his brows furrow together. I'm weirding him out.

Quick. Say something. Do something smooth.

I give him a thumbs up.

"This house is abandoned," he says.

I point to the SOLD sticker on the For Sale sign.

"Ah," he says. "Well… welcome to the neighborhood."

I give him another thumbs up.

Darting me a concerned glance, he resumes his jog, disappearing into the thicket of trees that line the running trail by the Connecticut River.

Milk waves her paws. Cereal drinks from her water spout.

"That went well…"

How much do I want to crawl into a hole and die? Let me count the ways.

Real life Nat Eaton's expression is forever imprinted in my memory. This isn't how I imagined my entrance into Wethersfield. Kit Tyler came to town in a silk gown and jumped into the freezing cold ocean to save a little girl's doll like a badass. Sure, she made a poor first impression to the uptight Puritans, but I'm pretty sure Nat was secretly mesmerized by her headstrong actions.

Meanwhile, I hid behind a hamster cage. The jogger didn't look bewitched by my badass actions. He looked like someone had cut the cheese.

This first impression makes it into the Awkward Hall of Fame.

Leave it to me to weird out modern-day Nat Eaton.

As I slump up the steps of my new home, I can't help thinking about a classic line from the book: "This town doesn't take kindly to strangers. And you be the strangest of them of all."

Story of my life.

chapter five

S haking off my embarrassment, I lug my hamsters up the porch steps and fish for my keys.

"Come on, Hammies. Let's check out our new home."

Cereal runs to her corner. Milk blinks three times and sniffs the air.

Hamsters are solitary creatures and vicious with their own kind. If left unattended, they might fight to the death. That's why their cage has a plastic divider, and even then I catch Milk eyeing Cereal like she's a snack. Cannibalism is not uncommon amongst hamsters. I learned that the hard way with my former pets Mr. Bubbles and Hamlet. Let's just say Mr. Bubbles made a meal of Hamlet and it was not pretty.

The front door squeaks. Making a mental note to oil the hinges, I burst into a coughing fit as a dust cloud settles over me.

My hamsters hiss and grind their teeth, a sign of agitation.

"Sorry guys!" I flip the cage around in a last-ditch attempt to shield my hamsters from the dust.

Milk has respiratory problems and Cereal is sensitive to pollutants. As much as I'm dying to explore the house, I jog back to my car, grab a microfiber cloth from the trunk and douse it with a flask of water. I cover the hamster cage with the wet cloth and return inside.

"Wow." I circle the living room, checking out the central fireplace and the dining room. The walls are a mix of peeling paint and grandma cabbage rose wallpaper. There's a boot-size hole in the partition between living room and dining room as if someone went on a wall-kicking spree.

"That can easily be repaired," I say, peeking through the hole.

In the living room, I admire the small section of oak flooring that has not been scuffed by foot traffic or ruined by water damage. I run my hand along the dusty wainscoting and marvel at the intricate carvings of leaves, chestnuts, and mushrooms on the banister.

"You can't find craftsmanship like this anymore," I tell my hamsters. "They just don't make houses like they used to."

Milk nibbles on a pellet. Cereal climbs into her wheel and runs one rotation before giving up. I think this means they're in agreement. Also, Cereal is looking a tad overweight. I might have to put her on a stricter regiment.

An avocado green fridge resides in the kitchen. I approach it with caution, knowing better than to open it. Beside the fridge is a matching avocado-green Kenmore range. A previous owner must have renovated the kitchen in the '70's.

The cabinets are relics from the 1950s (I can tell by the curved corners). Sometime in the last decade, another owner painted the cabinets a questionable mustard yellow.

I eye the gunk on the stove. "I can work with this, but this paint has got to go."

Making a mental tally of renovation projects, I turn on the faucet and jump back as red water gushes into the cracked porcelain sink.

"Rust." I clutch my pounding heart. "It's only rust."

The stairs creak beneath my feet. Upstairs, the boards groan even louder as the house rumbles like an arthritic old man settling into his recliner.

I count three tiny rooms in various stages of decay, a linen closet housing three crusty towels, and one '50's style bathroom with mint green tiles.

"I can work with this too," I say, figuring out how I'm going to salvage the bathroom.

And then I peer down at the toilet...

Someone — a long time ago — has left me a floating surprise. Except without running water, the surprise has *settled* and *spread*.

I slowly back away and shut the door. "Later. I'll deal with that later."

Onward and upward.

The master bed room boasts a quaint window seat. I can see myself curled up here and reading... after I remove this suspicious fungus from the wall.

I peer through the grime-caked window. There's a giant chestnut tree surrounded by fallen nuts and an old well covered with vines.

The backyard is huge, about three times the size of my parent's backyard, and flanked by a wall of trees. Everything is so green and lovely. Even the waist-high weeds are lush and wonderful.

By the time I return to the first floor, I'm still excited and overwhelmed. Most of the second story floorboards need to be replaced before it's safe to roam up there. There's an old raccoon's nest in one of the bedrooms and a damp spot next to a broken window where toadstools sprout from the wood.

I love this house already, but I have my work cut out for me. After years of abandonment, it's been reclaimed by nature and now it'll require a little elbow grease to take it back. I might keep the mushroom, though. They give the house an 'enchanted forest' charm.

I make several trips to my car, carting a broom, a plastic bucket, and a mop. Rolling up my sleeves, I move in an air bed and spend the rest of the afternoon sweeping and dusting a corner of the living room for overnight camping.

Tomorrow I explore Historic Wethersfield and visit all the points of interest in *The Witch of Blackbird Pond*. Today, I tidy.

By nightfall, I collapse in a dusty heap on my air mattress. My phone is plugged into a portable charger. My hamsters run around on their wheels. I've swept and mopped and batted more cobwebs than I would for an actual haunted house.

One point of interest: The Witch House is *not* haunted. I have the realtor's word.

How could a house with such an adorable 'cottagecore' vibe be haunted?

Even if the closets are full of ghosts, I'm too exhausted to care. I conk out the moment my head hits the mattress.

CREAK.

My eyes flutter open. "What was that?"

There's silence save for the creak of the hamster wheel. I check on Milk and Cereal. Milk is fast asleep. Cereal is getting an early start on her exercise regime.

The first floor is pitch black and dank despite my cleaning. Letting out my breath, I flip to my side and let the steady rotations of the hamster wheel lull me back into—

CREAK.

GROAN.

CREAK.

SCUFFLE. SCUFFLE. STOMP. STOMP. CRASH.

I jolt awake and gawk at the ceiling.

Oh my god. What's that? A rat? A ghost? A witch? A rat-faced ghost witch?

"Oh man." I draw my knees to my chest, my eyes swishing from side to side like the black cat clock in the kitchen. Okay. Maybe I'm just imagining things. There's no such thing as ghosts. It's got to be a raccoon or a stray cat that just snuck in through the—

BOOOOOOOOOOOOOO.

CRASH. STOMP. BOO.

I blink in surprise. "Boo?"

BOOOOOOOOO.

"Ahhhhhhhh!" I snatch up my hamster cage and run for the door. Parking myself on the porch, I start looking for a local Airbnb listing that can take me on short notice. It's either that or sleep in my car.

I take it back.

I *do* believe in ghosts, especially now that I own a haunted house.

chapter six

I spend the night at Bromley House, a bed-and-breakfast with dreamy grandma vibes.

By 'grandma vibes' I don't mean *my* grandma. My grandma kept her couch encased in plastic and never peeled the labels off her appliances. Whoever decorated this bed-and-breakfast shares my love for antiques, nautical oil paintings, and floral upholstery.

Bromley House itself is an ornate Victorian with bay windows, stained glass decor, and colorful floor tiles. Painted sage green with white exterior trim, the house reminds me of a Key Lime pie.

The chairs are cushy, the bedspread patterned in faded cabbage roses, and the carpets are a lush forest green. I count three oil paintings of old ships in my room and two throw pillows decorated with cross-stitched hens.

The stairs are steep and creaky. There is a weathervane on the roof. Honestly, I can live here forever. Considering the state of my own home, I might have to extend my stay for the foreseeable future. I should be more bummed, but as I wake up in a soft four-poster bed and stir to the aroma of strong coffee and frying bacon, I can't help feeling excited to start the day.

To think, just a month ago I dreaded waking up in the morning and slogging off to work. The only bright spot in my life were Friday afternoons, which couldn't come soon enough. And my weekends, which pass in a whirlwind of sticker cutting and order packing. Now my life has taken a complete 360 degree turn and I'm the proud owner of a haunted house. I know I should be concerned about the 'haunted' part, but with the robins chirping outside my window, I can't remember what I was so afraid of last night.

So I may have a ghost problem…

I'm sure I can sit down and have a grown up chat with whatever specter is haunting The Witch House and come to a diplomatic understanding. Maybe the ghost is friendly? Maybe he or she is Casper!

By the time I come downstairs, I've replaced the scary ghost in my mind with a friendly ghost with round cheeks and squat little ghost legs. I've also sketched out an entire sheet of Halloween themed sticker ideas featuring my new ghost friend and can't wait to start designing on my iPad. Maybe I'll sit outside, under the shade of a willow tree, and draw.

I run my hands along the oak banister, admiring the carving of a basket overflowing with grapes on the newel posts. The B&B has gorgeous colonial furniture from the china cabinets (expert dovetailing) to the demilune, a half-moon decorative table made from New England maple. There's even a fire screen dating back to 1753 when women used to knit by the hearth and needed protection from the flying embers.

I'm in furniture heaven, knocking on the coffee table, the sideboard, the bookshelves. I bend down to admire the flooring. Massive King's Wood planks. The original builder spared no expense.

Roaming around antique stores and estate sales to admire old furniture is one of my hobbies. Some might call it a quirk. What can I say? I appreciate wood and craftsmanship. While my specialty is Early Colonial furniture making, I spot some mid-19th century pieces and appreciate that too. I do not discriminate between time periods, though I admit to harboring a special abhorrence for particle board and laminate flooring.

31

"Breakfast is ready!" Mrs. Bromley, owner of the B&B, calls from the dining room where she's prepared a Continental style breakfast of scrambled eggs, bacon, sausage, orange juice, and coffee.

"Wow!" I gawk at the spread. "This is a feast for a king!"

"Good morning, Theodora," she smiles at me, ladling eggs onto my plate.

"Oh no, Mrs. Bromley," I say, taking the plate from her. "Let me do it."

"Nonsense!" She waves me away with a wrinkled hand covered in blue veins. "You're my guests. Sit down."

I linger behind her in case she needs my help. She's so tiny and fragile, I'm afraid she may overwork herself serving me breakfast. I don't know how old Mrs. Bromley really is (and it would be impolite to ask), but I guess her age to be around 80. Possibly even 90. Her skin is crinkled and thin, her hair a perfect white puff ball. She's wearing a peach-colored sweatshirt with a screen print of a grumpy cat.

Ooh. That's an awesome sweatshirt. I'll have to ask her where she bought it. She's also rocking a *huge* pair of glasses with tinted yellow lenses, and I not-so-secretly covet her peach frames. I'm getting so much fashion inspo from this woman!

As Mrs. Bromley adds a homemade blueberry muffin to my plate, my eyes suddenly fill with tears.

"What is it?" she asks, adding another wrinkle to her already crinkled forehead.

I have a soft spot in my heart for old people, and Mrs. Bromley is just *soooo* old and perfect. Pure Grandmacore. Even better: she has Hannah Tupper vibes. Would she be weirded out if I tell her I want to keep her? Not that I go around collecting adorable seniors… that would be insane. If collecting old people were socially acceptable, sweet little Mrs. Bromley is for keeps.

I help her sit down at a gingham-covered table inside a sunshine filled breakfast nook. Hanging plants dangle from ceiling hooks, casting vines against the window.

I assure her that nothing's wrong with me. "It's the blueberry cake," I say, gazing dreamily down at my breakfast. "The only thing that will make this day even more perfect is a kitten."

Mrs. Bromley studies my wistful expression and nods in understanding. "You're here because of *The Witch of Blackbird Pond*."

My eyes light up. "How did you know?"

"Your expression when I gave you the blueberry cake. Like you're lost in a dream."

I blush. "That's what my mom always says. That I travel through life in a rainbow-filled bubble and it's time to wake up."

"Well..." Her eyes twinkle. "There's nothing wrong with being a hopeless romantic. *The Witch of Blackbird Pond* is my favorite book, too. That's why I make blueberry cakes for guests. I make sure this old place is as homey as..."

I sit on the edge of my seat. "Hannah Tupper's cabin!"

She smiles. "I think you will love Wethersfield."

"I already do, and I haven't seen any of it."

She leans in and peers at the design on my T-shirt. "Isn't that the dearest little thing! What is it?"

"It's a sea sponge," I say, plucking at my shirt so she'll have a better view of the marine sponge amongst the coral reef. "I designed it myself."

"No!"

"Yes!"

"I have a friend who's a marine biologist. She inspired this design."

"How darling! You're a gifted artist." Mrs. Bromley polishes her bifocals. "Now let's see: there's a fish."

"Clown fish."

"And coral and oh! A squid! Look at their adorable faces."

Her encouragement is so different from my parents' skeptical reaction to my sticker shop side hustle. I glow under her praise and can't help boasting: "I make tote bags, key chains, clay pins, lanyards, and stickers too. And prints. Lots of prints."

Mrs. Bromley claps her hand in delight.

I beam. A part of me is always after a gold star.

"Do you sell on Etsy?" she asks.

"I used to," I say, "but now I run my own online shop. It's called *Vincent Van Sproot.*"

"My, my. How clever! What is a 'sproot'?"

"You know something," I tap my chin, "I don't know! I totally made it up. I wanted a business name that's both dorky and adorable. Adorkable."

"It suites you," she says. "Now let me ask you this: do you make anything with cats?"

"Do I!"

We chat over breakfast over spoonfuls of homemade raspberry jam. Her collection of hanging house plants curtains us from the late morning sun. The nook smells of coffee, bacon, and blueberries.

Mrs. Bromley's cat joins us midway through breakfast and weaves between my legs. She's a fluffy white Turkish Van breed with green eyes and a sour down-turned mouth. I bend down to pick her up and get three scratches to my forearm. The cat turns up her nose and struts away.

"Joan *Cat*ford doesn't take kindly to strangers," she says. "She's quite a diva."

"I know how that goes," I rub my scratches, "I own two very demanding yet enterprising hamsters."

The subject switches, as it inevitably does, to *The Witch of Blackbird Pond*. I tell her I discovered the book at summer camp and forced all my cabin mates to read it. They later became my lifelong friends and now we have an online book club called Cabin 13.

Mrs. Bromley read the book for the first time when she was twelve. She remembers sitting on the branch of a giant oak tree and snacking on Cracker Jack. She loves the part in the book when Kit Tyler, running away from a harsh Puritan reprimanding, plunges into the waist-high weeds of the Meadows. She meets Hannah Tupper and spends a delightful afternoon in the old Quaker woman's cabin, alongside the banks of Blackbird

Pond. The scene made Mrs. Bromley feel safe and at peace and she knew she had to visit the real life Meadows one day.

"… twenty years later, my Roger—may he rest in peace — and I bought this bed-and-breakfast and I've been here ever since."

I inhale a deep lungful of coffee-scented air, feeling a kinship with this stranger whom I just met last night.

This is what *The Witch of Blackbird Pond* will do to strangers. They change from strangers to lifelong friends.

She tops off my coffee. "How long are you planning on staying in Wethersfield?"

"Indefinitely. I just bought a house here."

She smiles. "Which house?" she asks, returning to her seat.

"The Witch House."

Mrs. Bromley pauses with her mug halfway to her lips. "Oh my. You're going to need to do a lot of work."

"The renovations are daunting." I wipe my brow. "But I'm great at DIYs and I have a degree in Early Colonial furniture making, not that I've ever made my own furniture. I appreciate wood and craftsmanship." I sip my coffee. "I'm talking too much, aren't I? I always do that. Tell me if I scare you off, Mrs. Bromley."

"'Mrs. Bromley?! Heavens! That makes me sound like I'm a hundred years old and I'm only eight-four. Edith," she says, laying her wrinkled hands on top of mine. "Call me Edith."

"Edith," I repeat. "Can I just say something? I think we're going to be best friends."

"Oh my. You are a burst of sunshine!"

"I don't get to be very friendly in my former job."

"What did you do?" she asks.

I wrinkle my nose, shuddering from the memory of working in corporate health insurance. "I was a Grievance Specialist."

"Good Lord! That sounds horrid."

"It was… it really was. I won't bore you with the details, only to say that I died a slow death for ten years until I finally decided to wake up." I sit back and bask in my cozy surroundings. "All that is in the past. I've got a new lease on life. I'm at liberty. I'm out there!"

Edith slides her chair away from the table and tries to get up. She shuffles (rheumatoid arthritis is no joke) and I can hear her joints creak as she tries to pick up the plates.

I jump up and take the dishes away from her.

"Hold that thought, dear," she says. "I have to run some errands this morning. Would you like to accompany me? I know you're eager to get out there and explore the town. I can guide you to the action."

"That would be fantastic." I feel like I've hit the jackpot. What better way to spend a day than touring Wethersfield with my very own Hannah Tupper.

"Theodora," she says, her lips hitching into a smile. "Do you like cheese?"

"*Do I like cheese?!* Every one in my family is lactose intolerant, but I lucked out. Why'd you ask?"

"I need to replenish my afternoon cheese board."

"*You have an afternoon cheese board?!*"

"The general store has the best gourmet cheese selection. All the fancy cheeses you can dream of and… let's see…" Her eyes become vague. "Dried fruit. Mixed nuts. Do you like nuts?"

"I enjoy all forms of nuts."

"I am partial to the macadamia nut. And sometimes, the humble pecan." She pauses. "Can your hamsters digest cheese?"

"They do! I give them a cube each as a reward for exercising on their wheel."

"Perfect," Edith says. "Then we shall buy extra cheese."

I clutch my heart. "I think I've died and gone to heaven."

Edith gestures to the front door. "Shall we?"

Grabbing her straw hat, I help her down the handicap ramp and into her motorized scooter. I've always thought scooters are Vespas for old people.

"Do you like it?" Edith asks. "My grandson got it for me."

"I love it," I admire the bright orange paint job, "How fast does it go?"

36

"Ten mph. Fifteen if I really push on the gas. I wanted the faster Sports model, but Carter didn't want me speeding on the sidewalk, the party pooper. I tell him, 'Honey, at my age… fast is the only speed I want to go."

"Your grandson sounds like a cautious guy."

"Carter's a real stick in the mud," Edith laughs. "Have you met him? He lives three doors down from the Witch House. You and he are neighbors."

I shake my head, recalling the hot jogger. Maybe that was Carter? Nah. Can't be. The jogger didn't look like a stick in the mud to me.

"Figures. He never leaves his house."

"Is he a hermit?"

"Do you remember Oscar the Grouch?" Edith asks. "That's my grandson. He doesn't live in a trash can, but sometimes he acts like it."

Okay. He's definitely *not* the hot jogger. "Does he like cheese? Maybe he would like to join us?"

Edith grumbles. "Too rich for him."

I can tell the subject of her grandson is putting Edith in a foul mood. "Hey," I say, patting the body of her scooter, "I have just the sticker for your ride."

A sparrow chirps in the trees. I spot a yellow leaf and two orange ones. The air is smoky and crisp, perfect sweater weather. Autumn in New England! It's happening!

It's my first full day exploring the setting of my favorite book and I've made, as Anne of Green Gables will call her, a 'bosom friend.' Even better, Edith is a bookish friend.

"Look out, Wethersfield!" I tilt my head up to soak in the autumn sun. "Here we come!"

chapter seven

E dith drives on the sidewalk. I walk beside her.
"I normally go faster," she says. "But I want to make sure you can keep up."

I hide a smile. "I appreciate it."

We loop around the Ancient Burying Grounds (it sounds spookier than it actually is), which is located at the center of Marsh Street.

"Reverend Gershom Bulkeley is buried there," Edith says, referring to one of the minor characters in *The Witch of Blackbird Pond*, who just so happens to be a real-life figure.

"The apple tart guy!"

"I remember him as the onion poultice guy. Do you want to visit his grave?"

I grin. "What do you think?"

We roll through the cemetery. Edith waits for me on the concrete path while I pick my way through the ancient moss covered tombs.

"This is my cousin Camille's idea of heaven," I tell Edith once I've filled up my camera roll full of faded gravestones. "She loves historical graveyards. The older the better."

"Is she a goth?" Edith asks. "I have a goth couple who books a weekend in October. They do a weekend here, a weekend at the Lizzie Borden Murder House, and then onto Salem."

"Camille doesn't dress like a goth," I say, thinking of my cousin's collection of designer handbags, "but she's a graveyard girl in her soul."

"Know a secret?" Edith asks as we leave the graveyard. "I am too."

"Aren't we all?"

As we round the corner, the colonial facade of the Buttolph-Williams House greets us. This house is the cherry on my geek sundae, the inspiration for the Woods' family home in the book. Its clapboards are painted an austere blackish color (a chef's kiss for mastering spooky Puritan vibes) and its four front facing windows resembles eyes.

"Oh my god!" I restrain myself from running in circles on the lawn. "Diamond-paned windows!"

I check the sign outside. They're closed for tours today, but you better believe I'll be first in line for tomorrow's tour.

"Do you want me to take your picture?" Edith asks. "You'll have to show me how to use your phone."

I hesitate, remembering the ghastly photos snapped by my mom and grandma over the last ten years.

"Let's take a selfie." I kneel down beside Edith's scooter and we mug for the camera with the house in the background. Not to toot my own horn, but I'm a pro at selfie composition and lighting. "Say cheese!"

Speaking of cheese, Edith *did* promise a cheese sampling.

We make a quick detour to the pharmacy to pick up Edith's arthritis medication. While we wait, Edith tells me about Carter.

I thought it strange that her grandson lived in Wethersfield. "What happened to his parents?" I ask, trying to piece together a profile from the snippets of information Edith drops about her family.

"They're in Manhattan. Upper East Side."

I whistle. "Wow."

"Carter used to live in the city too, but he moved back to Wethersfield two years ago."

I nod. "To settle down with his family?"

"He lives alone," Edith says. "More like to cut down on his living expenses. He was always complaining about the price of coffee and subway fare."

"What does he do now?"

"Do?" Edith shakes her head. "Nothing."

"Nothing? Nothing at all?"

"He founded a... What was it? 'Modern construction' company and then he sold it. He's retired now, enjoying the fruits of his labor and still complaining about the cost of coffee."

I'm already imagining a gray haired retiree who sits at home, counts his pennies, and has a cupboard full of Campbell's tomato soup. I recall Edith's Oscar the Grouch comparison. "Does he really live in a trash can?"

"Honey, Carter lives in the ugliest house in Wethersfield."

"Even uglier than my Witch House?"

"The Witch House is just run down, but it was glorious in its day. No, Carter's house was designed ugly, and he likes it that way." She snorts. "He designed it."

Now I'm really picturing a trash can, except with tin windows and a dented door. This Carter sounds like a real catch.

"Does he visit you?" I ask.

"Only when he wants free food, which is too much for my liking. That damn kid won't leave me alone!"

My lips twitch. "Cramps your style?"

"And my sex life."

"Edith!"

"I may be an old lady," she winks, "but I'm not dead yet..."

Centrally located in the middle of the action, Wethersfield Mercantile is a gathering point for the residents and hosts a number of events including a Heaving Bosoms Romance Book Club on Wednesdays, Knitting Tuesdays, and Wine & Cheese Murder Mystery Hour on Fridays.

I don't need to tell you that I sign up for all the events. I'm especially excited about the romance book club. It's run by Rachel, the owner of Wethersfield Mercantile, a nice lady in her early '50s with round tortoise-shell glasses and a green circle scarf. Rachel has lived in Wethersfield her entire life and used to date Edith's son.

As Edith and Rachel catch up on town gossip, I roam the aisle, gawking at shelves stocked with spices, locally made preserves, and over three hundred types of candy in old fashion glass jars. I come across plushies of the red onion, Wethersfield's staple crop and mascot, and gasp.

"Remember when Kit and Judith had to weed the onion fields in the Meadows?!" I call across the store.

Rachel shares a smile with Edith. "Another *Witch of Blackbird Pond* fan?"

"Why don't you pick out a plushie while I check out the new cheese selection," Edith says. "I may be awhile. I'm picky about my charcuterie."

Rachel walks Edith into the refrigerated storeroom at the back of the store, which is like a grocery store wine locker. Instead of wine, there are rows and rows of cheese: smoked gouda, brie, Camembert, gruyere, Harvati, goat, gorgonzola in chunks, wedges, and gigantic wheels.

Edith consults her shopping list and polishes her big glasses.

"Holler if you need help," Rachel says, shutting the door.

We can see Edith behind the frosted glass, studying a wedge of red wine soaked goat cheese.

"That's called 'Drunken Goat' from Spain. I think I have a sample here." Rachel beckons me to her sample table where there's a generous selection of prosciutto, grapes, dried apricots and cranberries, five sample cheeses, and four different types of crackers.

She pours me some wine. "Try this, Theodora. Edith just told me you bought the Witch House sight unseen."

I nod. "Have you ever been inside?"

"Never. We used to dare each other to run up to the front door as children."

"I camped in the living room overnight."

41

Her owlish eyes widen. "No!"

"Tried too, anyway. I think I met a ghost. It said 'Boo.'"

"The ghost actually said 'Boo'?"

"On top of making a lot of racket," I say. "Could it be the Widow Wolcott? I can't imagine she would want to haunt this house. She lived a long life and slipped on a chestnut in the backyard. I should think only murder victims become ghosts."

"Maybe she wants revenge against the chestnut."

We confer on the nature of the haunting. I show her a few illustrations I made of my ghost and her chestnut nemesis. The ghost is your typical white sheet variety, except I gave my version rosy cheeks. I also gave the chestnut a face. It looks pleased with itself for causing so much death and destruction.

"That's so cute! Edith also tells me you make stickers. Can you illustrate stickers for my store? I'm looking for cheese and the humble red onion."

"I already have tons of ideas!"

I love this town. I've made a new best friend and booked an art commission before lunch. As we hash out the design for Rachel's plans for local merch, we hear a racket in the cheese locker.

Rachel hops off her stool. "Looks like Edith's found my new inventory."

I follow her to the cheese locker in time to see Edith reaching for the biggest wheel of parmesan I've ever seen. It's the kind of specialty wheel chefs cook pasta in, and it's packed on the top shelf along with six other gigantic cheese wheels.

"Hold on, Edith," Rachel says, hunting for a step ladder. "Let me get that for you."

Edith cups her ear. "EHHHH?"

"Just hold on."

Edith continues to reach for the parmesan.

"I don't think she can hear you," I say. "Maybe her hearing aid isn't switched on."

"She can hear me fine enough." Rachel says. "She just pretends she doesn't. Edith! Oh no, Edith! Don't do that!"

Edith places her orthopedic shoe clad foot on the bottom shelf and reaches for cheese.

"Goddamn it, Edith!" Rachel tosses her hands in the air. "Now you're just pissing me off on purpose. This is why seniors have accidents," she mutters to me before rushing forward to pry Edith away from the shelf.

The shelf, unbolted to the wall, creaks.

My sense of danger is on red alert. "Edith! You really shouldn't be doing that!"

"Don't get your panties in a bunch," Edith says, her arms straining upward. "I can handle myself."

My gaze zeroes in on the top shelf. The parmesan wheels wobble. A wax covered Gouda topples over and hits the floor. A wedge of brie spills from the bottom shelf.

Rachel clutches her temples. She seems more stressed out about Edith than her damaged inventory.

"She's done this before, you know," Rachel says.

"Climbed your cheese self?"

"And then some. We went to a museum once — ancient Thai artifacts. She bangs on a thousand-year-old bell and argues with the guard. We were almost thrown out."

I nod in understanding.

I encounter this situation plenty of times as a Grievance Specialist. Edith, sweet as she may appear, is playing the old lady card and being purposefully obstinate.

A gorgonzola wheel bites the dust.

Cursing under her breath, Rachel picks up the fallen cheese. "I think we may need to tackle her to the ground."

"Okay, Edith." I step froward. "I think you should come down now. The shelf's not bolted to the wall and — "

The shelf rumbles.

SNAP.

One side of the top shelf splinters. Giant parmesan wheels wobble and one of them begins to roll...

Rachel clasps her hands over her mouth and screams.

"Edith! Watch out!" Acting on instinct, I rush forward and knock her out of the way.

Rachel screams again. "Theo! Watch out!"

I glance up. Too late. I've only just enough time to shield my face before the first of many cheese wheels topples off the broken shelf and whacks me on the head, knocking me out.

chapter eight

My world is filled with the sharp tang of parmesan.

It's raining cheese. I'm drowning in cheese.

Someone taps me on the cheek.

"Theodora?" *Tap. Tap.* "Theo?"

I swim out of my cheese ocean, groaning.

Rachel and Edith hover over me. A heavy weight presses against my chest, my back, my legs. I glance down. I'm buried under six big wheels of parmesan. Fun fact: during the Salem witch trials, nineteen of the accused were hung, but one man was pressed to death under gigantic stone slabs. Relatable.

"Are you hurt?" Rachel kneels beside me. "How many fingers am I holding up? What's your name?"

I mutter something that sounds like "cheese the day."

Rachel and Edith share a worried look.

"Theodora?" Edith tries to kneel down. Her knees creak so she settles for hunching. "Help me get this cheese off of her."

"Don't you move, Edith. Let me." Rachel lugs a cheese wheel off my chest. She pants and strains.

"Put your back into it, Rachel!"

"I'm *putting* my back into it."

"You have to leverage your weight."

"It's not easy. These wheels are heavy."

Rachel grits her teeth. She may be thirty years younger than

Edith, but she has spindly arms and legs. She can't weigh more than ninety pounds.

"Gaaaaah," Rachel grunts, then flops down on her rump. The cheese wheel barely budges. "Call an ambulance."

"Here," Edith says, reaching for the parmesan crushing my legs. "Let me help you."

A horrible image comes to mind: Edith tugging on the cheese and yanking her arms off just like that old man in the '90's *Got Milk* commercial.

"No Edith! Don't strain yourself. I'll do it."

I sit up.

The parmesan wheel on my chest slides off and lands on the floor with a *thunk.*

Rachel and Edith clap. "That's the spirit, sweetie! You're doing so well!"

I take a deep breath. I'm shocked, bruised, and my head hurts where the first wheel struck me, but I can handle myself. I topple the remaining cheese wheels while Rachel and Edith cheer me on.

"Goodness. You're very strong!" Rachel says, helping me up to my feet and guiding me to a chair behind the counter. "You've been very brave. Just sit down and relax and I'll get you some water."

"That was amazing," Edith says.

I wave off her compliment. "Pilates. It builds muscle strength."

Suddenly her fragile arms wrap around me. "You saved my life."

I flush, hugging her back. "No, no."

"Yes, yes. *You saved my life.*" Edith touches the bruise on my forehead. "Those wheels could have killed me."

She's probably right. I don't think she would have survived being crushed by six wheels of parmesan.

"I'm in your debt," she says.

"It's nothing."

"Not many people would rush under a falling pile of cheese

to save an old lady," she says. "Any favor you want, you've got it. Your wish is my command."

"I don't want anything." I crack my back and grimace. "Maybe a massage and an ice pack."

Her crinkled eyes lighten up. "Do you need help with renovating your new house?

I pause to consider. "I guess I need all the help I can get," I say. "But you really don't need to..."

"Oh no," she laughs. "I'm not volunteering to help you. I plan on buying you a housewarming plant."

My shoulders slump in relief. Good. I don't have to worry about Edith falling or breaking a limb in my house.

"But Carter will be happy to lend you a hand."

I start in alarm. "Your grandson who lives in a trash can?"

"Just because he lives in a trash can doesn't mean he'll turn your home into a trash can. He's quite good at woodwork."

"No. No. No. I don't want to trouble him."

"You're not." Edith takes me by the shoulder. "*I'm* troubling him. End of discussion."

Rachel returns with a glass of water, an ice pack, and a first aid kit. "What's going on?"

I shake my head, dazed. "I think Edith just made her grandson into my indentured servant."

Rachel's mouth twitches. "The cheese debt."

chapter nine

"*You sell cheese?!*"

I blow a strand of hair away from my eyes. "I told you already, Ma. I'm working on a commission for a nice lady who sells cheese. I'm designing cheese-related merch."

"What is 'merch'?" my mom asks over speaker phone. "I do not know this word."

I know for a fact that I've mentioned 'merch' around my mom before. She just chooses not to hear me.

I take a deep breath. "Stickers, spoons, labels for her jam jars, canvas grocery bags."

"Is she paying you?"

"Of course she's paying me."

Mom sounds relieved. "Then you have a job. Does it come with health insurance? A 401K?"

"It's a commission," I explain. "I'm freelance." I grit my teeth and explain to both my parents that my 'job' is a solo gig and no, it doesn't come with health insurance or a 401K.

"Whaaa! Did you hear that?" I hear a *thwack* and know that it's my mom smacking my dad on the arm. "She'll be out in the street by the end of the month. She'll be homeless and have to turn tricks on the corner."

"I'm not going to turn tricks on the corner, Ma."

"You won't be able to pay your mortgage and you'll be destitute."

"Everything will be okay."

I kneel down on my abandoned air bed and drop my hamster cage in front of me.

I'm back in the Witch House, waiting for Carter Bromley, Edith's grandson, who I'm meeting for a walkthrough of my house in order to assess the extent of my renovation needs.

I can't say I'm looking forward to meeting Carter. Edith didn't exactly make him sound like a pleasant person. I can't get the grumpy green muppet in the trash can out of my head.

Out of curiosity, I drove past Carter's home and while his home *does* have a lot of corrugated sheet metal and solar panels, I think Edith's trash can description was too harsh.

Carter lives in an ultra modern cube: tiny, minimalistic, devoid of welcome signs, weather vanes, and lawn gnomes. In fact, there is no lawn, a travesty in these parts, but a precisely landscaped garden of rocks and cement.

Behind the cube is a larger structure (also cubish), which I assume is the garage. Both cubes stick out like sore thumbs amongst its colonial neighbors. Given Wethersfield's love for historic homes, I can see why Edith and Rachel would think Carter's cubes are the ugliest structures in town. It's modern art in a town that adores the old masters.

As for me, I don't mind the cubes. I've seen plenty of them when I visit Lena in Seattle. The design is popular amongst tech bro millionaires, and I can assume by the Cube's drawn windows, that Carter Bromley falls somewhere in one or both categories. He certainly doesn't sound like someone who would want to spend his time restoring a historical home. Or socializing.

To calm my nerves, I distract myself by cleaning out my hamster cage.

I've been remiss in tidying Milk and Cereal's habitat during the move and it's getting pretty funky in there. Who knew two hamsters could poop so much?

I lay out fresh paper shreds from Edith's office shredder and scoop up poop pellets with the help of a tiny blue shovel. I've also neglected calling my parents, who have been exceptionally vocal about their disapproval of my life choices. Let's kill two unpleasant birds with one stone.

My mom is fixated on the subject of cheese.

"You don't even like cheese. You're lactose intolerant. What are you doing hanging around a cheese shop?" Mom asks.

I nudge Cereal aside so I can get at her buried poop stash. "I love cheese. *You're* the one who's lactose intolerant."

"Okay, Theo," Mom says in her trademark 'cut-the-crap' tone. "Your dad and I have been discussing…"

"Uh oh."

"We want you to come home."

"Ma!" I shoo Milk away. Usually she scurries aside when I open her side of the cage. She's an antisocial hamster, but today she's circling my hand, her buck teeth bared like she's protecting buried treasure.

"I'm not moving home. I *bought* a home."

"This is not a home. This is a crack house," Mom says. Did I tell you she nearly fainted when I showed her the listing photos? "You can't live there by yourself. It's not safe."

"I'm perfectly safe here. Wethersfield is like a town ripped straight from a Hallmark movie. Incidentally, not one but *two* Hallmark movies have been filmed here, and my new friends are extras in both."

Mom, an avid fan of Hallmark's *Countdown to Christmas* Marathon, calls my bluff. "I don't believe you. All Hallmark movies are filmed in Vancouver."

"Not true. Two were filmed here."

"Which ones?"

"*Christmas on Honeysuckle Lane.*" I pause. "I don't remember the other one."

"Ah. Eh… not my favorite."

"Not everything can be in the same caliber as *A Very Merry Mix-Up.*"

"That one is a classic. Did they use real snow in your make-believe Hallmark movie?" Mom asks.

I rub my temple. "Fake snow. Edith says filming took place during mid-summer and she had to wear a full parka."

I tell her about the antique wonderland that is Edith's bed-and-breakfast and Rachel's sample cheese board. I leave out the part about being crushed by six wheels of parmesan (that would only worry Mom) and tell her about the many clubs I've joined.

"Tuesdays we knit, and I've ordered my copy of *Ice Planet Barbarian* for Wednesday's romance book club."

"How much are you being paid for making this 'cheese merch'?" Mom asks, ignoring everything I've just said.

I roll my eyes. "Ma…"

"How much?"

I tell her a number that offends her accountant sensibilities and sends her into a full-fledged Vietnamese tirade.

I hold the phone away from my ears until she's finished.

"Tell her this is a stupid idea…"

My dad clears his throat.

"Hi Ba."

"Hi Little Cow," he says, calling me by my childhood nickname. My parents and relatives call me 'Little Cow' from birth, not because I'm chubby (I'm thicc in the hip-thigh-butt triangle), but because cows are considered lucky and prosperous animals in our culture. So is the pig, though I'm glad I didn't get that nickname. If there's anything my parents want for my future, it's financial security and good luck.

"Your mom wants you to come home." Dad pauses. "Are you getting enough to eat?"

I consider my meals since my cross-country move. A substantial breakfast, thanks to Edith. Four nights of takeout. One great lobster roll.

"Mostly American food," I say. "I get to eat free cheese."

"Tell her to stop eating cheese," Mom says in the background. "She is already too fat."

By now, I'm used to my mom picking on me about my

51

weight. It used to hurt, especially when she compared me to Camille. Camille is slender and petite and could eat like a hog without gaining a pound. I merely have to look at a hamburger and gain fifteen pounds. Then the *thicc* revolution happened and I've learned to accept my body. I'll never have Camille's svelte figure, no matter how much I work out or diet. I don't fully love all my squishy bits, but I've learned to dress for my figure and most of the time, I feel pretty confident.

Until I talk to my mom.

"She is *not* fat," Dad says, coming to my defense. "We will buy some snacks for you next time we go to ABC Market and mail it over."

"Okay!" My stomach rumbles, thinking of fried sesame balls and pandan madeleines.

"We miss you, Theo," Dad says. "Are you *sure* you don't want to come home? You can still get your old job back."

"I miss you, too," I say, my voice cracking despite my resolution to stay strong. "But I can't go back to that job."

I think about my old life. Living rent free with my parents. Going to the same job every day for ten years. I didn't exactly hate my life, but I never really felt alive.

But here, in Wethersfield, surrounded by my senior citizen friends and the excitement of walking the same streets as my favorite characters… I feel alive for the first time in my life.

That's enough to give up the security of a regular paycheck. Right?

My parents grill me about my finances. Outside of my impulsive house purchase, I've been very careful with my money. I still have tons of savings (can't recommend living with your parents until you're thirty-two enough) and vested stock options from my old company.

"I'll be fine," I say. "I don't need any money."

Mom spins the same old spiel about me ending up homeless.

"Uh-huh. Yup. I will ask you for help if I need it." I nod along, figuring it was easier to agree on the small things as long as I retain my freedom on the important things. "No, I don't want you to send me any durian. I'm pretty sure you can't send fruit through the mail. No, I don't know for sure, but I bet the postal service is against — OW!"

"What happened?" My parents ask.

"Milk bit me!" I rub the web between my thumb and forefinger, ready to reprimand Milk. "Milk?"

Where's Milk?

I stare in horror at the empty cage. That damn hamster must have scurried out of the cage while I was tending to my wound. "Oh shit…"

"What's the matter?" my mom asks, alarmed.

"I'll call you back. Love you. Bye!" I scan the floor. "Milk?"

Cereal stops running in her wheel and peers at me.

"Do you know where Milk is?" I ask, then curse myself. Why am I asking a hamster?

But Cereal hops to the edge of her cage and makes a nibbling sound. Maybe I'm imagining things, but it looks like her pink paws are pointing…

I turn my head. "Milk!"

The albino hamster scurries from side to side, sniffing the baseboard beneath the main staircase.

"Milk," I say, tip-toeing after her with my hand outstretched. "Come here, Milk." I cluck my tongue. "Easy now…"

Milk scurries in front of a giant hole in the wall. She eyes the hole, her whiskers twitching.

"Oh no you don't! I know what you're up to." I wave a pellet in front of her whiskers. "I know what you want. Delicious, huh? Come on… take it."

Milk sniffs the pellet. With a defiant twitch of her whiskers, she darts inside the hole.

"Milk!" I smack my hand against the floorboards. "You've been bad! Very, very bad."

My guess is that the hole leads to a closet tucked below the stairs. Sure enough, there is a dwarf-sized door. Locked. And of course… I don't have the key.

In order to retrieve Milk, I'll have to get down on my hands and knees and crawl through the hole in the wall. Can I fit? The hole is big enough to comfortably fit a toddler. For me, it'll be a squeeze.

"Great. That's just great."

I tie my hair back into a ponytail. "All right, Milk. No cheese for a week!" I poke my head through the hole. Pitch blackness assaults me from the other side. I ease my shoulders through and feel around in the dark, inching the rest of my body inside. A cloud of thick dust settles over me, tickling my nose. "Ah... Ah... Ahcooooo."

The clerk at the pet store sold me a bill of goods. I was told hamsters were easy pets.

"Milk!" I call into the dark void. "Where the hell are you? Just wait till I get my hands on you!"

As my eyes adjust to the dark, I spot a pair of eyes reflecting back at me.

"Eeeeee," Milk says.

That's funny. Milk is usually a silent hamster, unless she's scared. Wait. *Is* she scared? Poor little thing. She's never wandered outside her cage. This closet is probably a howling wilderness to her. She must be terrified!

As my hamster mom instincts kick in, my anger at Milk instantly disappears.

"Don't worry, baby. Mama's got you." Putting my weight on my elbows, I crawl closer to the pair of glowing eyes. I'm half-in, half out of the wall. Just a few inches and I can reach her furry body...

I grit my teeth, pushing and pulling myself forward. The bare boards clamp around my hips like a vise. "Ouch!"

I twist and turn, trying to back myself out. I can't move. I'm stuck!

Panicked, I wiggle my waist, my butt...

I twist my shoulders. No give. Perspiration builds on my forehead. The boards dig painfully into my hips. My mom's nagging voice echoes in my ear:

Shouldn't have eaten all that cheese...

I can see myself on the evening news. Crowds gathered around my big ass as firefighters try to yank me out. Reporters and cameras:

This just in. Woman trapped in wall after chasing her pet hamster. Her mother says she's eaten too much cheese. Tonight at 7. When being thicc goes wrong…

Something furry nuzzles against my hand.

"Oh Milk," I say, stroking her back.

Hmm.

Her fur is not so soft. She actually feels… coarse and greasy. As she continues to rub her slick body against my palm, her leathery tail swishes against my wrist.

Wait a minute.

Milk has a stubby cotton ball tail. She doesn't have a long, slimy, prehensile…

"Eeeeeeeeeeeeeeeee," this creature who is most definitely *not* Milk says.

This isn't a hamster…

Who or *what* am I petting?

"Eeeeeeeeeeeeeeeeeeee," goes the rat.

"Ahhhhhhh!"

chapter ten

"Ahhh!"

Knock. Knock.

"Eeeee!" The rat scurries and *hopefully* disappears.

"Ahhh!"

Knock. Knock.

I stop screaming. Wait. Is someone at my door?

Knock. Knock. The front door rattles.

"Are you okay?" A man shouts from the other side.

"Carter?"

"That's me," comes his muffled voice. "What's going on in here?"

"Help! I'm trapped! With a rat!"

There's a pause. "Are you hurt? Should I call the fire department?"

"The kitchen door is unlocked! Come around back."

"Be right there."

I'm in a cocoon of darkness. Tiny paws touch my wrist. Yelping, I snatch my hands back. "Hurry!"

Seconds later, I hear the sound of panicked footsteps. Old floorboards creak behind me.

The footsteps halt.

A pause.

I freeze, sensing eyes on my butt. I was wiggling before. No chance I'm doing that now in case he gets the wrong idea.

"Carter?" I squeak.

"At your service." His voice is deep, rich, younger than I expected and dripping with amusement.

Given Edith's age, I assumed her grandson was pushing fifty. She went on and on about Carter being retired. My Uncle Duc was the only retired person I know and he's *ancient*. Maybe I have to revise my mental image.

"Theodora." I sneeze. "Theo."

"Grans says you might need my help." Another pause. I picture him with his arms folded over his chest, head tilted to the side, checking out the situation. The situation being my ass. "I can see she's right."

A rush of blood surges to my cheeks. What's more mortifying? Getting myself stuck in a wall or meeting Carter while stuck in a wall?

Footsteps again. Carter comes closer. "How did you get yourself stuck beneath the stairs?"

"I was cleaning my hamster cage and one escaped." I wiggle my hips. "Into this hole. You get the picture."

A muffled laugh. "I think I can put two and two together."

"My other hamster... Oh shit! I forgot to shut the cage. Can you check on Cereal?"

"Cereal?"

"My hamster."

"What's your other hamster called?"

"Milk."

"Milk and Cereal," he repeats, and I sense he's trying hard not to laugh.

I don't see what's so funny about my hamsters. "Can you...?"

"Got it." *Creak. Creak.* The cage door shuts with a gentle *ting.* "He's all right. Just dozing on his back."

"She. Cereal's a 'she.'"

"Sorry," he says. "Is Milk a 'he'?"

57

"At first I thought so, but now I'm not so sure. I believe Milk is gender confused."

Silence.

I poke my head up. "What's going on back there?"

Carter sounds like he's choking. "N-nothing."

"Can you get me out of here now?"

"Right." Carter slaps his hands together. He kneels behind me. An awkward pause. "Sorry," he clears his throat, "I'm going to have to... touch your..."

I blow a strand of hair away from my eyes. "Just get it over with."

His hands grip my waist and tentatively settle on my hips. I sense him shift behind me, trying his best to maintain a non-contact hover. Despite his consideration, our position makes it impossible not to touch. His knee bumps against my butt, his chest presses against my lower back.

"You okay?" he asks. "Everything where it... should be?"

"Roger," I say, and immediately want to die. That doesn't sound as cool as when astronauts say it.

"Right. Here's the plan. We're going to have to work as a team. On the count of three, you push, I'll pull."

"I can't push! There's a piece of wood stabbing me in hip."

"Pretend you're giving birth."

Seriously? "Just because I'm a woman doesn't mean I know what it's like to give birth."

"All right. All right," he says, losing some patience. "Pretend you're on the toilet and pooping."

I shrug. "That I can do."

"One... two... three..."

He pulls.

I push.

We're a seesaw.

I grunt.

He sees my grunt with an even louder grunt.

If Edith walked in right now, we might give her a heart

58

attack. Rather than free me, our efforts only succeed in digging the wood more painfully into my hip.

"Ow!"

"Gah!" Carter collapses on top of me, and then immediately backs off like he's touched a red hot burner. "Sorry."

"It's okay."

He sounds out of breath. "You're really in there."

"You don't have to tell me twice."

"Okay. We'll try again. Ready?"

"Get me outta here!"

His arms wrap around my waist. This time he doesn't bother with non-contact. He grips me in a bear hug, his face buried in my spine, my ass bumping against his groin. I'm getting well acquainted with Carter Bromley, and I haven't even seen his face.

"Heave!" he orders.

I heave. He yanks.

"I'M BEING IMPALED!"

Carter curses.

I bury my face in my hands, smearing dirt over my cheeks "Ahhhhchoooo!"

"Bless you."

"Thanks." I hang my head in defeat. I'm never going to get out of there. We'll have to involve the fire department after all. I'll be the town laughingstock—not the first impression I want to make.

Carter paces behind me. "I've got it. Do you have any lube?"

"Come again?"

"Lube? WD-40? Canola oil? Olive oil?"

"Well… I *did* pick up some stuff at the grocery. I forgot what I bought. Check the fridge."

Carter runs to the kitchen and rummages.

"Yes!" He returns with a bounce to his step. "I found some butter," he says, clearing his throat. "I'm going to have to um… "

I sigh.

I think I know where this is going. I hang my head. "Do what you must."

"I just want you to know: I won't enjoy this." He sounds sincere.

"I'll enjoy it less than you."

"Right," he takes a deep breath. "I'm going in."

I squeeze my eyes shut like I'm about to get a flu shot. His hands dips beneath my T-shirt and gently lifts. Using the entire stick of butter, he rubs grease circles on my naked hip.

"Hey! That tickles."

"Sorry."

"Do you know what you're doing?"

"This is the first for me," he says dryly.

I'm grateful he thought to use the butter stick instead of his hands. "You mean you don't make a habit of buttering up girls?"

The amusement returns to his voice. "Can't say I have."

The butter stick travels to my front, working the crevice between my stomach and the wood.

"Whoa!" My body jerks. "Watch it."

"Sorry," he says, sounding as mortified as I feel. "But I have to cover all my bases." He globs butter on the small of my back. "There. Done."

"Thank God."

"Ready?"

"This better work!"

He grips my hips. "Heave!"

The boards creak and the clamp around my waist loosens. "I'm slipping!"

"Heave!"

SNAP!

We fly backwards.

Carter lands on the floor.

I crash land on his leg. I'm free! I'm free!

"We did it!" Cartoon birds circle my head. I might need a tetanus shot. All in all, I'm mendable. I stand up and brush dust off my clothes.

"Are you okay?" Carter asks. "It looks like you're bleeding."

"I'm — " I gawk at his shoes.

Black Allbirds High Tops.

An ancient pair of jeans.

A grey T-shirt hugging a leanly muscled soccer player's physique.

Toned arms that's seen their share of push-ups.

Sandy, sun-bleached blond hair, messy from our butter escapade.

Mocking blue eyes—Nat Eaton eyes — smile down at me.

Oh.

My.

God.

"Is something the matter?" Carter asks.

"You're him," I blurt out. "It's you!"

He frowns. "Who?"

"Hot jogger!"

chapter eleven

Carter blinks at my reaction, and I immediately regret my words.

"I do jog," he begins, "and it *does* get warm during the summers."

"I didn't mean it like that." I *did* mean it like that. Why did I say that aloud? Maybe I should stick my head back in the hole. "I mean, I've seen you before. You're the jogger."

Carter peers at my face. "I remember you too. You tried to offer me your hamsters."

He remembers?! "I wasn't trying to offer them to you. I was hiding."

Doh! Why did I say that?

Carter's lips twitch. "Who were you hiding from?"

You! I tip my head up and straighten my spine. "Wouldn't you like to know."

"Actually," he says, chewing on his inner cheek, "I would like to know."

Tough. I have no explanation. I've backed myself into a corner and can't string together a logical thought when he's gazing down at me with those mocking blue eyes.

"So you're Edith's grandson," I say, trying to change the topic.

"You were expecting someone else?"

"No, it's just that... I thought you were much older. Edith says you're retired, so I assumed you were my parents' age. She also told me you live in a trash can."

"I *am* retired." Carter jams his hands in his jeans pockets. "And I wish she'd stop telling everyone I live in a trash can. I'm starting to develop a complex."

My eyebrows shoot up. "How old are you?"

"Thirty-four," he says.

"And you're *retired*? Like 401K? Pensions? Done?"

"FIRE," he says with a proud lift to his shoulder.

"Ohhhh. *FIRE*."

So I spend a lot of time on Reddit at work. 'F.I.R.E.' AKA the 'Financial Independence Retire Early Movement' is a personal finance mindset of saving up to 80% of your income, making wise investments, and retiring before 35.

Of course, not everyone retires in the traditional sense of the word. FIRE followers don't sit around watching TV and playing bingo all day. They have a side hustle or two. They *definitely* have a lucrative source of passive income or even better: *multiple* streams of income so they're not tied down to one job and are free to live life on their terms.

He pokes his head up in surprise. "You've heard of it?"

"I'm part of it too."

"Really?" Carter eyes me with new appreciation. "I've never met a fellow FIRE follower. At least outside of the Reddit forums."

"I'm not exactly retired. But I have..." I shrug. "A sticker company."

"Stickers?" His lips twitches again.

I stiffen at his patronizing tone. "Stickers."

"Sorry," he says, sounding decidedly *not* sorry, "I didn't know there's money to be made in stickers."

"I do tote bags, charms, and earrings too. And T-shirts."

I regret mentioning T-shirts because Carter immediately nods toward the one I'm wearing. "Did you design that?"

I prop a hand on my hip. "I did."

"What is it?"

I glance down. "It's a potato."

His brows knit together. "It has a face."

"My customer base likes cute expressions."

Carter narrows his eyes. It doesn't help that the potato's face is located on my right boob.

"Crosses for eyes," he says.

"It's an artistic choice."

"Is it supposed to be dead?"

"He's exhausted."

He dips his head down, his shoulders shaking. At last, Carter resurfaces, his features schooled into a serious mask. "What's a potato got to be exhausted about?"

"If you were working 60-hour weeks, you'd be exhausted too."

Carter blinks. "Fair enough. What's your sticker company called?"

"Vincent Van Sproot."

Carter is silent for a long time. He crosses his arms and cups his chin, considering the name with a solemn nod. "Hm, right, right. What is a 'sproot'?"

"It's a word I made up," I say with as much dignity as I can muster. "But lately, I've visualized it as a cross between a sprout and a spud. Like the sprout becomes a spud, the spud becomes a potato, and the sproot exists in-between the sprout -spud stage."

"So it's like the adolescent spud?"

"You know what?" I narrow my eyes, seriously considering his suggestion. "I think you've hit the nail on the head."

"You do realize," he begins, "that a spud is a potato."

"It's a *pre*-potato. It's what the potato will be."

"No," Carter says. "No, no. It's an actual potato."

I tap my foot on the floor. "I think I know the life-cycle of a potato."

Carter cocks his head toward the kitchen. "There are a ton of stickers on your fridge. Yours?"

I nod.

"A bit cluttered, don't you think?"

Oh no, he didn't! "I like a personalized fridge. What do you have on *your* fridge?"

"Nothing. I hate clutter."

I wrinkle my nose. Now I know what Edith's complaining about. Carter *is* a grouch, and he's mocking my stickers.

"So stickers led you to financial independence?" he asks.

Never moving out of my parents' house was unintentionally part of my frugality. Skipping out on ten years of rent in Los Angeles helps. It's not a cheapness issue, it's a having-no-social-life issue.

But I'm not going to tell him that.

"I have investments," I say. "And I'm frugal, if I do say so myself."

Carter brightens up. "Investments?" He gazes around my dilapidated living room. "As in real estate? Are you planning on flipping the Witch House..." His mocking gaze transforms to understanding. Even admiration. "In that case, I can advise you on cheaper repair alternatives. This place needs a lot of work. You have one of two options—"

In two seconds, his attitude switches from skeptical to gleeful. I can tell 'cheaper alternatives' is a special interest for him and nothing gets his rocks off more than talking about saving money.

"I don't plan to sell," I interrupt.

"Sure. You're looking for tenants then?"

I shake my head. "I'm not planning on turning this into a rental property. I plan to live here."

"Live here?" He rubs his forehead, realizes he's got butter fingers, and wipes the residue on his jeans. "In the Witch House?"

"Yeah." I frown. Buying a house and fixing it up to live in isn't a very unusual concept. Why does he look so horrified? I'm planning to renovate, not start a cult.

Carter clears his throat. "I'm sorry, Theodora..."

"Theo."

"Theo," he begins. "I don't know you, but Gran sent me here to offer my professional opinion and I aim to give it. You can't live here."

"I thought she offered your help in my renovations." My shoulders lift in a humble shrug. "You know, because I saved her life, I get you…" I look him up and down. "You're like my indentured fixer-upper."

"*I'm* indentured to *you*?"

"You're in my debt," I say. "Technically your grandmother is, but she can't exactly help me with the roofing, so she gifted you to me. I know it sounds weird, but there it is."

He narrows his eyes at me. That's right. He knows I speak the truth. Family obligations compel people to do strange things and puts them in situations they don't want to be in. And that's how I acquired a handyman for free. It works out for me.

"She told me you saved her from a falling pile of cheese," he says.

"That's right."

Carter steps forward, head tilted at a skeptical angle. "She's exaggerating. How can anyone be crushed by cheese?"

"*I* was crushed by cheese."

He snorts. "I heard about that, too. What's the matter? Can't handle a wedge of brie? A few piles of Kraft?"

"You're thinking about American cheese slices. That's not what we're dealing with here. Edith could have been crushed under six wheels of parmesan. The kind you cook noodles out of."

"I've never eaten noodles that came out of a cheese wheel."

"Just because you haven't done it doesn't mean it isn't done."

"Sounds expensive."

"It's on the pricy side," I say.

"Why not just sprinkle store-bought parmesan on your noodles rather than go to the trouble of having someone cook it out of a wheel?"

I rub my temple. "Because you're at a restaurant and you're paying for the ambiance."

"I wouldn't pay for the ambiance."

"That's why you live in a trash can!" Okay. Low blow, but Carter is really pissing me off. I feel like I'm in a tennis match against a machine who keeps serving fast balls and I just want a break.

"So you pushed her out of the way?" he asks, ignoring my 'trash can' jab.

"I took the hit."

Carter chews on his inner cheek. "Hm…"

I can tell he won't believe me unless I show proof. I fish out my phone and look for the photo Rachel texted me. It's a snapshot of me buried under the parmesan wheels. Most of my body is covered by cheese, but my unconscious face is visible *and* identifiable.

I hold out my phone. "See for yourself."

Carter squints at the picture. "Jesus. Those wheels are huge!"

"And heavy."

"Who makes cheese that large?"

I enlarge my unconscious face.

"Wow, that would've killed Gran!"

"Uh huh…"

Carter has the decency to duck his head in shame. "Sorry I doubted you and um…" he clears his throat. "Thank you for saving Gran's life."

I acknowledge his apology with a nod. "Can we get back to the house?" *And your indentured servitude.*

"Right, the house," Carter rubs the back of his neck, blinking away the image of me buried under all that cheese, "I guess I'll help you, but speaking as a former contractor… are you *crazy*?"

I stiffen. Hot jogger? More like hot asshole. "No, I'm perfectly sane. This is where I'll retire."

"Are you rich?"

"What?"

"Are you rich?"

"That's a very rude question."

"Why is everybody so touchy about money questions?" he

asks. "I just need an honest assessment of your financial situation so we can move forward, bearing in mind that you're getting my very expensive services for free because of... cheese."

I sniff. "Well, if you have to know... I do okay."

"Good, because you're going to have to be rich to restore this place." He glances around the Witch House like a man before Mt. Everest. He'll choose to walk away. I'm the madwoman they find dead at the summit. "Believe me, you don't want to go down this road."

"Ever heard of the road not — " Something white and furry materializes in my peripheral vision. "Milk!"

Carter frowns. "You want milk? Now? This is hardly the time for—"

"No! Milk is my hamster, remember? She got out of her cage, which is why I..." I gesture to the hole beneath the stairs. Sure enough, Milk scrambles over the hole, kicking her stubby legs, and darts across the living room. "Help me get her!"

Milk pokes her pink nose in the air and sniffs. She scurries along the baseboard, searching for treats. I tiptoe toward her, careful not to make a sound. "Come here, baby. Come to Mamma..."

With a twitch of her nose, she darts into the kitchen. "Get her before she runs under the stove!"

The kitchen has two entrances. "I'll go right, you go left. We'll cut her off."

He salutes me. "Yes, ma'am."

I roll my eyes.

Forming a tag team rescue squad, I approach Milk from one direction. Carter creeps from the other end.

I spot Milk sniffing at a slimy, unidentifiable substance by the range. Oh dear God. "Milk! Don't you dare eat that!"

I meet Carter's gaze. "Do it. Do it now," I mouth.

Milk sniffs the air, then turns her stout body toward Carter. Her whiskers twitch. A tiny pink tongue appears.

"Your fingers," I whisper. "The butter. She wants to lick your fingers."

"If that's the case, she should be drawn toward your hips."

Milk scuttles toward Carter, sniffs. "She likes fingers better. Give her what she wants."

"What if what she wants is to bite me?" Despite his reluctance, Carter opens up his hands anyway and Milk inches toward him. "Come on... Come on..."

Carter pounces and grabs Milk by the middle. "Gotcha!" He wraps my hamster up in the hem of his T-shirt, revealing a yummy swath of stomach.

"That was easy," he says, smiling down at me.

"Thank y — "

CRACK.

We flinch.

A piece of ceiling plaster falls onto floor behind Carter, splattering him with dingy flakes.

I bite my bottom lip. "That will probably need repair."

Carter hands Milk over to me and brushes plaster from his hair. "From one frugal FIRE follower to another," he says, "This house is a money pit. If you're smart, you'll tear it down."

chapter twelve

"Tear it down? Are you crazy?!" I can't believe what I'm hearing. The Witch House is history. It's a piece of art!

"Money pit." To demonstrate, Carter heads toward the kitchen sink, which has seen better days. "Does this work?"

"The water's turned on. I've let it run so there's no more rust."

As Carter washes his hands, I drop Milk off in her cage and level her with a warning stare. No cheese for her tonight.

I turn around, startled to find Carter behind me, drying his hands on a sheet of paper towel I brought with me that morning.

"Shall we?" He gestures to the dining room.

"You still want to do a house tour?"

"I'm giving *you* a house tour."

I arch an eyebrow. "It's my house."

"I was born in this town," he says. "I know this house better than you. I know enough to convince you to sell this place and get out while you can."

I scoff. "We'll see about that."

"After you." He leads me to the dining room and halts, scanning the peeling Victorian wallpaper. "Trash."

"Excuse me!"

"Don't get riled up." His tone is all business. "It's just a house."

"It's more than just a house. It's my home."

"And everybody thinks *I* live in a trash can," he mutters.

"I heard that!"

We're back in the living room. He bends down and eyeballs the hardwood floor. There's a slight incline in the corner. I just know he's going to call me out on that.

Carter looks up at me, his intense blue eyes stopping my heart for a beat. "Got a quarter?"

"I don't carry change."

He hesitates. "Wedding ring?"

"Not married."

Carter ducks his head. Am I imagining things? Did his lips just twitch?

"Here." I yank off a rose-gold signet ring I bought from an *extremely* persuasive Instagram ad and dropped it in his palm. "What are you going to do?"

Carter studies the ring under a shaft of daylight and rolls it across the floor. The ring travels down a slope and settles into a depression in the corner.

"Un-level foundation," he says, like a doctor diagnosing a terminal disease.

"Old houses settle unevenly. Gives it a kooky charm."

Carter grimaces at the word 'kooky.' I don't think he's ever heard the word in his life.

"In addition to the uneven floors," he says, "you have a crack along the northern most wall and a series of cracks here." He points to the opposite wall. "The hardwood is warped and buckled in some areas, and I have a strong suspicion of a slab leak." He shakes his head, his face grim.

"But it can all be fixed with some spackle, right?"

"You're going to need a lot more than spackle and prayers. The house is sinking."

"Oh no!" I gulp. "How do we… raise it back up?"

"It can be done, but it's going to cost."

"How much?"

He gives me an estimate. I stagger backward, stepping into a

71

shallow crater in my floor. "You're joking! Please tell me you're joking."

"You're going to have to sell more potato stickers," he says. "As I said: money pit."

I frown as he retrieves my ring. The word 'money pit' makes me want to hurl. I wish he would stop saying it.

Can I afford it? Vincent Van Sproot sales are killing it recently. I'll just have to amp up production and do a massive shop update. It'll be tight, but with a little elbow grease—okay, a lot of elbow grease—I can make it work. I *must* find an extra sixty-thousand via sticker sales.

Feeling more optimistic already, I dart forward. "Have you seen the pocket doors? See the detail? Expert craftsmanship."

Carter nods begrudgingly. He slides the doors out, it sticks. "Not enough meat on the bones to save. Money pit."

He leaves me for the stairs. I stick my tongue out at his back. I'm starting to believe 'money pit' is Carter's favorite motto.

The main staircase is steep and narrow, pockmarked every other step with a hole. We tread carefully, side-stepping land-mines, our footsteps creaking on old wood.

This is definitely where the strange noises I heard during my first night came from.

I point out the craftsmanship along the banister. Carter points out wood rot.

"Money pit," he mutters.

I roll my eyes. "What about the banister? These grapes leaves are a work of art. They don't make details like this anymore."

Carter gives the carvings a passing glance. "Too much going on for my taste."

"What *is* your taste?"

"Less, but better. I like modern architecture."

"Then what are you doing in Wethersfield? Every house here is at least two-hundred-years-old."

"I have fond memories of growing up here. Gran lives here, and she feeds me on occasion. Cheaper cost of living." He smiles over his shoulder. "Every house is old here, except my house."

"Ah yes. The trash can."

"I inherited my childhood home. The house looked like every colonial on the block until I tore it down."

My eyes widen. "You tore down a historical home?!" What kind of *monster* am I dealing with?

"It was built in the '80s."

"What about your childhood memories?"

"The memories are not in the thing." He taps his temple. "It's in here."

"What do your parents think?"

His eyes crinkles at the corner. "We had words," he says. "In the end, if they wanted to retain the house, they shouldn't have signed the deed over to me."

On the second floor, Carter nudges me away from a weak spot on the floor where water dribbles through an old roof leak. He says nothing, but I can read his thoughts. "Money pit."

Water damage is ten times worse in the master bedroom. We trace the expanded floorboards to a basketball sized hole in the ceiling. Standing under the hole, we tilt our heads up for a great view of the sky.

Carter frowns. I know what Mr. Doom and Gloom is going to say. So there's a giant hole in the ceiling? So what? The sky is blue and the clouds are especially fluffy today.

"I slept in this house on the first night," I say.

He gazes down at me with some surprise. "So you enjoy camping?"

"It was fun."

"Is that why you've permanently booked a room at Gran's?"

I leave him in the master bedroom. There are two bedrooms in similar states of disrepair. We haven't even peeked into the attic. Carter joins me in the hallway.

"I'm staying at Edith's because this place is haunted," I say.

He rolls his eyes. "Don't tell me you believe in ghosts."

"If you heard what I heard that night, you'd be a believer too."

"What did you hear?"

73

"Strange creaks and groans all night. *All night!*"

"Sinking foundation, water damage, expanding wood." Carter glances up at yet another rotting ceiling. "You might also have a nest of raccoons in the attic and God knows what's in the basement. It's a—"

"Money pit," I say, beating him to it. "The ghost said 'Boo.'"

Carter studies my face with a quizzical expression. "What are you? In preschool? No ghost say 'Boo'?"

"Then you admit there's a ghost?"

"I admit no such thing."

"I heard Eliza 'Boo' all night long."

"Eliza? Your ghost has a name now?"

"Widow Eliza Wolcott. The 'witch' this house is named after," I say. "The old lady who tripped on a chestnut."

Carter opens his mouth to say something when another piece of ceiling falls on the floor behind me, along with a rain of chestnuts from the tree outside. It must be a sign from Eliza, the chestnut ghost witch.

Carter picks up a chestnut and holds it up, bewildered.

"So what's the prognosis on the house, Doc?" I ask. "You can keep your opinions about my ghost to yourself."

"I don't think you're a true FIRE follower," he says, taking me by surprise.

"Wait a minute!" How dare he doubt my frugality! What do I have to do? Show him my credit card statement? Better yet, flex my outstanding FICO score?

"A true FIRE follower would never make such an unsound investment. If you're practical — "

"Trust me, I'm practical to a fault."

He narrows his eyes. "I doubt that."

"Sometimes you just have to stop and smell the roses and follow your dreams."

Carter arches an eyebrow. "Your dream is to live in a tear down?"

"My *dream* is to restore a beautiful historical home and live in

Wethersfield." I give an embarrassed shrug. "I did it because of *The Witch of Blackbird Pond*."

He blinks.

"It's my favorite book. I presume you've never—"

"I've read it," he says. "You can't grow up in this town without reading it." Carter raises a finger, then takes a moment to collect himself. "You moved here, bought a money pit sight unseen… because of a book?!"

I smile. "It's romantic, isn't it?"

He shakes his head in disbelief. "Nothing good ever comes of romantic ideas."

Sounds like something that should be carved on his tombstone. "So I guess your answer is No."

"No?" He tilts his head.

"You're not going to help me with the renovations."

With a hassled sigh, Carter rubs the back of his neck. "I'll help you."

My eyes widen. All this talk about money pits and bad investments, and he's still in. "Why?"

"You saved my Gran from… death by cheese. She told me I had to help. I don't think I have a say in the matter."

"The cheese debt," I whisper.

He nods. "The cheese debt."

My mood instantly brightens. I have a handyman-contractor-hot indentured servant! Thanks Edith! "I'm designing cheese stickers for the owner, ya know."

"How many stickers do you need to sell to pay for the uneven foundation?"

I stiffen. "I've got this."

His eyes crinkle at the corners. "I should have known when I heard the cheese story what kind of person I'm getting mixed up with."

I can't help smiling. "What kind of person is that?"

"A kooky one," he says, his blue gaze almost meeting mine before flickering away. We don't like eye contact around here.

"That doesn't sound like an insult," I say.

"It's not."

"It almost sounds like a compliment."

"It's not."

"Maybe you're not such a grump after all."

"Oh, I am," he says. "What did you do before you 'retired'?"

"Appeals and Grievances at a health insurance company."

"Good. You better believe I'll have grievances and I *will* be airing them."

"I'm sure you will."

With one last disapproving glance around the first floor, he says, "You sure I can't convince you to tear this place down?"

"Nope."

"Then it's your grave," he says with a shake of his head. "I'm only helping you dig it."

chapter thirteen

On my front porch, Carter glances down at his clipboard. He tears off a sheet of paper. "Your estimate."

"Thanks." I take the invoice reluctantly, fold it in half, and stuff it in my back pocket.

"You're not going to look at it?"

"I make a point never to deal with bad news on an empty stomach." I'd skipped breakfast today and my energy levels were depleted.

"I could use a coffee break myself." He tries to lean against one of the unstable porch columns, thinks better of it, and jams his hands in his pockets instead. "D-do you want coffee?"

This is where I assumed Carter would leave me, but he throws me a curveball.

"You want to have coffee?" I blink. "With me?"

"It's just a suggestion. You don't have... I mean, we don't have to," a shy, boyish shrug, "you know... together."

It was the shrug that sold me. "I can use some coffee. There's a place on Main St. that serves nitro cold brew. The Chilly Bean? Have you been there?"

Carter shakes his head. "Too expensive. Eight bucks for a medium black? Come on!"

"A Starbucks then?"

"I don't do Starbucks."

"The Heirloom Market serves coffee... and sandwiches." My stomach rumbles. Sandwiches sound like just the ticket.

Carter tucks his pencil behind his ear and smiles down at me. My heart spikes despite my sluggish state. He doesn't smile often, but he lights up a room when he does.

"I have a better idea."

"Where?" I ask.

"My place," he says, gazing carefully away.

"Your place, eh?" I follow him out to the driveway and check out his car: a black Tesla S-series in desperate need of a wash. "Wait. Is this a pick up?"

"A pick up?" He sounds genuinely confused as he opens the passenger side door for me. "I just want coffee that doesn't cost an arm and a leg."

"Eight dollars is hardly going to break the bank."

"Says a fake FIRE follower. A coffee a day adds up. If you invest eight dollars a day in a high yield savings account or broad index fund, in twenty years you'll have..."

Okay. I take my suspicions back. If Carter's trying to hit on me, he's chosen the least romantic way to do it.

Buckled in, I check out the soft leather seats as he goes on about compound interest. "If you're so into saving money, why do you have a Tesla then? Shouldn't you be driving a used Toyota or something?"

Carter looks aghast. "And pay more for repairs than the car is worth?" He shakes his head. "I save more with a Tesla. No gas bills. No smog check. I can charge at home. The supercharger rates are incredible if you charge during off-peak hours."

Makes sense. Is there nothing he can't skim a few dollars off of? "Mary Poppins is practically perfect in every way," I say. "You're perfectly practical in every way."

"It's the FIRE way," he says, pulling out the driveway. "I live three houses down."

I know. I checked out your place. "No way."

"We're neighbors."

"I can't believe I'm finally going to see the trash can."

"Funny."

"So tell me about this coffee," I say. "How good is it?"

He takes his eyes off the road and shoots me another one of those intense gazes. "Life-changing."

My knees turn into noodles. "Are you sure you're not a serial killer? I'm not going to find seven bodies buried in your basement?"

"Nonsense," Carter says, without missing a beat. "I doubt you'll find seven. I abhor clutter."

"Are you sure this is not a pick up?"

He chews on his inner cheek. "Would I be showing you my trash can if it were?"

chapter fourteen

"So this is what you transformed your childhood home into," I say as we pull inside his state-of-the-art garage.

"Do you like it?"

I shrug. I don't hate it. "How long did it take?"

"Two weeks." Carter laughs at my shock. "After we razed the foundation of the old house, plumbing and electrical took one week. Then it was just a matter of waiting for the house to arrive from Germany. Every piece comes prefabbed and fits like a jigsaw puzzle." He eyes my reaction. "If you change your mind, we can have you moved in to a brand spanking new house before Halloween."

"No. Are you crazy? I love the Witch House."

"So you keep saying." He shakes his head. "It's easier to build from scratch than restore something old."

"So *you* keep telling me."

He leads me in through the kitchen and before I knew it, I've infiltrated the 'trash can.'

The interior couldn't be larger than 750 square feet and looks like a photo spread from Architectural Digest. I gawk at the sparse furnishings and minimal decor.

The house is tidy and clean, light and airy. Golden sunlight bathes the warm cedar floors. Floor-to-ceiling windows opens to a thicket of trees, half their leaves turning rich autumn colors, and a blue slice of Wethersfield Cove.

A rowing machine.

A standing desk tucked in the corner. Instead of a sofa, Carter has a custom built-in window seat that could fit two people. No throw pillows. No decoration that I could see. A short flight of steps leads up to a loft. From my vantage point, I can see a full-size futon, no box spring or headboard.

"Where do you keep all your stuff?"

He shows me cleverly designed storage built into the walls and an impressively deep area for a washer and dryer beneath the stairs. Overall, Carter just doesn't have much stuff.

"You're a minimalist?" I comment.

"I don't like clutter."

I nod at his stainless steel refrigerator. "No magnets?"

"Why would I need magnets?"

"As souvenirs from your travels."

He grimaces at the mention of souvenirs. "I take pictures."

"Do you ever print out your pictures?"

"No. I'm not a good photographer."

"I can give you some stickers," I offer as a joke. "Vincent Van Sproot originals."

He wrinkles his nose. "I'll pass."

"Not even one sticker?"

"Only if you take a picture of the sticker."

"Don't you worry about digital clutter?"

Carter thinks for a moment. "I have tons of server storage space."

"Noted." I circle the living room. How can a house that seems so cold on the outside and is *actually* bare on the inside feel so cozy? Could it be the large windows which makes you feel like you're surrounded by nature? Or the warm gleam of wood (real cedar, not a laminate) that radiates peace and light. See? This is why I appreciate wood.

"What are you thinking about?" Carter asks, leaning against

his kitchen counter. His hands are tucked under his armpits. His eyes track my every move.

It startles me to find myself under such blatant scrutiny. "The trash can... sorry, your house reminds me of Hannah Tupper's cottage on the edge of Blackbird Pond. Hannah is the old Quaker woman in the book whom the townsfolk believe is a witch."

He nods. "I remember. So I'm the town outcast?"

"In a way."

He snorts. "Do they gossip about me at the cheese shop?"

"Sometimes."

"All good things I hope?"

"Your grandma thinks your life choices are odd." A thirty-four-year-old single retiree who lives in an ultra modern home and never participates in any community events... tongues will wag, but all in good faith. "I think Edith wishes to understand you better."

"Understand why I live in the 'trash can' you mean."

I shrug. "Your words, not mine."

"The 'trash can' is built with fire-resistant materials in case a mob decides to burn it down like Hannah's cabin." His eyes glimmer with amusement. "Any more gossip from Gran and her hens you want to share?"

I whirl around and stroll to the window. "They talk about how handsome you are," I say, glancing over my shoulder.

Carter straightens. "Do they now?"

"And what a shame it is that you're a hermit." I smile at his teasing tone.

Is he flirting with me? Am *I* flirting with *him*? I sense a mutual attraction stirring in the air.

"I'm not a hermit, but I *do* like my alone time."

I look at the front door. "Should I leave?"

"I don't want to be alone all the time."

Oh my god. I chew on my bottom lip. He *is* flirting with me. "The trash can is gorgeous," I change the subject, "Every West Coast tech bro would kill to live here."

82

"Yet land is cheaper here," he says with a hint of smugness. "I'm getting more bang for my buck."

"You like a good deal," I observe.

"Nothing gets me more excited than saving money."

I gesture to my sparse surroundings. "Obviously furniture doesn't excite you."

"Again," Carter pokes his chest, "minimalist."

"No dining table."

He does a palms up. "No entertaining."

"Not a social creature?"

"I'm an introvert."

"Me too," I say, wandering to the blank wall before the couch. "No TV?"

"I have a projector when I need it," he says, pointing to the opposite wall. "I don't watch much TV. I like to read."

"What's your favorite book?"

"*Think and Grow Rich* by Napoleon Hill."

Oh dear. "I haven't read that one," I say.

"It's no *Witch of Blackbird Pond*. Tell me, what is it about this book that obsesses you so?"

"Where do I begin? Are you ready to block out the afternoon?"

"I have time," Carter says.

I turn around so he can't see my face. I can talk about *The Witch of Blackbird Pond* until the cows come home, but I find myself strangely tongue tied around Carter. He actually listens to my every word, waiting at every opportunity to catch me off guard.

Carter's brows furrow in concern. "What's wrong?"

"What do you mean?"

"Your face is red."

"No, it's not." I clear my throat. "Look, I don't want to talk about the book now."

"Why not?" The ever-attentive tilt to his head makes me feel like I'm on stage.

"I don't know you well enough yet."

"Gran says the book is all you talk about."

"It's different with her."

"Why is it different with me?"

I shrug. His hotness scares me. His resemblance to Nat Eaton scrambles my already scattered thoughts and decimates my composure. I'm most comfortable around him when we're chatting about nothing. He can make fun of sproots and cheese wheels and my witch house all he wants. But *The Witch of Blackbird Pond* is my whole heart, and I'm not ready to have him make fun of that.

"That exciting of a book, huh?" Carter fills a kettle with water and sets it on his high-end electric stove. "Maybe I should reread it and see what all the fuss is about."

The image of Carter reading my favorite book sends an unexpected shiver through my body. Would he really read it again? Is he just amusing me?

I peer out the window. "You have a second unit," I say, suddenly curious about the cube structure, identical in design to the main house but about half the size. A mini trash can. "Is that a guest house?"

"No. I don't have guests. It's where I keep my model trains."

"Model trains?" I blink. I wasn't expecting that. "Can I see them?"

Carter regards me with a weary notch between his brows. "You're the first person who has ever asked to see them."

"Why? What do other people say?"

"They never say anything mean, but I get a general feeling of disapproval."

"Much like how you reacted to my sticker business."

"Touché."

"So can I see them? Your trains? Do you have a tunnel? Mountains? Tiny trees?" Gasping, I clasp a hand over my mouth. "A tiny village?"

"I might."

"How cute!"

84

"Cute?" Carter says, affronted. "There's nothing cute about trains. They're manly things."

"Do you have a bridge?"

He presses his lips together. "A covered bridge."

"Adorable."

"No, no. Not adorable. Nothing adorable about bridges."

"So when can I see them?" I ask, deriving joy from making him grumble.

Carter hesitates. "I don't know you well enough yet," he says without a hint of mockery.

"Touché."

I guess some things you don't share yet.

"So coffee," I suggest, steering us to neutral ground.

"Coffee!" Remembering the kettle of hot water he set to boil, Carter pops open his pantry.

I turn around with a relieved smile, expecting to find him deftly working a high-tech espresso machine. Carter has two gray stoneware mugs on the counter and is spooning instant coffee into one of them.

Instant coffee? So this is the delicious cup of coffee he promised?

"Do you take cream?" Carter asks, rummaging in his cupboard.

It takes me a while before I can find my voice. "Uh huh."

I join him in the kitchen to wash my hands. The small space necessitates we sidestep each other. He shoots me a shy smile as our shoulders bump.

"I took you for a 'plenty of cream and sugar' girl," he says, and I watch in horror as he opens his very expensive stainless steel fridge and takes out a container of creamer.

I clear my throat. "Is that Coffee Mate?"

"I would *never* buy Coffee Mate. Store brand does the job *and* its twenty cents cheaper."

"You sure you don't want to grab some coffee in town?" I gulp. "I'll pay."

He looks at me as if I've lost my mind. "Why buy coffee when you can make it at home? Here, try..."

I take the cup from him and take a sip. I swish it around in my mouth, wishing I could spit it out.

"Tastes just like Starbucks, right?" Carter asks.

I force myself to swallow. This tastes nothing like Starbucks. Maybe it's my own LA coffee snobbery speaking, but this doesn't even taste like bad diner coffee. It's what bad diner coffee *wants* to be.

"Are you hungry?" Carter asks, pleased by my answer. "I can mic up some Healthy Choice steamers. I have Penne alla Vodka and Chicken Alfredo. If you're into sandwiches, I just bought some bologna."

Oh dear Lord. He's trying to feed me.

"You know," I say, setting down my mug. "They have great sandwiches in town. Pizza, too."

He waves off my suggestion. "I never eat out if I can help it. Do you know, Theo, how much money you can save if you cook at home?"

I blink. "Never eat out...*ever?*"

"Never ever."

"Not even at McDonald's?"

Carter thinks about this. "You've got me," he says, holding his arms wide. "Sometimes I treat myself to a cheeseburger off the Dollar menu, but only for special occasions."

I turn around so he can't see my expression. So far I've been trying to understand why a gorgeous modern day Nat Eaton doppelgänger — tidy, funny, well invested, well read, and with great taste in architecture—is still single. Or why his own grandmother talks about him like he's a lost cause.

Now I know why. It's not because he's introverted or grumpy or would rather tinker with model trains than socialize.

Carter Bromley would make one hell of a catch if not for one small problem...

chapter fifteen

"He's cheap."
        Three shocked faces stare back at me from my laptop screen.

Sadie rubs her upper lip, taking off a good portion of her green tea clay mask. Her curly hair, a luxurious combination of auburn and cinnamon, is gathered in a massive topknot. Her ZOOM background is an interactive coral reef with schools of tropical fish.

My background, by the way, is a lush New England autumn scene. There's a cozy cabin with smoke curling from the brick chimney and a jewel toned carpet of crunchy leaves. Our group loves to personalize *everything*.

"When you say cheap," Sadie begins, "you don't mean..."

"Cheap."

"How cheap is cheap?"

I tell them of our casual coffee break, including the tidbit about how I offered to pay for the both of us. "He said he'll make better coffee at his house."

Camille chokes on her tea. "Whoa. Whoa. Whoa! You went to his *house*? This guy you just met?"

"Yeah, but he was at my house first. I figure if he hasn't killed me yet—"

"He'll kill you in time," Camille says. Her background is her

87

bookshelf in her Austin studio apartment, and by the looks of the haphazard stacks of Urban Fantasy paperbacks, she desperately needs to tidy up.

"I'm friends with his grandma," I say. "She'll be pretty disappointed if he kills me."

Moving on, I tell them of his 'trash can' house: "… a modern tiny house."

And the actual coffee Carter offered me: "Instant."

A collective groan.

Lena sets down her half-finished macrame plant holder and cleans her glasses on her T-shirt. Her background has changed from 'hanging pothos' to a jungle scene with vines and wild orchids. "When you say 'instant,' you mean 'Folgers'?"

I lower my head. "Store brand. It's twenty cents cheaper. And he treated me to… " The words stick to the roof of my mouth. "Penne alla Vodka for lunch."

"That doesn't sound so bad," Lena says.

"It's from a Healthy Choice microwaveable steamer."

Groan.

"What did he have?" Sadie asks.

"I wasn't very hungry, so we…" I swallowed, thinking of the meal that will live in infamy, "… shared one."

Camille buries her face in her hands. "Oh my god." Once everyone has collected themselves, she yanks the towel from her damp hair. "And he really looks like Nat Eaton?"

"Sandy sun-bleached blond hair, tall and slim, with mocking blue eyes and nimble hands." I sigh. "And a six pack."

"Wait, I read the book too," Camille says, "I don't recall Nat Eaton sporting a six pack."

"He totally had a six pack."

"How's a sailor from 1687 going to acquire a six pack? Unless there's a gym on his ship."

"He does crunches during the trip up the river. A few reps on the bow. Push ups on the rigging."

Lena and Sadie are in hysterics.

"What does he listen to when he works out?" Lena asks.

"Songs of the sea, of course!" I say.

I hold up a finger and flip through my battered copy of *The Witch of Blackbird Pond*. "See here? Page 114. Wood chopping scene. Kit stumbles upon Nat chopping firewood, his 'wiry tanned body bared to the waist.'" I arch an eyebrow in challenge. "What does that tell you?"

"I don't see a six pack," Camille says. "Show me the six pack."

"It's implied. You have to read between the lines. But Carter? He not only has a six pack, he has an *eight* pack..."

Lena pats her stomach. "Maybe I should switch to Healthy Choice too?"

"Did he show you his eight pack while wooing you with bad coffee and microwavable lunches?" Camille asks.

"No, I saw him jogging shirtless before I met him, though when he reached for the mugs, his T-shirt rode up and I caught a slice of stomach." I flopped back on my bed with a dreamy sigh.

Sadie, who knows a thing or two about fictional crushes (her bae of choice is Jamie Fraser from *Outlander*) joins me in sighing. "Your dream man!"

"And he's rich?" Camille blurts out.

"Well invested." I jolt back up. "Not that I want a sugar daddy."

"We know," Camille says.

All of them know I don't care about material things. My purse is from Target. The only pair of designer shoes I own are Nike runners. After the thrift store, Old Navy is my second favorite place to shop. I have a basic Banana Republic suit (thrifted) for meetings only, which I later sold online for a decent profit now that I won't be attending office meetings anymore.

"I don't care if he's rich, but I *do* want him to have a sense of adventure, even if it's something as mundane as going out for coffee. I mean, come on! I offered to pay!"

"Does he have any hobbies?" Lena asks. "How's his house plant situation?"

"He has a fern," I say. "And I think... a ficus."

"How are they doing?"

I haven't given a thought to the condition of Carter's house plants. "Thriving, I suppose. Plenty of natural sunlight. He watered them while I was there."

Lena, whose apartment is overrun by plants, straightens up. "Marry him."

"Come on…"

"If you won't marry him, I will."

"I worry about you, Lena. You can't impulsively marry the first man you see."

"Sure you can," she says. "If he's Mr. Right everything will take care of itself."

"I foresee multiple divorces in your future."

Lena shrugs. "Or a ride off into the sunset and a happily ever after."

"I barely know Carter," I say, thinking of the man-shed in his backyard. "He won't even give me a tour of his second unit."

I describe the back house, a smaller version of the trash can. The three of them lean in, mouths agape.

"Maybe he's hiding something in there he doesn't want you to find?" Sadie asks.

Camille's eyes sparkle with morbid curiosity. "Bodies?"

"Shade plants?" Lena offers.

"Model trains." I say.

They blink at me like they hadn't heard me right.

"I can only imagine miniature mountain passes and villages," I say, "tunnels and bridges and those cute little trees. He has a whole set up."

"An entire man cave dedicated to model trains?" Camille shakes her head. "Uh oh."

"He likes to tinker. I get the impression he tinkers a lot." I purse my lips, considering the path I want to take. Do I like him? *Should* I like him? "Do I want to be with a guy who tinkers? Is he dateable?"

"Model trains are expensive," Camille strokes her chin, "and he serves you instant coffee… Seems like he'll spend all his money on his hobbies and give you the leftovers." She snaps her fingers. "Un-date-able."

"But he looks so much like Nat Eaton!" Sadie, my hopeless romantic ally, lists on her fingers. "He takes care of his grandma, rescued you from the hole in the wall, helped you catch your hamster. And lest we forget the eight pack abs?"

"And he takes care of his plants," Lena adds. "Marry him."

I laugh. "Slow down, Lena. I think we're all reading too much into things. Who's to say he's even into me?"

"She's got a point," Camille says. "He offered her half a Healthy Choice steamer. That doesn't exactly scream 'wooing.'"

I wrinkle my nose. Camille has a good point. If I were a guy and I was trying to hit on someone, I would wine and dine them at the fanciest restaurant. We're talking restaurants with four dollar signs and dessert. I certainly won't treat them to half a Penne alla Vodka unless I was actively trying to make myself undesirable.

"I don't know about this guy," says Camille.

"He's sending all kinds of mixed signals." I hug my pillow to my chest. "Okay, I've made up my mind. He's un-date-able."

"Seems to me you're pretty picky, Theo," Sadie says.

I stiffen. "What's that supposed to mean?"

"I know your dating history. Whatever happened to the hot claims adjuster? Andy, Andre — "

"Anthony?"

"You went out with him for what? Three dates tops. He takes you to Maestros and you drop him like a hot potato."

I purse my lips. "He's completely un-date-able."

"Why?" Lena grills me.

I share a glance with Camille. "Theo has an issue with his personal grooming," she says.

I hold up my right hand. "He has an excessively long pinky nail."

Lena and Sadie narrow their eyes.

"He clips all his nails, but grows out the pinky nail like a raptor claw. It scratched my arm!"

"Okay, fine," Sadie says. "That's kind of gross. But what about the orthodontist?"

"Paul?"

"You seemed to like him and then BAM... dumped. What happened at Disneyland, Theo?"

I chew my bottom lip. Okay. Paul snuck a fast one on me. He wore a dress shirt and tie to our first date at the Cheesecake Factory, and I was impressed. But then, one Saturday in late April, he surprises me with tickets to Disneyland and...

"He wore a Ralph Lauren polo shirt," I began.

"So?"

"It was a *huge* polo player. The logo took up half the shirt." I shake my head, shuddering from the memory. "What's he trying to prove here?"

Lena giggles. "So he makes one wardrobe mistake."

I lower my voice. "He has a closet full of giant logo polos."

"What did Carter wear?" Camille asks.

"Solid blue T-shirt and jeans."

"What's the state of his fingernails?" Sadie asks.

"Clipped to the bed."

"Did you look at his feet?" Lena asks.

A guy's feet are a deal breaker for me. Nothing grosses me out more than a dry heel and long yellow toe nails on anyone, but *especially* on a potential boyfriend. "He never removed his shoes."

Sadie holds her palms up. "Then you need to check out his feet before you mark him as un-date-able."

"You think so?"

"A real life Nat Eaton? Your almost-perfect man?" Sadie nods. "I think he deserves a re-consideration."

"How do you know Nat Eaton has nice feet?" Camille interrupts. "He's a 17th century sailor. I don't know what kind of socks he wears — if he wears socks at all — and don't get me started on the ventilation of sailor shoes..."

"He's Nat Eaton," I say, scandalized. "Of course he has perfect feet. He has perfect everything."

"Theo, you're dreaming!"

For the next half hour, we argue about the condition of Nat Eaton's feet: what his heel situation's like, how often he clips his toenails, what kind of tools he would use to clip his nails. And realistically, it's not looking good for Nat.

"… I'm thinking everyone in *The Witch of Blackbird Pond* must have funky feet," Lena says. "When will you have time for self care?"

"Carter has every opportunity to get weekly mani pedis," I say.

"But is he too cheap to get them?" Camille rains on my parade. "I think you know the answer."

I open up a carton of cookies n' cream ice cream and shove a big spoonful in my mouth. "Ladies, my mission is clear: I need to get him to take off his shoes."

chapter sixteen

Edith and Rachel were waiting for me by the homemade jam section before our Wednesday night smutty book club meeting. Their heads were joined in hush whispers.

"Evening, ladies. What's the gossip?"

"Evening," they said, jumping apart.

They seem dazed. I don't blame them. I was up *all night* with our book club selection and I've got one hell of a massive book hangover.

"How about those ice planet barbarians, huh? I don't know about you but I was shook. We have *a lot* to talk about, but I'll wait until the others get here. I'm itching to discuss the…" I lower my voice. "The barbarian's *spur,* if you know what I mean."

"Ah yes, the cock spur," Edith says. "That's my favorite part."

"Edith!" Gathering her embroidered cardigan together, Rachel darts a fretful glance at the entrance.

"Oh, don't be such a prude," Edith says. "Didn't your husband have a penis piercing in the '80's? Don't act like this is your first rodeo."

Rachel's face turns white.

"That's my cue to get to work." I grab a jar of locally made apricot preserves from the shelf, shaking the picture of Rachel's husband's piercing from my mind. I've seen the man, a kindly silver fox with a fondness for cable knit sweaters and Dockers. You can never tell with some people...

I volunteered to come early to help style a cheese spread for the bookclub meeting. "I'm thinking Manchego and Camembert for the board, Rachel. What do you think about adding Stilton? Mrs. Thornberry is pretty picky. Do you think she'll object to Stilton?"

"Up to you," Rachel says, leveling Edith with a warning death stare. "You know your cheese."

"She's been known to eat more than her share, and the other ladies never get enough. I think I'll add some goat cheese. She doesn't care for goat—" I whirl around to find Edith peering up at me with an expectant smile on her crinkled face. "Edith, dear. You're in my way."

My eyes shift to Rachel, who smiles at me with the same eager expression. I step back. "Is something going on?"

The hamster wheel in my mind turns, landing on the worst-case scenario. I gasp. "Am I fired from snack duty? It's because I ate all that smoked gouda the other day, isn't it?"

"No, no." Rachel touches my shoulder. "Whatever gave you that idea? You can eat all the cheese your heart desires."

My shoulders slump. "That's a relief."

Edith takes my hand. "Theo."

I frown. "Edith?"

"Is there something you want to tell me?"

"Um... no. Is there something *you* want to tell *me*?" I walk her to the nearest chair and crouch down until we're at face level. "Are you okay, Edith? How's your heart? Was the book too much for you? We don't have to continue with the Ice Planet Barbarian series next time. We can read something milder. I've heard good things about the new Debbie Macomber. It's a seaside Christmas story with pen pals."

She waves off my assistance. "Bah. I'm fine. I'm *fine*."

"Then why...?" I glance between the two women. Why does it feel like I'm in the middle of a set up?

"You met Carter?" Edith asks.

"I did," I reply cautiously.

"How did the walk-through go?"

"Fine."

"And?" Edith grasps me by the shoulder and peers into my eyes. "What happened?"

"He doesn't think the Witch House could be saved, but he's agreed to help me renovate."

"Yes, yes. I know that bit already."

"Then what — "

"What do you think of him?"

I shrug. "He's nice," I say, recalling his 'money pit' mantra. "Sometimes."

"And handsome?" Edith's face brightens with hope. "Don't you think my grandson is a ten?"

He's an eleven.

I turn my head away to hide my blush. "I think that goes without saying."

"So what happened?" Edith says. "I want to know everything."

"Edith!" Rachel chides. "Leave the poor girl alone. You're being pushy."

"I'm not pushy."

"They just met and you're practically counting your grand-children."

"Oh hush!" Edith rolls her eyes. "I just want to know the juicy details."

"Wait…" I glance from one woman to the other. "What's going on here? Are you trying to set me up with Carter?"

"Honey," Edith cups my hands in her wrinkled ones, "I don't know what happened this weekend, but you've made *quite* an impression on Carter."

"I have?" My heart leaps to my throat. I stagger backward. Rachel pushes a chair behind me. I plop down on it, winded. "Did he say something?"

"It isn't so much what he said as how he said it."

Rachel rubs her temples. "You have to be more specific than that, Edith. She's not a mind reader."

Edith leans forward while Rachel and I hang onto her every word. "He told me he's thinking of showing you his model trains."

I blink. "Yeah, I asked to see his collection. He refused to show me."

"But now he's considering..." Edith gives me a meaningful nod. "Seriously considering."

"Okay... well, I'll love to see them."

Edith turns to Rachel and *they* share a meaningful look. "You would?" Edith asks, perplexed.

"Well, yeah. I enjoy trains. I don't own any myself. Never had the space. One time my parents and I went to an estate sale where this guy has a garage full of them: stations, mountain passes, a ski lift, even a mini conductor. Is that what Carter's collection looks like?"

Edith beams like she'd won the billion dollar lottery.

"Edith, you're creeping me out. Can someone tell me what's going on here?"

"Carter is very precious about his trains. He never lets anyone into his station except for these strange train enthusiasts he met online. Definitely no girls." She clears his throat. "Well, one woman from the club, but she came with her wife. Left the wife outside."

Carter is part of a model train club?!

"What about you?" I ask. "Have you been inside?"

"Once," Edith grumbles. "I'm banned for life."

My eyes widen. "You? But you're his grandmother!"

"Yes, yes. I moved one of his precious trees and he freaked out on me." Edith shakes her head. "Anyway, the fact that he's willing to consider letting you into his precious man shed, and you not even being a train enthusiast, means he likes you. When's the wedding?"

"*Wedding?!*" I stand up.

"Look what you've done!" Rachel steps in. "You've terrified

the poor girl. Don't mind her. She doesn't know what she's saying. She doesn't know the meaning of subtlety."

"Yes, I do. I just choose not to be subtle. Honey, when you're my age, you can't beat around the bush. Do you like Carter?"

I pace back and forth, chewing my thumbnail. "I just met him."

"That doesn't matter," she waves me off. "I met my first husband a week before I married him. My second husband? Met him three days before we eloped. Between you and me, they were both *great* in the sack."

"Edith!" Rachel's eyes widen, scandalized.

"Aw, don't act like you haven't heard that story before."

The flush in my cheeks travels to my hairline. Rachel notices my discomfort and offers me a glass of water.

"Edith," I begin. "Carter is very nice and cute… I don't mind being friends."

"Friends?!"

"Stop it, Edith," Rachel shakes her head. "Young people like to weigh their options. They don't jump into marriages like your generation."

I mouth 'thank you' to Rachel. She's hit the nail on the head.

"Options?" Edith grumbles. "Kids these days have too many options if you ask me. Don't you want to jump his bones?"

"Edith!" Rachel says.

"I'm not suggesting marriage," Edith says, defending herself. "I'm with the times. They can still have children *without* tying the knot. Now tell me, Theo," she cups my hands, "why aren't you head over heels in love with Carter yet?"

I will never get over Edith's bluntness.

"Well…" How do I break this to her? I'm saving myself for Nat Eaton. Carter is a good runner up, but he isn't my dream man. "I suggested we get coffee and he…" I scratch my nose. "He insisted on brewing a homemade cup."

Edith pinches the spot between her eyes. "The instant coffee?"

I nod. "Instant coffee."

Rachel shakes her head. Something tells me Carter's cheapness isn't news.

"And he treated me to a frozen meal for lunch," I say.

Edith grimaces. "What kind of meal?"

"A Healthy Choice steamer. Penne alla Vodka."

"Oh no." Rachel clasps a hand over her mouth.

"Well…" Edith begins feebly. "That's a good sign. Those are his *best* TV dinners. He usually saves the Penne alla Vodka for himself. If he hadn't fallen madly in love with you, he would have served Hungry Man. So does that earn him points in your book?"

I shake my head. "Ehh…"

Edith sighs. "Suppose he got better coffee?"

"We'll see," I say. "Food is important in my culture. I need to be with someone who appreciates good food."

Edith's face is the picture of disappointment. "Well, that's not Carter… He has no taste buds and the only thing that wets his whistle is money and model trains." With a dramatic sigh, she slams a fist on the counter, disrupting the cheese board. "That damn kid and his damn coffee! I'm never going to have great-grandchildren now."

Rachel and I jump back. Who knew Edith had it in her! I right the jam spoons and straighten the crackers. "I know I'm picky. I didn't use to be, but I'm thirty-two years old."

What can I say? I was at my most open-minded in my early twenties, but after a string of bad dates (the long pinky nail guy and the big Polo logo guy were just the tips of the iceberg) and disappointments, I can't afford to wear my heart on my sleeve again. My biological clock is ticking. I don't want to waste my time or lead anyone on when I know it's not going anywhere. I'm financially independent and I'm not desperate to get married. What I want is a beautiful romance, preferably with the perfect man. And by perfect man, I mean Nat Eaton.

Except he doesn't exist.

"I'm not writing Carter off yet," I say. "I need to think things through."

A hopeful light returns to Edith's eyes. "What can I do to help you?"

I chew my inner cheek. "Have you seen his feet?"

Edith blinks. "Not since he was ten."

"He never wears flip flops at the beach? By the Cove?"

"He never goes to the beach."

"This may sound like a strange request," I begin.

"Honey, at my age, no request is too strange…"

I take a deep breath. "Can you help me get his shoes off?"

chapter seventeen

Carter is waiting for me at my front door. It's 6 am on Saturday and of course, I'm not at the Witch House to let him in. I'm still rooming at Edith's and overslept my alarm.

I can see Carter scowling all the way down the block.

"Sorry, sorry!" I run down the sidewalk, balancing a carrier of coffee in one hand, my hair still wet from a shower.

"You're late," he says as I run up the rickety front porch. He's wearing a faded navy blue T-shirt, a well-worn pair of jeans, and construction boots.

"I know! I know! There was a rush at the cafe and their latte machine wasn't working. The barista had to hand blend." I jostle my bundle. Hot coffee scorches my thumb. "Ow!"

Carter grabs the caddy before I drop the coffee.

"Here's your cup. Americano. Black. Cream and sugar on the side. I figured you for a black coffee kind of guy, but if you don't like it, we can swap and you can have my pumpkin spice latte. Oh, I got you breakfast." I fish into my tote bag and hand him a paper bag. "It's a chocolate croissant. Crushed but edible."

"I already had coffee," Carter says.

I roll my eyes. "Instant coffee, again?"

He nods.

"Then you've never really had coffee. Try it."

"You don't need to buy me coffee."

"Just drink it."

Carter reluctantly brings the cup to his mouth and blows on it. Steam curls over the rim. His blue eyes pierce mine. My stomach flip flops as I recall Edith's ridiculous theory of Carter having a crush on me. Is that why he's making eye contact over coffee? What's going on here? Is his stare a seductive message or is he just staring off into the middle distance?

I break eye contact and take a big gulp of my pumpkin spice latte. I choke as the coffee scalds the roof of my mouth.

"You okay?" Carter pats me on the back.

"I forgot to blow." I make the mistake of glancing up to find those blue eyes laughing down at me.

"Here, bite into this." He holds the croissant to my mouth and I take a bite.

Oh my god. Chocolate croissants tastes so much better when fed to you by a hottie in tight jeans. A smudge of chocolate melts on his thumb and I nearly choke again as I watch him lick it off.

Is that a sign?

A sign for what? An invitation to nibble?

Now Edith has me second-guessing myself and reading too much into things. Then again, Carter could have used a napkin instead of licking his thumb.

This is crazy.

I *am* reading too much into things.

If there's one thing I learned from *The Witch of Blackbird Pond*, it's that love doesn't happen instantly. Love is a work-in-progress, taking place over many chance encounters in the Great Meadows (and once in the stocks). For love to blossom, it takes time and effort, compassion and understanding. Love takes at least a year.

I don't believe in insta-love. I believe in friendship.

Even if the guy *does* have an eight pack.

While I try to get a grip on myself, I catch Carter sneaking a second sip of coffee.

"Better than the tar you drink, isn't it?" I ask.

Carter swishes the coffee in his mouth as he contemplates the difference between gourmet beans and store brand instant.

He swallows. "You paid too much."

My jaw drops. "You're lying. You love it."

"It's overrated," he says, taking another sip.

"Then why are you having seconds?"

"I don't like waste." His eyes twinkle with merriment. "In that spirit, I'm taking the croissant to the roof."

I'm calm on the outside, freaking out on the inside. Did he re-read the book already? How else would he know my all-time favorite scene? I call it the 'rooftop scene' when Kit helps Nat thatch up Hannah Tupper's roof. After the work is done, they bask in the sun and bond over their shared love of books. Kit saw a side of Nat Eaton that day, a dignity she never gave him credit for.

"The roof?" I ask. "Is that what we're working on today?"

"It's what *I'm* working on." Carter nods at the eaves, oblivious to my excitement. "We'll never beat the mold if we don't patch up the leaks. You'll thank me later when it rains."

"Okay. I have some work gloves stashed in the kitchen. I'll join you."

Carter rips his gaze from the roof. "No."

"No?"

"It's too dangerous up there. You'll fall through or fall off. Can't chance it."

"How clumsy do you think I am?"

He narrows his eyes. I can read his mind. He's remembering how he first found me.

"That was the first time I've ever been stuck in a wall!"

"That's one time too many."

I prop my hand on my hip. "I know what I'm doing," I say haughtily.

He tips his head to the side, scrutinizing me until my cheeks turn red. "If you did, you wouldn't have bought this house in the first place. No. My word's final."

I cross my arms across my chest. "I only want to help."

"And I appreciate that. I just don't want you to help me into an early grave."

Well!

"What should I do instead?"

"Grab a mop, a respirator, and bleach," he says. "Clean up the mold."

Edith was wrong. If Carter has a crush on me, he sure has a funny way of showing it.

Having given his command, Carter finishes the croissant and turns to the locked front door. He shoots me an expectant glance, waiting for me to let him in.

I eye his boots.

Here's my cue:

I point to my new Welcome Mat. It's the cutest thing. There's a collection of forest mushrooms and it says, 'Come on in! There's mush*room* in here.'

"You'll have to take off your shoes," I say.

"Take off my shoes?!"

"In my culture, we take our shoes off before entering someone's house."

Carter shakes his head, incredulous. "I'm about to work on your roof. You want me to do it without shoes?"

He's got me there. "I just um… mopped the floors. So if you can take your shoes off before stepping into the living room, then feel free to slip them on in the dining room."

I just need a sneak peek at the feet. Again, this is not a foot fetish. I'm just… curious.

Carter frowns. "You're comfortable walking across a living room with water damaged flooring?"

Damn. Why does he have to be so observant?

With my head held high, I open the door, pausing to check over my shoulder. I take a final glance at his boots, laced tight and firmly on his feet.

Until next time…

chapter eighteen

B y noon, all suspicions that Carter might be into me vanished with the last bit of wall mold.

I've got fans working full blast in one corner of the master bedroom. My hair is tied up in a messy bun and my hands are encased in rubber gloves. I'm breathing like Darth Vader through my respirator mask, my eyes stinging from bleach fumes.

I can hear Carter ripping up rotten shingles and hammering a temporary replacement. He joins me fifteen minutes later, navy T-shirt plastered to his chest. His jeans are filthy, his tanned forearms covered in grim. He's dirty. And hot.

Very, very hot.

My breathing is shallow for a different reason.

With a curt nod at me, he heads into the kitchen to wash up. I join him after he's dried his hands. Lurking in the doorway, I watch him stand in front of the open fridge, guzzling a bottle of cool water. Droplets splash his already sweat-drenched T-shirt and yes… okay. That T-shirt is looking pretty wet. Maybe he should take it off.

Carter turns just as I'm licking my lips. "Water?" He holds out a second bottle. "You look thirsty."

If he only knew how thirsty I really am.

"I need fresh air."

"Good idea. The bleach is making me dizzy too."

Carter follows me out to the porch just in time to meet the FedEx guy coming up the steps.

"Theodora Dy?" FedEx guy scans my package.

"That's me."

He hands me a cube-shaped Styrofoam box. "Sign here," he says, passing me the scanner. "Whew. I'm glad to get that thing out of my truck."

Carter sniffs the air and eyes the package dubiously. "Is it me or does this package smell like..." he sniffs again. "Onions?"

"It's not just you, buddy," FedEx says. "Have a nice day!"

I cart the package to the porch. One glance at the return address on the shipping label and I know what's inside.

"It's from my parents."

"What is it?" Carter asks, sitting on the step beside me.

"Do you have a knife?"

Carter pulls a Swiss army knife from his back pocket and slices the packing tape.

I pop off the lid and we peer down at the temperature-controlled contents. *Two* spiky, soccer ball sized green fruit. A sudden blast of homesickness hits me. Sometimes my parents can be so sweet.

"What is it?" Carter cautiously picks up one of the spiky fruit. He sniffs it, grimaces. "It smells awful."

"Durian," I say. "It tastes better than it smells."

"It looks like a Medieval mace."

"You can definitely use it as a weapon," I say. "You won't like it."

"Why wouldn't I?"

"From my experience, every white friend I've ever had hates durian. The smell repels them. Most of them won't even try it, and the brave ones who attempt a taste test only nibble the teeniest tiniest bite before freaking out. They guzzle a gallon of water. Fake vomit. It's a whole show. Come to think of it, most of my Asian friends don't like it either. It's an acquired taste."

"But that doesn't mean I won't like it."

106

I eye him up and down. "You're *exactly* the type of white guy who will freak out."

Carter rears his head back, offended. "I *never* freak out."

"Hmmm. You're not culinarily adventurous."

"I'm adventurous," Carter says.

"No, you're not."

"How do you know?"

"You drink instant coffee and eat TV dinners. Do you travel?"

"I used to live in New York."

I snort. "New Yorkers think it's blasphemy to put pineapple on pizza."

Carter makes a face of disgust. "It *is* blasphemy!"

I smile, point made. "From my observation, you have the culinary palette of a Midwestern Boomer."

"All right," he holds up the durian and glares at it like his arch-nemesis, "how do we cut this open?"

We take the durian into the kitchen and I hack at it with my only kitchen knife. The smell cuts through the bleach fumes. If there's a ghost haunting this house, the durian would be a great weapon for exorcism.

The fruit is buttery yellow on the inside and comes in pods with giant seeds.

I hand Carter a tiny sliver.

"Oh, come on," he says. "That's barely a bite."

"It's what I think you can handle."

He holds it suspiciously, sniffs, jerks back.

"You don't have to try it," I say, expecting another freak out. Personally, I love durian and there was a time when I had put more effort into coaxing my friends to try it. After seeing both Lena and Sadie freak out at camp, I've given up. They couldn't be in the same cabin while Camille and I snack on our favorite fruit, sent to us via mail by our Vietnamese parents. "I know you won't like it."

With a flash of defiance, Carter shoves the slice in his mouth. He chews. And chews. And chews.

"Well?" I ask, waiting for him to spit it out. "What do you think?"

Carter surprises me by helping himself to seconds. "Not bad."

I nearly choke on my own mouthful. "Really?"

"Yeah. It's great. It really does taste better than it smells."

I take a bite and regard him with a frown. I thought he had no taste, or at least bland taste. He's proved me wrong. My mom, lover of durian, would definitely approve of him. He's passed the durian test.

Suddenly my favorite line from *The Witch of Blackbird Pond* pops into my mind:

What a contradictory person he was… surprising her, letting her peek through a door that always seemed to slam shut again before she could actually see inside.

"What's the matter?" Carter peers into my face. "You look concerned."

"Why do you have to be so contradictory?"

He frowns. "Me?"

I shake my head to clear it and a brilliant new plan hatches. "Do you think your grandma would want to try some durian?"

"She'll try anything at least once."

"Let's take some to her!"

He blinks in surprise. "Now?"

"Yes! Now! Help me pack this back up. I'll let her know we're dropping by for lunch."

"We don't need to call. Gran never minds when I drop by."

"It would be rude to just drop in," I say, and before he could protest, I run out to the porch, phone pressed to my ear. "Edith!" I whisper. "I need your help with something…"

chapter nineteen

"If it isn't my two favorite people in the world!" Edith says, opening the door. She seems out of breath. *Oh no.* I hope she didn't run to the door to greet us.

We had hashed out a rough script over the phone. Something in the vein of a basic 'Oh Hi!' would suffice. Frankly, I think Edith is laying it on a bit thick.

"Hi Gran." With a blink of surprise, Carter bends down to kiss Edith's cheek. "Is something wrong?"

"What could be wrong?" Edith gives me a quick hug.

"You're happy to see me," Carter says.

"I'm always happy to see you," she says.

"No, you're not. You usually want me to go away."

"Because you eat all my food."

Carter narrows his eyes and surveys his tiny grandma. "That's why it's so odd you're inviting us over for lunch."

Edith turns to me. We never counted on Carter turning this simple get-together into a police interrogation.

"I-I didn't invite you," Edith says. "I invited Theo and you came along."

Unconvinced, he nods to the front window. "I saw the curtain move. Were you waiting for us?"

Oh, he's good. Police detective good.

"B-because I'm... I'm... hungry!"

"Famished!" I jumped in, holding up the durian. "So let's go in and eat."

Edith sighs. "Yes. My legs are killing me. How long are you going to make an old lady stand?"

She opens the door wider. Our eyes meet. This is my cue. I slip off my shoes and place them next to the Welcome Mat.

We turn to Carter expectantly.

For someone so observant when we don't want him to be, he's certainly oblivious when it counts. He stomps his boots on the Welcome Mat and attempts to enter.

"Whoa, whoa, whoa." Edith slaps a frail hand to his chest. "Where do you think you're going with those filthy shoes?"

"What's the matter?" Carter asks. "I always come in with my shoes on."

"Not anymore." Edith winks at me. "I'm adopting a new rule. No shoes in the house."

"But the other guests," Carter surveys the front porch, "where are their shoes?"

"I-I'll um… I'll give them a piece of my mind later. Shoes off."

Carter side-eyes me. "Is this your doing?"

I hold my palms up.

"Don't blame poor Theo. She respects my rugs, and I just had the floors oiled. I took a look at her customs and I thought, 'looks good' so now her are *my* customs." She gestures to Carter's boots. "Shoes off."

Defeated, Carter bends down on one knee and unties his laces.

Edith winks at me. I wink back.

I peer down at the unveiling, my nerves taut with anticipation.

After much grumbling, Carter yanks off his boots and steps onto the Welcome Mat. I let out my breath. Damn. Socks. Of course he would be wearing socks. On the bright side, his socks were blue and grey stripes, much more Tim Burton-esque than I ever gave him credit for. I pegged him as a plain white crew kind of guy.

He edges past his grandmother. "Can I come in now?"

Edith nods, disappointed. "Don't worry," Edith whispers as I pass through, "we'll get those socks off him yet."

chapter twenty

E dith reacted to the durian taste test as expected with an explosive gag reflex. "Water!" *Cough. Hack. Choke.* "I need water!"

I nearly knock my cheese plate onto the carpet. Oh, my god! What if she's allergic? I heard of people having violent reactions to nuts. What if it's the same with Edith and durian? Wouldn't it be a sick twist of fate that I saved her from cheese only to kill her with durian?!

"Carter get some water!"

"Hang on, Gran!" Carter approaches with his half-filled cup of water.

"No!" Edith says, sounding remarkably clear for someone choking, "the pitcher of iced tea in the fridge. I need the whole thing."

Carter rushes into the kitchen. I kneel before Edith, patting her on the back as she choke-gags. "Everything will be fine, Edith," I say, wondering if I'll have to perform the Heimlich maneuver on her if she keeps this up. She's so old and frail that I'm afraid I'll break her rib cage. "Maybe I should call an ambulance and—"

Still choking and wheezing, Edith winks at me.

I do a double take.

Wait. "Are you *faking*?" I mouth.

"You bet your ass," she whispers and explodes into a fresh choking fit.

Edith, you sly dog.

Carter appears with a giant pitcher of iced-tea and pours Edith a glass. "Here, Gran. This will help."

He brings the glass to her mouth. With one big whooping cough, Edith knocks the tea from his hands. Tea splashes the carpet just shy of Carter's feet. Another flailing fit and the pitcher bites the dust, splashing Carter's jeans and drenching his socks.

"Oops." Edith is suddenly back to normal. "Well, that was an episode."

Carter steps away from the puddle. "Are you all right?"

"I'm fine," Edith take a sip of water, "but it looks like I made a mess. Better take off those socks. You don't want wet feet."

Dazed, Carter sits back down in his arm chair. His socks are soaked through. With a shake of his head, he leans down and begins peeling off his left sock.

I suck in my breath. Moment of truth.

Edith and I tilt our head as Carter reveals his foot.

I nod in appreciation. I like what I see. Well groomed toenails, exceptionally moisturized heels, a little pale, but what can you expect from a New Englander?

Carter bares his other foot and slaps his wet socks on the ground. Oh man. This one is nice, too.

Beside me, Edith arches a suggestive eyebrow. "Everything checks out?" she whispers, except when Edith thinks she's whispering, she's actually using her outdoor voice. "See? Nice feet runs in the family."

"What checks out?" Carter pokes his head up and catches us staring at his feet.

Oh shit. He heard her!

He glances down and, growing self-conscious, stacks one foot on top of the other. "I knew it! Something fishy's going on and it has something to do with my feet." His intense blue gaze pins me to the spot. *"You've* been trying to get me to take my shoes off all morning. What's going on?"

Oh no. The gig is up. I whirl on Edith. This is all her fault. "You said you were an actress."

"I was an actress!" Edith shouts. "I was in a Coppertone commercial in '72. I didn't have any dialogue, but if you saw the bikini I was in, I didn't *need* dialogue."

I slap a hand to my forehead.

"Gran?" Carter stands up and walks (barefoot) in front of us. He crosses his arms. "Theo...? Somebody better start explaining."

"We were..." I tug at my collar. Is it hot in here or is it just me? "It's a funny story, really."

"Try me."

"You see," I begin, shrinking under his judgmental stare. "Shoes. What are they good for? Absolutely nothing."

Carter scratches his scalp. Edith cringes.

"I have a fear of shoes. Shoe-phobia." *Oh god. Why am I still speaking?* "Don't need 'em. Can't stand 'em. You know, we were never meant to wear shoes. The human foot is very resilient to the earth."

"Oh, for Heaven's sake!" Edith interrupts. "This is painful to watch. I might as well tell you the truth: Theo has a foot fetish —"

"Edith!" I whirl on Carter, my eyes wide with horror.

He surveys my red face with frank interest.

"A full-blown, freaky foot fetish," Edith continues. "And she's taken an interest in your feet. Had to see 'em bare. Gets off on it."

Kill. Me. Now.

"Traitor!" I'm fighting the urge to tackle an eighty-four-year-old woman to the ground.

"So now you know," Edith says. "Show her your feet. Maybe let her touch a toe or tickle the arch. It'll do you both good." With a sympathetic pat on my arm, Edith mutters "you'll thank me later," and heads to the kitchen, leaving me alone with Carter.

Thank her?! I want to kill her!

Blood pounds in my ears. I keep my gaze adverted to the ground, but then... oh no, I don't want to give Carter the wrong idea. Summoning up all my courage, I look up.

Carter still has his arms crossed and his cheeks are slightly flushed from holding back his laughter. "So feet, eh?"

A tidal wave of mortification hits me. "I don't have a foot fetish!"

Before he could respond, I shoulder past him and run out the door.

"Theo!" I hear him call from the porch. I squeeze my eyes shut, racing down the street. At least one good thing came of this humiliating incident: without his shoes, Carter can't chase me.

chapter twenty-one

O kay. Don't panic.

So Carter thinks I have a foot fetish.

No big deal. What do I care what he thinks? In the scheme of things, a foot fetish misunderstanding is just a tiny drop of water in the pond.

He probably won't remember in a day or two. Much like when the Puritans of Wethersfield put Kit Tyler on trial for witchcraft, then, after she's found innocent, invites her to a Christmas wedding. Forgive and forget. Water under the bridge. When compared to a witchcraft accusation, my embarrassing episode is tiny.

So why am I *still* running?

Because I'm mortified!

I dash past an enclave of colonial houses (in better condition than mine) and cut through a narrow dirt path flanked by shrubbery. I run until I burst upon the calm blue waters of Wethersfield Cove. Panting, I pick my way across the pebble beach and plop down on a log.

I draw up my legs and bury my face between my knees. A breeze blows through the Cove, rippling the still waters and stirring the fallen leaves.

I lose track of time. I might have dozed. One moment I'm alone, the next moment a shadow yawns across the ground.

I poke my head up and immediately want to die again. Carter sits down beside me. His boots are back on. He sheepishly hands me a drink while keeping his eyes fixed on the thicket of trees on the opposite bank.

"What's this?" I take the drink from him.

"Starbucks. Venti Hibiscus Iced Tea. Half sugar with a splash of almond milk," he says, staring down at his clasped hands.

I almost fall off the log. "You bought me a drink?"

No answer.

"How did you know I liked this flavor?"

An embarrassed shrug.

I take a sip of the iced tea. Refreshing. Delicious. I would have never thought to add almond milk, but it works. "You sure know your way around a Starbucks for someone who never buys coffee."

"I used to work there in high school," he says, matter-of-factly.

I'm so surprised by this Starbucks gift that I momentarily forget why I ran off in the first place. Hibiscus tea can only distract me for so long. My mortification comes flooding back.

"H-how did you know where to find me?"

Is it my imagination or are his cheeks red?

"I'm," he clears his throat, "a quarter of the way through the book."

My eyes widen. I'm glad I'm sitting down. "You're re-reading *The Witch of Blackbird Pond?!*"

A curt nod. "Kit fled to the Meadows," he says. "Since the Meadows is now a Xerox office, I figure you'll come to the next best thing."

We gaze out at Wethersfield Cove. The golden afternoon light touches the trees and pebbled banks, lending a silver gleam to the still waters. At this moment, the Cove fulfills the magic of the fictional Blackbird Pond I've carried with me in my imagination.

"I know all about you now," he says, his lips twitching at the corners.

Oh God. I regret asking him to re-read the book. Now he

knows all my secrets and fantasies. Attention men: everything you know about dating is wrong. Just listen to your girl when she talks about her favorite book. She's given you the key to her heart.

I didn't actually think he'll re-read *The Witch of Blackbird Pond* or pay attention to my flights of fancy.

"You know," he says when I don't respond, "don't pay too much attention to what Gran says. She a meddler. I get the feeling she's trying to set us up."

I look carefully away. "Yeah, well, it's not working."

Carter rubs his palms together. "Ridiculous, right?"

"Maybe back in her day people hook up at the drop of a hat, but we can't all be 'flower children and free love,' can we?"

He clears his throat. "Our generation has standards."

"That being said," I say, staring at a pile of yellow leaves by my shoe. "I don't have a foot fetish. I don't know where Edith gets this idea."

He nods. "Right."

I look up. "You don't believe me?"

Carter holds his hands up in self defense. "I'm agreeing with you," he says, suppressing silent laughter. He nudges my foot with the toe of his shoe. "Just to be safe, I put my shoes back on. I can take them off if you're still curious — "

I take a big sip of my Hibiscus iced tea, stopping him mid-sentence with my laser death stare.

"Changing topics," Carter clears his throat, "I have a new train coming in. The Cannonball Express. Maybe after we work on your house next weekend, you may want to..." he rubs the back of his neck, "come check it out."

I swallow my tea. "You're inviting me to see your trains?"

Carter's ears redden. "Only if you want to. You don't have to. I just thought — "

I touch his wrist. "No! I want to."

His smile is big and hopeful.

My heart skips a beat. "But I can't next weekend. I'll be out of town. In fact, I'll take a raincheck on the renovations too."

"Oh?" Carter frowns. "Where are you going?"

"I'm headed up to Salem," I say. "I'm seeing a man about a couch."

chapter twenty-two

I bought a couch.

All things considered, it's a very ordinary thing to do. I have a new home. I want to furnish said home. I don't know why Carter is treating this news like a bad decision.

"Where are you going again?"

"Salem." Seriously, sometimes he could be so dense.

"That far? For a couch? You do realize there's an Ikea in town."

I'm personally offended he thinks I'll settle for Ikea furniture in my colonial home. "It's not just any couch. It's made by Jacques Le Fèvre, the French colonial furniture maker. I got the deal of a lifetime."

"How much?"

I tell him the price and watch his eyebrows shoot up to his hairline.

"That's highway robbery!"

"I should think so. The owner is practically giving it away. I even offered to pay more, but he refused."

"Sounds like he's trying to get rid of it. What happened? Someone die on it?"

"Jack the Ripper himself could have done his business on it. I'm buying it."

I tell Carter about falling down a crazy rabbit hole of

browsing Craigslist and Facebook Marketplace for colonial furniture, which led to the listing for a Jacques Le Fèvre original. Maple frame. Claw feet. Reupholstered in luxurious yellow brocade. The moment I saw it, I knew I had to have it. It *belongs* in my newly renovated living room. I can imagine Marie Antoinette lounging on this couch. Or to a lesser extent, Benjamin Franklin.

As I geek out about my new furniture purchase, Carter rubs the spot between his eyes. I don't care for his reaction.

"How do you know it's a Jacques Le Fèvre original?" he asks, as we leave Wethersfield Cove behind.

"I asked for detailed photos."

He scoffs. "I suppose you're an expert on 18th century couches."

"As a matter of fact, I *am*. I have a degree in Early Colonial furniture making."

Carter halts. "You're making this up." He studies me. "Nobody has a degree in Early Colonial furniture making."

"Well, I do. Do you want to see my diploma?"

He shakes his head and asks to see the photo of the couch. "Not worth it. Have you browsed Wayfair? You can probably get a dupe for a fraction of the price."

"I don't want a dupe. I want the real thing. Here," I enlarge the photo, "look at the frame. That's American red maple with gold acanthus leaf inlays. You can't find that at Wayfair."

"It's just a couch," Carter says.

"It's not a couch. It's a piece of history."

He sighs. "Romantic ideals will only screw you in the end."

"Motto of your life," I say. "Not for me. Romantic ideals are the only ones worth living for. I'll see you on Monday."

We walk partway down the block. I wave goodbye. Carter lingers with his hands jammed in his pockets. "You're really going to do this? Drive all the way to Salem for a couch? Your house is not even ready for furniture."

Jesus. He sounds like my mother. "Edith says I can keep it at her B&B."

"Why can't the seller ship it?"

"The shipping costs more than the couch," I say.

"Salem is a long way from Wethersfield…"

"It's a just a hundred miles and change."

"That's a two hour drive!"

I roll my eyes. "It's the same amount of time it takes me to come home during rush hour in Los Angeles. Really, you New Englanders are so afraid of driving. Besides, this is *my* holiday. Salem is on my bucket list of places to visit, and it's the first weekend of October. Are you a *Hocus Pocus* fan?"

He tips his head to the side. "What do you think?"

I roll my eyes. "What is your favorite movie?"

"*The Big Short.*"

"Hm." I wrinkle my nose. Typical. "Well, *I* watched *Hocus Pocus* every Halloween since I was eight, and now I'm going to check out all the filming locations. The seller lives right in town and he promised to give me a tour."

"*He?*" Carter narrows his eyes. "What does this guy look like?"

"What does it matter?"

"You're touring Salem with a complete stranger."

"Just a week ago, *you* were a stranger."

"But I'm not a serial killer."

"The jury is still out on you," I say, earning a reluctant smile from him. "Anyway, strangers are just friends I haven't met yet."

"So says the many hitchhikers that end up in ditches."

Seeing that Carter wasn't going to let up, I show him the seller's Facebook profile picture: a middle aged man with a nicely trimmed beard and half-rim glasses. He's standing on a fishing boat and holding up the trout he just caught. He looks like an upstanding fellow.

"It's worse than I expected," Carter says, "Serial killer."

"I think he's in IT."

"I can't believe you're even considering stepping inside this guy's house. Next thing you know, you're locked in his dungeon."

"Everything will be okay." Geez. Look at the imagination on him. Who knew Carter was so paranoid. "I'm a big girl. I can handle myself."

"Won't you need somebody to help you move the couch?"

I pat him on the arm. "I'm not going to rope you into helping me move if that's what you're worried about. Your weekend's free. The owner, Matt..."

"Matt," Carter scowls.

"*Matt* will help me. I'm renting a U-Haul."

"But—"

"I moved all the way across the country, didn't I?" I notice his tense shoulders. "Edith's right. You need to relax."

Carter runs his fingers through his hair. Wow. My impromptu couch purchase is really bothering him.

"Thanks for the drink!" I say, swatting him on the back. "And maybe look into a getting a massage."

"Theo! Wait..."

I turn around.

Carter casts his eyes to the ground. "Need an extra pair of hands?"

"*You* want to come with *me*? To Salem?"

His lips hitch into an embarrassed grin. "I could use a vacation."

chapter twenty-three

Our rented U-Haul burns rubber along the highway to Salem.

I'm behind the wheel, singing along with the radio. The highway stretches before me, flanked by autumn trees as far as the eye can see. The air is crisp and smoky. Our truck interior smells like pumpkin spice latte and raspberry danishes. Life is good. Until I glance over at the passenger seat...

I roll my eyes.

Carter is as pale as a ghost and does his best to look like death warmed over.

He wipes away the perspiration from his brow. "Are you sure you don't want me to take over? It's no problem. No problem at all."

"I'm fine."

"I don't mind," he says. "You look tired. Why don't you take a nap?"

"I'm wide awake."

"Studies show that most people who are tired don't know they are tired."

"What studies?"

He scratches his nose and mumbles. "Studies."

I take a sip of my latte.

Carter braces himself. "Eyes on road!"

"I can drink coffee and drive! I've done it before!"

"You were swerving!"

I take a deep breath and pray for patience. Why can't he just shut up and eat his danish? "Carter… I get the feeling that you don't like my driving."

He makes a grab for the truck's Oh-Shit-Handles. "Watch out!"

I tap on the breaks. "What?!"

"You're too close to the Camry!"

"Wrong. The Camry is too close to me. He's going fifty."

"That's the speed limit," he says.

"Is it? I thought it was a 'suggestion.' Like the freeways in California 'suggest' a 65 mph speed limit, but everyone does 80. If you go the speed limit you'll be run over."

"Oh God." Carter crosses himself.

Seriously? "You're laying it on a bit thick, don't you think?"

"You're driving a bit too aggressively, don't *you* think?"

"That's how we drive in LA. You don't know driving until you've tried to take someone to the airport. Here," I crank up the radio. "Listen to music. Meditate. Eat your danish. Take a nap. Just stop bothering me."

Carter crosses his arms like a petulant child. "I'd feel better if I drove. Let's swap."

"I'm not turning it over to you."

"Why not?"

"It's sexist." I lower my voice in a poor imitation of his, "'Move over little lady, let the big strong man handle this.'"

Carter snorts. "I don't know what you're talking about. I just want to live through this trip."

"Don't make me regret taking you."

Despite our bickering, nothing could dampen my mood. It's the first weekend of October. I'm dressed in a cozy cable-knit sweater, corduroy pants, and stripy socks. I look like an extra out of Harry Potter, which is all I want in life.

I have a weekend in Salem to look forward to, the *literal best*

Halloween costume inside my overnight duffle bag, and a Jacques Le Fèvre couch with my name written all over it.

"In October," I say, quoting one of my favorite lines from *The Witch of Blackbird Pond*, "any wonderful unexpected thing is possible."

Carter arches his eyebrows at a quizzical angle that's becoming all too familiar. "How many times have you read this book?"

"Too many to count. It's my desert island book."

Carter glances out the passenger side window. "So what are you searching for when you read it?"

"What do you mean?" I ask, keeping my eyes on the road.

"You don't read a book so many times unless you're searching for something. What are you hoping to find?"

I laugh. "Are we playing twenty questions now?"

"It keeps my mind from death by fiery car crash," he says, loosening his grip on the Oh-Shit-Handles.

Okay. I'll play along. Anything to keep Carter from backseat driving. "I'm looking to recapture a memory."

Carter eyes my profile. "A memory of what?"

"Being young and impressionable." I think for a moment and add, "warm and cozy."

"Being tried for witchcraft is warm and cozy?"

I refuse to let Carter grump over my favorite book. "It all worked out for Kit Tyler in the end." I sigh. "The ending…"

"Ah yes," Carter nods in understanding. "The ending. So what is it about this Nat Eaton, anyway?"

"Only that he's the most perfect man ever! He saves cats and takes care of old ladies and reads! Shakespeare! He reads Shakespeare!"

"Don't forget that he speaks only in nautical metaphors," Carter points out.

"That's sexy stuff!"

"He's borderline pirate."

I consider the image. Nat Eaton, pirate. "I'm okay with that," I say, "so long as he has a puffy white shirt."

126

Carter hides a grin. "Is that what you're looking for? Nat Eaton?"

He's hitting a little too close to home. "I'm looking for a beautiful romance," I blurt out.

He snorts. "What does that entail? A romp through the meadows with a guy in a puffy pirate shirt?"

"Don't tempt me," I say, and we both laugh.

"Seriously, Theo," Carter asks, "define this 'beautiful romance'?"

"I think we've covered it. Someone who saves cats and takes care of the elderly and reads and — "

My hands tighten on the wheel as a shocking new realization dawns on me. Swap 'cat' for 'hamster' and I've just described Carter. But does he realize he's Nat Eaton?

"And?" he presses, sensing my sudden fall into silence. Fortunately, Carter doesn't put two and two together.

I gulp down a cold mouthful of coffee. "Enough about me. It's my turn to ask the questions. I'm entitled to three since you put me through a literal interrogation."

The notch hasn't completely disappeared from his brow, but he leans back in his seat. "Make it count."

"How long was your longest relationship?" I ask and immediately start to blush.

"You've been gossiping with Gran," he says after a long silence.

"You're evading the question."

Carter rakes a hand through his hair. "Three months," he turns to me. "To save you the questions. Yes. She dumped me. No. I'm not bitter. Yes. It was over the instant coffee and the food sharing..."

"Food sharing? You mean you made her share your Healthy Choice steamer meals?"

"Worse," he says, proud of his cheapness. "You know how large the portions are at Cheesecake Factory? I can't eat an entire wet burrito by myself so I suggested we split a plate—"

I hold up my hand to stop him. "I can see why she dumped you."

"Why is sharing a meal a relationship ender?" Carter sounds genuinely confused. "She never finishes her Chinese chicken salad, and she always forgets to eat her leftovers. A half plate at Cheesecake Factory is equivalent to European portions."

I gape at him, horrified. I take it back. He checks all the boxes as Nat Eaton. Sadly, he's no Nat Eaton. Would Nat ask Kit to split a wet burrito at the Cheesecake Factory to save a couple of bucks? Or what's the 17th century equivalent? Treat her to half a blueberry cake and share a glass of milk? I don't think so... A girl's gotta eat!

"No good?" Carter asks.

"No good. Carter... we need to have a long discussion about women."

Carter grumbles. "I'm not looking for a beautiful romance."

"With habits like that," I mutter, "you'll never have one."

The U-Haul bounces over something on the road and I swerve toward the grassy island. I right my course, cool as a fighter pilot under attack. I'm back on the road in no time.

"That's a big log," I say, checking over my shoulder. "Whew! For a moment I thought it was a raccoon."

I make the mistaking of glancing at Carter. His entire body is clenched in terror. His eyes are wide, traumatized. He's probably clenching his ass.

"Carter?" I roll my eyes. "You okay?"

He makes a feeble goat bleat. "I think I'm going to be sick."

"Good thing you're too cheap to eat breakfast."

He crosses himself. *Actually* crosses himself.

I roll my eyes. "Oh, for Heaven's sake!" With a sigh, I pull over on the side of the road and snap off my seatbelt. "Fine. You drive."

128

chapter twenty-four

Getting into Salem was a lot more difficult than I anticipated. The traffic to enter was horrendous, the line twenty cars deep.

I gawk at the hordes of costumed revelers roaming the quaint New England sidewalks. A man in a Jason mask. A group of elementary school girls dressed as witches. The Bride of Frankenstein.

"Salem is busier than Disneyland! I know Salem takes Halloween seriously, but we're still a month away."

"Folks here like to get Halloween started early." Carter steers us slowly through a mob of tourists. "I could have told you coming here in October is a bad idea."

"It's not a bad idea!" I bounce in my seat in excitement. "It's a great idea. The more the merrier!"

"I hate crowds," he says. "Where's this guy's address again?"

"He won't be there to meet us until noon. In the meantime, we enjoy ourselves."

"Enjoy ourselves?!"

"Soak up the spooky season vibes." I press my nose to the window, drinking in the kitschy gift shops selling tarot cards, black witch hats, and cauldrons. "Stop and smell the candy corn."

Carter mumbles something about annoying tourists under his breath.

I hide a smile. Call me a sadist: I enjoy pushing his buttons. We're balancing on a seesaw. The more he sinks into grumpy quicksand, the higher I fly. It's fun being on a road trip with a man who has a permeant storm cloud over his head.

"Street parking is going to be a bitch," he says.

I point to the looming three story structure. "Turn into the parking lot."

"No way. I'm not parking there," he says, and drives right past the entrance.

"Why not?"

"Did you see the price? $30!"

I frown. "The parking lot says there's an $8 flat rate."

"*Unless* you visit in October. Then they milk you for everything you're worth," he says. "Keep your eyes peeled for a spot."

"All right," I say, keeping a look out. "But I doubt you'll find parking."

"I'll find it."

"There are no sidewalks and the streets are all one-way."

"I'll find it."

I chew my inner cheek. "That's the Halloween spirit!" I say, blossoming under Carter's withering glare.

Thirty minutes and five circles around Salem later, Carter pulls into the parking structure. He was right. The rate has skyrocketed to $30.

I hand over my credit card. "I'll pay."

"Put that away. I'll pay."

"Don't be silly. It's my idea to come here and you hate spending money."

He pushes my card away and shoves his card into the slot.

"Well!" I sit back in my seat, feigning offense. Inside, I'm happy to add a cherry on top of his shit sundae. I know. *I know.* I have a problem. When I was a kid, I used to love picking scabs. Consider Carter Bromley a giant scab. Just wait until he gets a taste of what I have up my sleeve…

The U-Haul is probably not the best vehicle to take into a jam-packed parking structure during Salem's busiest month of the year, but Carter manages to find a parking spot. I dig inside my duffle bag as he maneuvers us in, grumbling about 'romantic ideals' and 'impractical trip planning.'

"What are you doing?" Carter side-eyes me and nearly side-swipes the car next to us as I tug my sweater over my head.

"Changing into my Halloween costume," I unzip my corduroy pants, "turn around."

"Why am I not surprised?" Carter shifts his entire body so he's facing the opposite window.

I wiggle into a black sheath fringe dress. Black and white stripped stockings come next, then three long strands of pearls and a black pointy hat. "Carter?"

"Yes?" he asked, still turned away.

I reach behind me, tugging on a zipper that I'm only able to pull halfway. "Can you zip me up?"

"Are you decent?"

"Everything but my back."

Carter tentatively turns around, his cheeks red as he assesses my naked back. He swallows.

I laugh. "You can be such a Puritan sometimes."

"Runs in my blood."

Our eyes meet over my shoulders. His gaze roves over my black dress and pearls. "What are you supposed to be?"

"Isn't it obvious? I'm a flapper." I prop my pointy hat on my head and cock it at a rakish angle. "And a witch."

"Well, which one are you?"

"Both. I'm a witch from the Jazz Age."

"Yeah," he rolls his eyes, "that makes sense." He smacks one of my fringes. "There's a lot going on with this dress."

"The Roaring Twenties were an age of excess." I shoulder shimmy. "I thrifted this dress years ago. The pearls are from Edith, a gift from one of her past boyfriends. What do you think?"

His gaze lingers on my bare shoulders and travels down my

naked back. "You'll be cold." He gestures for me to turn around. "Don't shimmy."

"The dress compels me to shimmy."

"Control yourself," he says before grasping my zipper with steady hands.

A shiver shoots up my spine as his warm fingertips graze my back. He pauses at the top, unsure of what to do. "The eye hook. Do you want me to — "

I nod, my breath hitching as he brushes the hair away from my neck and deftly clasps the eye hook together. His hand lingers for a fraction of a second, long enough to radiate heat.

"T-thanks."

"Uh huh." He drops my zipper like a hot potato and backs away.

I fuss with my pearls. Sometimes I think the only benefit of wearing excessive costume jewelry is to have something to do with your hands in awkward moments.

The parking structure is cool and cave-like. The space between us becomes uncomfortably silent and charged with an electrifying energy that makes my forearms erupt in goose-bumps. All because of a silly zipper!

In need of a distraction, I dive into my duffle bag. "Now it's your turn."

"My turn?!"

"To change into your costume. I figured you wouldn't dress up for our Salem trip. Don't worry, I got you."

"That's what you think," he says. "I do have a costume."

I blink. "You do? Where is it? Did you pack it?"

Carter straightens his shoulders, smug. "I'm wearing it."

I eye his black turtle neck, light washed jeans, and white runners. "I don't see it."

"Ah!" He holds up a finger, reaches in his pocket, and slips on a pair of rimless glasses with circle lenses. "Can you guess who I am now?"

I stifle a giggle. Carter without glasses is hot. A bespeckled Carter is adorable. "Someone's '90's dad?"

"I'm my hero. Steve Jobs! What do you think?"

"Eh…"

"What? It's ironic!"

"No one will get it," I say. "You'll just look like a regular Joe in dad jeans."

"Hence the irony."

I shake my head. "What if you try on the costume I made for you? It's super simple and you can wear it over your Steve Jobs get-up."

"You *made* something for me?" Carter regards me wearily. "What is it?"

I beam. "Bet you didn't know I dabbled in paper mâché," I say, lugging out my new creation and presenting it to him like a gift. "Surprise!"

"Ahhhhh!" Carter yelps and bumps against the driver's side door. "What is it?"

"It's a jack-o'-lantern head." I frown. "I might have smooshed it with my foot, but I don't think it warrants that kind of reaction. It's not even supposed to be scary."

Carter regards the paper mâché pumpkin with a weary expression. "It's the stuff nightmares are made of."

Okay. My foot caved in one side of its face and the grin is a bit too ghoulish. Overall, I think it's still cute.

"It's vintage. People in the '20's used to make masks out of paper mâché all the time. It'll pair perfectly with my flapper witch costume. Here. Try it on."

Carter holds the pumpkin head at arm's length. "You sure I'll be able to take it off?"

"What do you mean?"

"Remember the haunted mask in *Goosebumps*?"

"I made it with old newspapers and back issues of Edith's *Better Homes and Gardens* magazines. I didn't curse it or hex it. In fact, I may consider adding paper mâché masks to my *Vincent Van Sproot* shop update."

Carter scowls down at the mask. "How do I get myself into these situations?"

chapter twenty-five

A flapper witch and a pumpkin-masked man dressed as Steve Jobs walks down the street.

Children scurry out of the pumpkin man's way.

We stop to peer through a vintage tarot card display at Coven's Cottage. A woman gets a gander of Carter's paper mâché head and yelps. Her baby howls.

"I told you I'm going to give children nightmares." Carter's voice is muffled and echo-y beneath his pumpkin mask, making him sound like a demonically possessed Darth Vader.

"Stop it. Your dad jeans are scarier than the mask."

"Everybody is staring at me."

"That's the hallmark of a good Halloween costume."

We stroll through the narrow streets, gawking at the Frankensteins, vampires, and ax murderers in the Salem monster parade.

"I wonder if they have a prize for best costume," I say. "We should march. I bet you'll win if you cool it on the watch checking and do a little more lurching."

Carter yanks off his pumpkin head, revealing a sweat-drenched face and blond hair disheveled into a damp cowlick. "I can't breathe in there," he says. "It's a quarter till noon. Let's get the couch."

I glance with longing at a window display of dry sage,

potions, and a selection of macabre oddities. "Oooh, a shrunken head!"

"Theo! The couch."

With a sigh, I let him lead me away from the main drag and into a quieter street lined with stately colonial houses and sprawling maple trees.

"Our Airbnb is on this street," I say, distracted by pumpkins on the stoop of a cheery red door. "But we can't check in until after 3."

Did I tell you we're staying overnight? You may think it would be like pulling teeth to talk Carter into splitting a studio room. He's not the type to splurge on a weekend trip. I had him pegged for a 'let's get the couch and go' kind of guy.

Carter was surprisingly open minded. I didn't even have to pull his arm to get him to agree to a sleepover. Come to think of it, it didn't take that much effort to get him to wear my pumpkin head.

I halt in my step, consumed with a creeping new suspicion.

"You check to see if he's home. I'll bring the U-Haul around and — " Carter notices me studying him. "What's wrong?"

I narrow my eyes. "Is this a pick up?"

"Yes. We're about to pick up the couch, remember?"

"No…" I stop him in the middle of the street. Two bright red spots burn my cheeks. Ever watch anime when the characters get unnecessarily bashful? That's me. "Are you trying to pick *me* up?"

Carter glances down at my curly witch shoes. "If your feet hurt, take off your shoes. No way are you roping me into giving you a piggyback ride."

"I didn't mean — " Actually. A piggyback ride sounds kind of… hot.

Wait.

I'm confused.

I'm getting all these mixed signals.

"Haven't you put me through enough for one day?" With a

135

shake of his head, Carter leaves me on the sidewalk, strolling away with my pumpkin head tucked beneath his arm.

chapter twenty-six

"It's *gorgeous!*" I circle my new couch. It's even more exquisite than in the picture. No photo can do it justice. That's it. It's over for me. I'm in love.

With a stupid smile plastered to my face, I run a hand across the carved red maple back and the brand spanking new upholstery. Yellow. The color of sunshine. I sink down in the cushions, and my bones protest.

"Uncomfortable?" Carter asks, watching me grimace. He's standing by the seller with his arms folded over his chest. Matt (not a serial killer, but a member of the Masonic Lodge of Salem *and* a hobby fisherman) is counting his money.

"The stuffing is... minimal," I say, settling into the center of the sofa and lounging like Cleopatra in her sedan chair. "But that's expected. Aristocratic 18th century people didn't like to be comfortable. Slouching was a sign of ill-breeding as opposed to inbreeding, which was frowned upon, but not uncommon."

"My wife is my third cousin twice removed," Matt chimes in.

Carter and I turn to him with matching horrified expressions.

"I need to take a leak," Matt says, sensing nothing amiss. "Call me when you're ready to move it."

Carter waits until Matt leaves for the bathroom before kneeling beside me. "What did I tell you?" he whispers. "Now you know why I had to come."

"Relax," I say. "He's engaged in a little light incest. Never killed anybody. Besides, third cousins twice removed doesn't even count as incest." I pat the cushion beside me. "Sit down and help me test drive this beauty."

Ever the grump, Carter sits down on the edge of the sofa, his gaze never straying far from the hallway where he's probably anticipating Matt returning with an ax.

"What do you think?" I close my eyes, imagining my friends and family gathered around the yellow couch for the holidays. With a bit of elbow grease, my house will be semi-livable by Thanksgiving. "Isn't it lovely?

Carter shifts from side to side. "There's a piece of wood poking me in the ass."

"That's American red maple," I point out. "Luxury wood."

"I'm honored."

"Do you think we can get the Witch House ready by Thanksgiving? I'm throwing a party and a couch viewing."

He snorts. "Theo, there's a thing called reality…"

"Reality?" I wrinkle my nose. "Don't want to go there."

Carter studies my dreamy expression with a frown. He looks me over for so long that I'm forced to turn away. I pick at the sofa's wooden backing with my thumbnail, pretending to inspect a scratch.

"*Candy Land*," he says softly.

"What?"

"I bet your favorite board game growing up is *Candy Land*."

I sit up. "How did you know?"

"Lucky guess." Carter shrugs and stares down at his clasped hands. "I imagine that's how you see the world: bright and colorful and sweet. Skipping along lollipop lane, snatching up gummy bears and biting off their heads."

I tilt my head to the side. "Are you making fun of me?"

A grin ghosts his lips. "A little," he says, sounding almost sad.

"What was your favorite board game? *Monopoly*?"

His smile broadens. He nods.

"Bet you were good at it. Hoarding your play money while your parents splurged on that Fifth Avenue mansion."

"I never lived beyond my means," he says, "and I played to win. It's just that…" Carter ducks his head. "Sometimes it would be nice to live in *Candy Land*."

He seems like he needs a pick me up. "Here." I hand him a small waxed packet with a black cat on it.

"What's this?" Carter asks, perplexed.

"Candy corn."

"Where'd this come from?"

"My pants."

His lips twitch. "You keep candy in your pants?"

We both glance down at the modest hem of my flapper dress.

Carter clears his throat. "You're not wearing pants."

I arch a smug eyebrow. "Formerly my pants. This dress has pockets."

The toilet flushes and Matt returns with a magazine tucked under his arm. "All right, let's get this show on the road."

The two men angle the couch through the narrow foyer, down the front steps, and onto the sidewalk. I offered to help, but I was told (by Matt) to 'stand aside, little lady. Let the men handle it.' No comment.

"Mind my pumpkins!" Matt shouts. "Pivot!"

A sweat breaks out on Carter's brow. "Why is this thing so heavy?"

"Because you're used to Ikea furniture," I say, running ahead of the moving team. "Maple is heavier than particle board."

"Heave!" Matt grunts, backing Carter onto the ramp leading to the truck. "Heave!"

"Yes! Yes! I know!" Carter grits his teeth together.

By the time they lift the couch into the U-Haul, Carter is a wreck. He collapses on the sofa in a sweating heap. I've never felt better.

Matt shakes my hand. "Wait right there!" He jogs back in the house, returning with an old lamp with a stained glass shade. "I'll throw this in for free."

My knees threaten to buckle. "Is this a real Tiffany lamp?"

"No. It's from Amazon. Want it?"

"Thanks!"

Everything is coming up Theo! I have a new couch and a cool knock-off Tiffany lamp. I plop down next to Carter with a dreamy sigh. My hand accidentally lands on his thigh, causing him to jolt like someone poured iced water on his pants.

"Sorry!" I snatch my hand back. "I got excited about the lamp."

"It's fine," he says, sitting up straight and scooting away from me.

See? There it is again! Mixed signals. He's enticing me with talks of *Candy Land* one moment, treating me like a leper the next. What's a girl supposed to think?

A blanket of awkwardness descends over us until I clear my throat. "Lunch? I'll pick somewhere cheap."

chapter twenty-seven

We're hit with the mouthwatering aroma of marinara sauce, warm gooey cheese, and garlic the moment we set foot inside Witch City Pizzeria.

The restaurant is packed for lunch.

Servers dressed in head to toe black zigzag between tables and the open kitchen where the chefs sling dough and slide pizzas into the many industrial wood-fire ovens behind them.

Carter requests an outside table where we can watch people in costumes march by.

I'm already suspicious when we're shown our table.

Red and white checkered tablecloth?

A tea candle?

A vase with a single red rose?

This looks like the setup to a romantic Italian dinner.

It's not until the server hands me the menu and I glance at the pizza options that I know something is up.

Pear and gorgonzola?

Neapolitan with handmade mozzarella fired in a wood oven? Black truffle drizzle? When Carter suggested we get pizza, I thought he meant sharing a medium pepperoni pizza at Domino's. This was *fancy* pizza. Prosciutto instead of pepperoni. San Marzano tomatoes instead of canned tomato sauce.

"Are you sure you want to eat here?" I peer at Carter over

my menu. "This is a four-dollar sign place according to Yelp. There's a McDonald's down the street."

A casual shrug. "When in Rome," he says, peering at his menu. "Do you want appetizers? We can start with garlic bread and... stuffed mushrooms? A Caprese salad?"

When in Rome?! Appetizers?! This coming from a guy who gave me instant coffee?

"We can share a pizza," I offer.

Carter takes a sip of water, oblivious to my surprise. "How about we order two and split it family style?"

Whew. Okay. That sounds like Carter. Two pizzas. Leftovers for tonight.

The server drops by and asks if we're interested in seeing the wine menu.

"No, we — "

"Yes, please," Carter says.

I almost fall out of my seat. Now I know aliens from outer space have abducted Carter and reprogramed his brain.

"Do you like red or white?" Carter asks. "I guess that depends on the pizza. Why don't we order a glass of each and — "

"Whoa! Whoa! Stop! Time out. Who are you and what did you do to Carter?"

He frowns. "What do you mean?"

"Gourmet pizza? Appetizers? Wine?! The Carter I know would never blow this much money on lunch!"

He smiles at my outburst. "You've only known me for two weeks. I'm capable of splurging for special occasions."

"Special occasions? This is lunch."

"Lunch with a friend on vacation," he says. "Also: lifestyle inflation."

Are we friends?

"I'm hope you don't think of me as just your indentured servant," he adds, his eyes laughing at me over the table. "Seriously, don't worry about the bill. I can afford it."

"You're paying?! I thought we were splitting."

"You bought me coffee twice. I'm returning the favor."

"But coffee isn't fancy pizza and wine…" I stop talking and narrow my eyes. Carter rakes a hand through his hair. His gaze is fixed on the menu, but he isn't reading a damn thing. His ears are red. There's a scarlet streak down his left cheek. I nod in understanding. Oh, he's good. He's *very* good. "I see you."

"W-what do you see?"

"Carter Bromley…" I shake my head. "This is a date!"

chapter twenty-eight

"It's not a date." Carter's laugh is a little too loud. He turns to the table next to us and snorts. "Preposterous."

"You know who says 'preposterous'?"

He arches an eyebrow.

"Liars!"

"I'm not —"

"Super slick. Dating without asking. You should write a book."

Who knew Carter had so much game? All this instant coffee + TV dinner + shirtless jogging business seems so innocent at first. Next thing I know, I'm being wined and dined, possibly seduced. That's the endgame, isn't it? So when he mentioned *Candy Land...* it's really a metaphor for sex.

"I've got my eye on you, Carter."

"I don't know what you're talking about."

I snap my fingers. Why didn't I see it before? "This is just like in *The Witch of Blackbird Pond.*"

He rolls his eyes. "All roads lead to that book."

"That's right. It's like when William Ashby decided to court Kit without directly telling her he's courting her. Instead, he counts his growing pile of wood. That's what you're doing. Growing your wood."

"I assure you. I don't... Excuse me." He ducks his head and mashes his lips together. "... have wood."

"*Oh*," I wag my finger, "I see your wood."

Scrubbing a hand over his face, Carter turns away. His jaw tightens as he struggles not to laugh. "What did William Ashby do with all that wood?"

"Build a house," I tip my chin up at a haughty angle, "to bone in."

He takes a deep breath. "I don't want to build a house."

"But you *do* want to bone."

He explodes in laughter.

I tap my foot under the table. "That's right. Laugh it up. I don't think it's very funny."

"I'm sorry." He clutches his stomach. "House... to... bone??"

The server chooses this moment to take our order, prompting Carter to wipe the tears from his face and get a hold of himself. We order two pizzas: pear and gorgonzola and triple truffle with spicy Italian sausage, two glasses of wine (Bordeaux and Chardonnay), a Caprese salad...

I slam my menu down. "And duck."

Both Carter and the server stares at me.

"Duck?" Carter repeats.

"There's a build your own pizza option."

The server clears his throat. "How would you like your duck, Miss?"

"Pressed," I tip my chin up like I know what I'm doing, "in a Peking sauce and what the hey, add Thai peanut slaw and pineapples. Do your pineapples come in rings or chunks?"

"We have both."

"Rings, then. Pile it on." I meet Carter's perplexed gaze. "Can I really combine this dish with four types of cheese? Even blue cheese crumbles?"

"Your wish is our command," the server says.

Carter makes a face of disgust. "That's a strange combination of flavors."

"Asian fusion."

He lifts a brow. "It fuses something alright. I'm not touching it. That's *your* personal pizza."

I wait until we're alone before leaning forward. "If you're going to try to seduce me, I'm going to get my money's worth. Think your wallet can handle a $32 dollar pineapple-duck-blue-cheese pizza?"

"I think I can afford it," Carter says, eyeing me over his water glass. "I'm not trying to seduce you."

"That's too bad…" Dropping my gaze to the table, I straighten the crease of my napkin with a shaky fingertip, "because I may let you."

chapter
twenty-nine

C arter chokes on his water and spits it all over my face.
"Oh shit." He rushes over with a napkin and dabs me.
"Sorry. I'm so sorry." He's so mortified he can't look me in
the eye.

"My fault. I should have waited till you were done with your
drink," I say, blushing under his attention. "I'm the queen of bad
timing."

"That's a good one." He clears his throat and utters a laugh
that sounds like a goat bleating. "You really got me going for a
minute."

Okay.

Moment of truth. I've been given an out. I can either play this
up as a joke or commit to my original trajectory.

I grab his wrist to stop him.

Carter freezes. He doesn't exactly look at me so much as
concentrate on my knee.

"It's not a joke," I say softly.

As if his ears and cheeks weren't red enough, Carter has
turned into a stewed tomato. Glancing around the crowded
patio, he lowers his voice. "Do you mean what I think you
mean?"

I nod.

"When did you... um..." he tugs at his turtleneck collar, "how did you arrive at this idea?"

"Just now. Five seconds ago," I whisper. "Though I suppose it's been brewing for at least a week."

He narrows his eyes. "Are you joking?"

"I'm dead serious."

"Are you sure?"

I nod, feeling like I'm committing a crime. "I'm sure."

He considers my indecent proposal with grueling silence. Slowly, Carter gets up and returns to his seat. He blinks as if he's in a daze and carefully folds his napkin.

Our food arrives. Is it just me, or is our server taking an excruciatingly long time to set everything on the table?

Our eyes meet as the server pours our wine. He frowns. I see the wheels in his head turning, his dazed thoughts churning.

It's quite the bombshell to drop over lunch. In keeping with this year of big, bold moves, I figured I'll make the first move and grab life by the balls again. It can't be any more scary than quitting my job, buying a house sight unseen, and moving across the country, right?

Suppose I made a terrible mistake? I've misread him completely and he isn't attracted to me at all. Or maybe he *is* attracted to me, but like any rational person, he's not ready to move this fast whereas I'm speeding things along like a sex crazed maniac.

Oh. My. God. That's it isn't it? He's going to reject me. Worse, he's going to say 'you've got the wrong idea' and make sure I stay firmly in the friend zone.

At long last, we're alone with three pans of steaming pizza stacked in front of us. Wordlessly, Carter dishes a slice of spicy Italian sausage on his plate. I plate three slices of my duck-pineapple-blue cheese pizza onto my plate. I don't know what I was thinking. It looks and smells disgusting, but I don't waste food. I'm going to eat every bite. At least it's personal pizza sized and a thin crust.

"You don't have to eat it," he says, watching me hesitate. "You can change your mind."

I arch an eyebrow. A challenge? I take a big bite. Oh dear god. Why did I add blue cheese? I take a hearty swig of red wine.

Torturous silence. I finish my slice and tackle the other. Vile as it tastes, my Franken-pizza gives me something to focus on.

"Once I make a decision," I say between mouthfuls of food, "I stick to it. No take backs."

"Suppose you regret it?" He looks carefully away. "The morning after?"

"I won't. I like this pizza so long as…" I shrug and pick all the blue cheese crumbles off my slice. "The pizza likes me."

Carter leans forward and faces me in earnest. His blue eyes pierce through me, electrifying my every nerve. His voice is huskier than normal. "The pizza likes you."

"That's good to know."

"I thought you were saving yourself for a better pizza," Carter continues. "One you read about in your book."

"What book would that be?" I ask, playing along.

"*The Witch of Blackbird Pond*. You know, the perfect pie that," Carter frowns, "came from the sea."

"I'm still saving myself for that one, but I figure I might as well sample other toppings in the meantime."

Carter downs his entire wine glass and pours himself another. "When does the 'sampling' begin?"

"As soon as we've finished eating," I say, smiling at his flustered face. "The Airbnb should be ready by now and I figure we'd — "

He flags down a passing server. "Check please."

chapter thirty

We stand in the middle of the sidewalk without a plan. Carter's holding a stack of leftover pizza boxes. I turn this way and that for no particular reason. My inner compass is out of whack. I jumped through the hurdle of proposing a one-night stand or whatever you call our evening plans. Where do we go from here?

I glance up at his flustered face. "Things just got weird, didn't it?"

"It's just unexpected," he says after a curt nod. "I'm down for whatever you have in mind. You make the call."

I begin walking toward a line of old shops. There are fake cobwebs on the door and plastic skeletons climbing the lamp posts. Normally I would stop and gawk at the Halloween decorations. My stomach churns. I plow ahead without paying attention to my surroundings. I have tunnel vision, all my worries centered on tonight. I should have planned this better. Packed sexier pajamas. Oh God… what's my underwear situation look like?

"Theo!" Carter calls me back. "The Airbnb's this way."

"Ah." I whirl on my heels and follow him.

"Just so we're clear," he asks. "Are there any ground rules to this, um… to tonight?"

"What do you mean?"

He keeps step beside me, his gaze fixed ahead. "Do you have a plan?"

My sensible flapper heels jams into a crack, forcing me to halt. "Like positions?" I ask, yanking myself out of my rut. "I thought we'd try whatever comes naturally. I'm flexible. Er, I don't mean 'flexible' as in..." I've won a blue ribbon in the most awkward contest. "You know what I mean. *But* that doesn't mean I'm up for *anything*, so don't get any funny ideas."

"Good to know," he says with a cough. "Can we do it multiple times?"

My eyes widened. A shot of heat zips through my body at the suggestion. Images of our bodies intertwined in a variety of creative positions—all night long—sounds enticing.

The possibility that we can do it multiple times hadn't even crossed my mind. I'm just trying to jump the first hurdle and Carter's thinking ahead.

"I'm open," I say with as much dignity as I could muster. No point getting flustered. We're both adults here.

"And tomorrow?" he asks shyly.

"We leave Salem tomorrow," I frown. "I suppose we can squeeze one in before check out."

A secretive smile. "Or two?"

I step back. "How many times are you planning on doing it?"

"Does *this*," he makes a strange circle with his hands, gesturing to space between us, "carry over to next week?"

"What's 'this'? You mean the sex?"

He casts his eyes to the pavement. "Meaning where do we stand when we come home?"

"I hadn't thought about that either," I say, a little less certain about my big bold move. "Are you worried that sleeping together will put our friendship in jeopardy?" I frown. "*Are* we friends?"

"I'd say we are."

"We've known each other all of two weeks. If this ends in disaster, you'll still work on my house, right?"

"It won't end badly. I won't let it." Seeing that his rationality

151

was putting him in danger of not getting laid (and believe me, he looks like he's desperate to get laid), Carter backtracks: "We don't have to think about that now. Let's just say what happens in Salem stays in Salem?"

"One night and a morning?" I take to the idea. "Let's establish some deadlines. *This* ends when we return to Wethersfield. At the stroke of midnight."

"Why midnight?"

I shrug. "It worked for Cinderella. Actually... let's aim for 6 P.M. Cinderella isn't in her thirties with night routines to maintain. We can also catch dinner at 7 and binge the new season of *The Crown*."

"That's premiering tomorrow!"

"Yeah it is!"

"Practical. I like it. Okay," Carter nods, getting accustomed to the terms. "I like deadlines. It makes me work harder." He glances around the busy town. We hadn't moved from the sidewalk. People in Halloween costumes stream past us. He holds out an arm for me to take. "Let's not linger. We've got a lot to do."

"Don't you want to sight see?"

"NO!"

I take his arm. His skin is warm through the thin cotton of his turtleneck. His forearm is (Oh Hello!) sturdy and firm. I could squeeze it all day. Another surge of heat bolts through me. I wonder what other part of his body is this firm and squeezable.

"Do you like how my arm feels?" Carter asks, sneaking a glance down at me.

"I approve."

He bumps my shoulder. "What are you thinking about?"

"Thoughts."

"What kind of thoughts?"

"Dirty ones." I hide a smile until a crucial detail occurs to me. "Shit! Condoms. You don't happen to have — "

"I'll buy some!" Carter says, pulling up the location of the closest pharmacy on his phone. "I'll buy whatever you want."

I prop a hand on my hip, amused. "Carter Bromley, I've never seen you so eager to shop."

He levels me with a hungry gaze that makes my knees weak. "There's never been anything I've wanted until now."

chapter thirty-one

In the pharmacy, I drop two bags of Hot Cheetos into my basket, sour gummy worms, and three mini containers of ice cream. I join Carter in the condom aisle where I left him to do his thing.

"I'm ready," I say, lifting up my basket.

Carter checks over his shoulder before slipping two boxes of Trojans into my basket.

I arch an eyebrow. "Two boxes? Really?"

"Not enough?" Flushing, Carter tosses in a third box.

"You do realize this is for one night?"

"I know."

I lower my voice. "When was the last time you've been with anyone?"

"Too long."

"Should I be afraid?" *Should my vagina be afraid?*

He leans forward until his mouth is inches away from my ear. "Yes," he says in a low growl that makes my toes curl. His eyes sweep over my flushed cheeks to the basket. "Hot Cheetos?"

"Snacks."

"We have leftover pizza."

"I want something to nibble on." I bite my bottom lip. The action doesn't escape his notice. His breath quickens and he sways a little closer.

"Carter?" I lift my eyes and meet his smoky gaze. "Don't you think we're doing things out of order?"

"What do you mean?"

"We're skipping straight to boning." I glance up at him through my lashes. "You haven't even kissed me yet. Of course, people can bone without—"

My eyes widen as I see him approaching me, his attention intensely focused on my lips. Whoa. So much blue steel.

My back bumps against the shelves. "What are you doing?"

"I'm going to kiss you," he says in the sexiest grumble growl ever.

I'm in danger of melting. "Okay," I squeak.

"Are you ready?"

I nod. "Uh huh."

"Here I come."

Three. Two. One. Touchdown.

My eyes widen as his lips meet mine.

Oh.

Oh.

Hello. What have I been missing? Dropping my basket, I shut my eyes and melted into him like warm butter folded into chocolate.

Had I known he could kiss like this, we should have been doing it sooner! I would've devoured his mouth the moment he freed me from that hole in the wall. His hands had been slick with butter, slipping and sliding over my waist… *That's* when we should have first made out. Who needs introductions? We should have gone at it like… hamsters.

Carter pulls away to study me. "What are you thinking about?"

"Hamsters."

His lips twitch. "My kissing you reminds you of your hamsters?"

"In a different context," I swallow, "Yes?"

His mouth seeks mine, soft and gentle nibbles that had me on my toes. "You're adorable."

I wrap my arms around his neck. His arms encircle my waist and his kisses take a hungry turn. His lips are no longer gentle and unsure, but questing for answers. My answer is yes. Yes. Yes. Hell yes.

One moment we're two calm adults, the next moment I'm knocking a stack of Trojans to the floor.

"Ahem."

It takes several 'Ahems' before I realize we're not alone in the aisle. Before I can un-hook my arms from around Carter's neck, his lips brush the side of my jaw, triggering a full body shiver.

"Um…" A skinny stock clerk stands before us with a cart of inventory.

We blink at him like moles in daylight.

He holds up a new pile of condoms and points to the ill stock shelf behind us. "I'll come back."

"Don't worry," I say, sharing a secretive smile with Carter. "Just put them in my basket. We'll take them all."

chapter thirty-two

I 've longed to come to Salem all my life and partake in the Halloween festivities.

Normally I would want to visit the old cemeteries, lighthouses, and take a haunted tour of everything associated with the witchcraft trials.

This was before I knew I was about to enter into a sex marathon with Carter.

I'm ashamed to admit that my libido takes precedence over my carefully laid sight-seeing plans. Come to think of it, I can't even remember my original itinerary. My brain swims in a fog that can only be cleared when I've scratched my itch to bone a sexy man with eight-pack abs.

Our Airbnb comprises the entire second floor of a cozy colonial home. The cheery red front door is decorated with a wreath of Indian corn. I take a second to appreciate the cozy decor and punch in the key code into the lock.

My fingers fumble the numbers. BEEP. Access denied. I glance over my shoulder and give Carter a nervous smile.

His lips curl at the corners. "Something wrong?"

"Stop watching me."

"I'm not watching you," he says, but I can sense his eyes on the nape of my neck. A rush of heat blazes through me like a wildfire as I try again.

BEEP. Access denied.

He steps forward, bracketing me between his arms. "Let me," he speaks in my ear with the hungry growl guaranteed to turn anyone into a puddle on the doorstep. I arch backward, my back curving into his front. Oh God... He feels so good.

"Do you even know the code?"

"No," he says, nuzzling into the crook of my neck. His arm comes around my waist and—

"Get a room!" A man shouts.

We both check over our shoulder. A pack of families pass by our house. A mother covers her daughter's eyes and glares at us. Another woman tells her kids to move along and shames us with a shake of her head.

Carter lets me go. "What's the code again?"

Feeling chastised about almost committing a public sex act, I mutter the four numbers.

A few deft punches with his fingers and the door opens. He levels me with a dangerous look. "Inside," he says.

As soon as the door shuts behind me, I hitch in my breath. The oxygen is sucked out of the room and replaced with an electrical current. I sense the charge in the air, the fire risk... all I can do is draw out the impending backdraft. All the ambient sounds of life, the ticking of the kitchen cat clock, the whirl of the air conditioner, and the street noises outside have been drowned out by the erratic pulse of my anticipation.

Keenly aware that Carter is watching my every move, I drop my duffle bag off at the entrance and take a turn around the room to calm my nerves.

Thankfully, the host is gone for the weekend and has left notes to help ourselves to her pantry. Our room is small and cozy with a view of Salem Harbor and the Derby Wharf lighthouse at the end of the jetty.

A wax melt burns on the dinette table, perfuming the room with the scent of lavender Earl Grey tea. We have one Murphy bed, already pulled out from the wall and decorated with the largest collection of throw pillows I've ever seen, and a pull-out couch.

I check over my shoulder. Carter has not moved from the entryway.

"Two beds." My lips curl into a tentative smile. "In hindsight, I guess we won't need two."

My words are met with weighted silence. Carter's overnight bag hits the ground and the next thing I know, he wraps his arms around me from behind, enfolding me into him like warm butter.

"You're goddamn right," he says, nuzzling my neck and scratching me with the bristles of an early five o'clock shadow.

I arch my back against him—my rear to his front — and *ohhhhh...* someone is happy to see me. "Aren't we going to unpack first?"

"No."

He feels like he's about to unpack something all right.

His hand slides up my abdomen, ruching up my fringe flapper dress. His lips imprint a hot brand on my neck and leave a trail of searing kisses on my collarbone.

Carter slides my spaghetti straps off my shoulder, one after the other. He undresses me slowly, his touch gentle yet intense, demanding yet attentive to my needs.

I squeeze my legs together. My chest rises and falls with each raspy breath as he kisses and caresses my bare skin with infuriating patience.

If a simple kiss on my shoulder can get me this worked up, imagine how it'll feel when we're naked and entangled in bed.

"Carter?" I squeak.

"Turn around," he says in my ear.

My stomach twists at the command in his voice. I gulp and turn around, sighing as he presses his hand to my lower back. He rests his forehead against mine. He is fevered, his breathing erratic.

"Last chance to change your mind," he says. "Once I get going, I don't think I can stop."

"You've been going since lunch," I say, eliciting a slow smile from him.

Not waiting for his reply, I stand on my tiptoes and kiss his jaw, his mouth, my fingers bunching up his black turtleneck, desperate to touch skin. My palms slide down his washboard abdomen and it's every bit as warm and hard as I imagined. Edith once told me her second husband was a David amongst men. He had the most perfect six-pack abs in the world.

I was unimpressed.

Our generation has to work harder for everything. We need a college degree and five years of experience to qualify for an entry-level job and be quarter millionaires to own a tiny starter home. The bar is set higher in every aspect of our lives, including abs. Leave six pack abs for the boomers. Our millennial men need to have eight packs now. Not that I'm complaining…

"Where did you have time to get these?"

"I can't sleep at night," he says, sounding strangled as I trace his hip dips with my fingers. "So I do crunches until I tire myself out."

Thank God for insomnia. Feeling courageous, I bend down and plant a kiss on his stomach and work my way up inch by delectable inch to his chest. A moan rumbles in his throat as I use my teeth and the next thing I know, I'm being swept off my feet and carried to the Murphy bed.

Carter dumps me on the mattress and falls on me like a hungry dog. Throw pillows tumble to the floor. The bedspring squeaks.

I wrap my legs around his waist, luxuriating in his kisses and the heavenly weight of his body atop of mine. My body responds, grinding my pelvis not-so-tamely against his.

My stomach responds too, rumbling loud enough that Carter pokes his head up and smiles down at me.

"You can't still be hungry," he says.

"No, I…" How embarrassing.

My stomach grumbles again, louder, grittier, prolonged. We both glance down. Can stomachs fart? This sounds like a fart.

160

And this time…

Oh my freaking God, no…

A quick stab of pain followed by a dull churning ache—a spinning cement mixer in my gut.

"Nerves?" Carter asks.

I swallow. "Perhaps."

My stomach quiets. The churning subsides. *Whew.* I say a silent prayer that the ache isn't what I thought it was. I can rest easy.

"I'm nervous too," he says with a smile.

"I have the perfect remedy for that," I say, running my hands under his shirt.

"I like the way you think." Straddling me, Carter reaches behind his neck and yanks his turtleneck over his head in one fell swoop.

I unbutton his jeans and we're off to the races in a contest to see who can get naked faster. I kick my witch shoes across the room. My black flapper dress puddles on the ground, joined by Carter's dad jeans and my strapless bra. He slips out of his boxers and plants a kiss on a new part of my body.

I wiggle my hips. "Help me with these tights," I say, and yelp with shocked delight as he tugs me to the edge of the bed by the ankle and peels my stripped tights off of me. I hear a tear.

"Oooh," he grits his teeth, "sorry."

"That's okay. I have a drawer full of witch tights."

He peers at me over my bare knees. "Witch tights?"

I shrug. "I love Halloween."

My tights, along with my panties, top off the pile of discard clothing.

Carter stands before me for a moment, worshipping my naked body until I self-consciously scoot to the head of the bed. A flush steals across my skin. I eye the nightstand and hide a smile. He's managed to place our condom supply within arms' reach without my knowing.

I settle down against the throw pillows and check out his goods as he takes an unsteady step toward me. It's now or never.

Sucking in a ragged breath, I open my legs and crook a finger for him to come closer. My other hand wanders down my stomach, curious, playful. I touch myself, uncertain at first…

And then, when I take in his tortured expression, his pupils a black pool of lust, his own hand stroking himself, pumping faster, I settle back and become more comfortable.

My stomach clenches for a bit, a pang of anticipation accompanied by a small rumble. My brows knot and I clamp down on my bottom lip. Hm… This is worrisome. My stomach is doing that funny grumbling thing again.

Carter takes my frowning as a sign that I'm close. "Oh no, you don't."

My stomach quiets and I slump in relief. Okay. What was *that* all about? One thing I know for certain: we need to get this show on the road before my stomach churns again and kills the mood.

"Maybe I *am* hungry," I say. "Get over here and let me suck on that big, delicious c—"

My laughter rings through the small room as he pounces and the bedsprings squeak beneath our weight.

It's GO time.

chapter thirty-three

I won't get into the lurid details.

Okay. Maybe a few important ones.

Carter's abs feel great, especially when pressed against my bare breasts and if I thought a kiss on my shoulder was electrifying, imagine how that mouth feels on my knee, my inner thigh, and my…

"Carter… Oh God!" My back arches off the bed. "Don't stop." My legs are draped over his shoulders and I'm climbing higher and higher, twisting handfuls of his hair, lewdly grinding myself against his marauding mouth, his wicked tongue.

I'm so close… so *so* close to seeing stars.

And then.

It happens.

Again.

My stomach rumbles.

Huh?

My eyes snap open. I'm staring at an ancient ceiling fan. No stars. Where's the stars? The fireworks? I was soooo close and now… nothing.

My stomach growls.

I glance down at the top of Carter's mussed up blond hair. Did he hear it? He's still slaving away between my legs, unaware of anything amiss.

I release his hair and press a hand to my abdomen. The dull ache has returned.

My stomach churns, bubbles actually, and the pain is sharper and more insistent, hinting at the mother of all stomach aches.

Oh no. Please don't do this. Not now.

I break into a cold sweat.

Okay. Breathe. Calm down. Mind over matter. I am one with the Force and the Force is with me. I clench my hands, my body, my ass. *Especially* my ass.

I'm just going to have to will the stomach ache away and use the bathroom afterward. Now, instead of luxuriating in what was shaping up to be the best foreplay of my life, I prop myself up on my elbows and watch him work. He's really diligent, making sure he covers every surface area. My skin is clammy and I shift in discomfort, wishing he'd wrap it up already.

But he seems to be intent on drawing this out.

"Carter?" I tap his shoulder.

"Hm?"

"How long is this going to take?"

He pokes his head up. Our eyes meet over the plane of my stomach. "I thought you were enjoying it."

"I was. I mean, I am."

He plants a kiss on the heart-shaped mole on my hip. "Let me take care of you..."

"No! You really don't want your mouth there!"

He returns to doing his thing. Instead of aroused, I feel irritated and bothered. I cover my face with my hands.

After a while, Carter stops pleasuring me and hovers over me on all fours.

His face looms over me. "Are you okay? You kind of... dried up in the middle of—"

In reply, my stomach lets out the loudest, *wettest* rumble yet and that's when I knew...

No amount of willpower or ass clenching can stop it. The Force is *not* with me. With a whimper, I push him over and scramble off the bed. "Get out of my way! I have to use the bathroom!"

chapter thirty-four

There's tap on the door. "Theo?"

Oh God. "Yeah?"

"Are you okay in there?" comes Carter's concerned voice.

"*Uh huh.*" I clutch my stomach and curl my toes, but there's no disguising what's happening in this tiny, ill-ventilated bathroom.

What moron thought it was a good idea to order a pressed duck-blue cheese-pineapple pizza with extra duck fat? I was tempting fate.

At least I made it to the bathroom. It could have been worse. I could have gone on the bed. Or on his face. He was dangerously close to that region and—

Another wave of stomach pains rolls through me. I dip my head between my knees and groan. It's a bowl filler. My head droops to my chest. I squeeze my eyes shut.

Carter clears his throat. "I'm heading back to CVS. I'm actually not feeling well either, so I figure I'll pick up some Pepto Bismol and Gatorade." He pauses as my body makes a very loud, un-sexy sound. "Is there anything else you want me to bring back?"

Kill me now. "Matches."

chapter thirty-five

At one point during the night, it was coming out of both ends.

Too much information? It's important to note that our room is tiny, the walls thin, and the overhead fan inside the bathroom doesn't circulate worth a damn. I used up a pack of matches. We burned the candle all night. Mortified doesn't begin to describe how I feel.

I spend the remainder of the night in the bathroom.

Sex is out of the question. A sex marathon? Ha! I doubt Carter would want to touch me after this.

We never touch our giant supply of condoms, but I sure as hell got acquainted with the bottom of my Pepto Bismol bottle.

I'm curled upon on the sofa, wrapped in a throw with a trash can in arm's reach. My head is propped on Carter's thigh as I absently re-watch *Hocus Pocus*.

I'm sure there are places Carter would rather be, things he'd rather do. Heck, there are better things *I'd* rather do. Whoops and hollers, laughter and drunken ghoulish howls echo from outside. We're missing quite a Halloween party.

Resigned to being my nurse instead of my lover, Carter strokes my hair. "This is a very noisy movie," he says, cringing at the movie's sound effects.

"It's a Halloween classic. Didn't you ever watch it as a kid?"

"Never."

"What did you watch as a kid then?"

"If it didn't win an Oscar, I didn't watch it."

"Snob." I roll over and peek up at him. He grimaces as Winifred, flying atop her broomstick, has Max by the throat and is trying to suck the life out of him.

"This movie is the audio equivalent of someone banging pots and pans over my head," he says.

I smile for the first time since my food poisoning. "You don't suppose we can still catch that ghost tour? It takes us through graveyards, the Ropes Mansion, and all the filming locations of *Hocus Pocus*."

Carter glances down at me like I've lost my mind. "Do you have to use the bathroom?"

"I — " *Gurgle.* I clutch my stomach, my mouth twisting into a grimace. "Hold that thought."

I run to the bathroom, returning ten minutes later weaker, paler, five pounds lighter. "Don't go in there."

chapter thirty-six

The next day, I update my status from 'curled up in fetal position on sofa' to 'pathetic potato in passenger seat.'

I'm bundled from head to toe in a flannel throw, clutching a half-drunk bottle of Gatorade in my claw. A CVS plastic bag is chilling by my feet in case there's more duck I have to chuck during our drive home. I'm dressed in a sweatshirt with a stain on the front (just a little puke) and chunky socks. My hair is greasy and gathered in a messy bun which, thankfully, is covered by the flannel throw. All in all, I look very attractive. The picture of seduction.

Carter is behind the wheel of the U-Haul, his attention focused on the road. His hair is tousled, but he's wearing fresh clothes from his Normcore wardrobe: a nondescript black puffer over a grey sweater and black jeans. Non-branded black running shoes, which I recognize from a bombardment of Instagram ads, are *Allbirds*.

"What are you thinking about?" he asks.

"That you're dressed like a serial killer."

He glances down at his outfit and frowns. "I don't see a killer clown outfit."

"You're talking about John Wayne Gacy," I say. "I'm thinking more 'Ted Bundy.' You can blend in anywhere and no one will bat an eye."

He gives me a funny look. "That's the dehydration talking. Are you afraid I'm going to kill you?"

"No," I hide a smile, "but I had my doubts about your backyard shed."

"My train shed?"

"You never got around to giving me a tour. Suppose you have something to hide? Bodies of your victims in various stages of dismemberment, perhaps?"

"Nope," he says. "Just model trains. I can show you around tonight, if you like. That is, if you're feeling better."

"I do feel better." I swallow the lump in my throat. He's nursed me through the night, making sure I'm properly dehydrated and had the good grace not to remind me of the incident. He *may* be a keeper. "Thanks to you."

Sensing my gaze on him, his eye dart to me before quickly returning to the road.

"Did you eat all your crackers?" Carter asks, changing the subject.

I glance down at the packet of Saltines that came with my soup. "I don't like crackers."

"Tough. Eat."

Reluctantly, I nibble on a dry cracker and chase it with a mouthful of lemon-lime Gatorade.

"You can do better than that," he says. "Finish the bottle."

My lips twitch. "Yes, Mom." I drain the Gatorade and polish off my Saltines. I'm 60% back to my old self, though I would never admit that Carter's fussing is the reason for my speedy recovery.

"Here's a question," Carter begins, eyes still on the road. The skies are grey and crawling with distant storm clouds. A light sprinkle coats the windshield.

I hold my breath, expecting him to broach our now-weird relationship status.

What are we? Friends? Lovers? Lovers, right? We've seen each other naked, and he's given me oral pleasure... even though he hasn't finished it. Plus, I'm pretty sure he's smelled my poop. If that doesn't say 'intimate' I don't know what does.

Oh God. I want to die every time I think about the last bit.

"Is it an important question?" I ask.

"Very."

"Shoot."

Carter takes a deep breath.

"Would you rather fight one horse-sized duck or one hundred duck-sized horses?"

I blink, overcome with relief and... disappointment. Okay. So he's ignoring talking about our relationship status altogether. I can do that.

"What would you do?" I ask.

"The choice is obvious. I'll fight the duck. One adversary is better than a hundred smaller ones."

"A giant duck will peck you to death."

"True," Carter chews on his inner cheek, "but if I win, I can eat him."

I roll my eyes and take a hearty swig of Gatorade. "I will never eat duck again. Bring on the tiny horses."

chapter thirty-seven

The trip passes in a blur of naps and irrelevant chit chat. Twenty questions has saved many an awkward situation, but as we pull up to my driveway, I knew we could no longer tiptoe around the elephant in the room.

Wait.

What am I talking about?

Yes, I can!

We still have to move the Jacques Le Fèvre couch inside. That should bide us some time and believe you me, I plan to milk the chore out for as long as I can.

Carter's eyes me dubiously as I take my place on one end of the yellow couch. "Are you sure you're strong enough to help?"

I roll up my sleeves. "You can't lug this thing in yourself and I'm much improved."

"It's unnecessarily heavy," he says, tapping the toe of his sneakers against the claw foot. Tossing unnecessary shade on American red maple, I see.

"Then you can shoulder most of the weight."

"You should probably eat more crackers before you attempt hard labor."

"Enough with the crackers!"

We bicker until the sun slants behind my backyard chestnut

tree and a gloomy shadow yawns over the Witch House, making it appear more creepy than cozy.

With gritted teeth and low curses, we haul the yellow couch into my living room. I'm huffing and puffing, secretly cursing the density of American red maple.

"Urgh," I grit my teeth, "this thing weighs a ton!"

"Told you so."

"I guess colonial people kept their furniture rearranging to a minimum."

"Colonial people who can afford this type of sofa would have their servants arrange furniture," Carter says, "much like you had me do in Salem."

"Oh right," I smile sheepishly, "I forgot that you're my indentured servant."

Carter shakes his head. "How do I get myself into these situations?"

"Cheese, remember?"

"I never forgot."

At last, the claw feet slam against the sturdiest part of the hardwood floor.

Night draws a curtain over the sagging corners of my living room. I switch on the light and nothing happens.

"For the love of—"

"What's wrong?" Carter asks.

"I forgot that not all rooms have electricity. The light works in the second-floor bathroom and the attic, but not in, say, important rooms."

"You don't really need electricity in the... kitchen."

I roll my eyes. "I give up."

Out of breath and sweating bullets, we slump onto opposite ends of the couch. Carter lolls his head against the maple backing. I gather my knees to my chest and squeeze my eyes shut.

Now what?

The couch has been moved. The trip is over. I've seen his dick. It's a nice dick. Dick-a-licious. Question is: do I want to see it again? Do I want his dick in my life? Where do we go from here?

It's some time before Carter glances my way. "How are you feeling?"

"Disappointed in myself," I blurt out. "I wrecked the weekend." And by weekend, I mean our sex plans.

"You didn't wreck the weekend. You got to see some of Salem."

"Which part? The parking lot?" I grimace. "Nothing good ever comes of 'make your own' anything. I make awful Subway sandwiches."

Carter shifts to face me, his lips twitching at the corners. "Did you add duck to your meatball sub?"

"I would if they had 'duck' as an option. It's more like teriyaki sauce over my bacon ranch chicken. Black olives in everything, even though I hate olives. I knew it would be gross, but I couldn't help myself. I've ruined many a sandwich and now... pizza. Why do I do this to myself?"

"Because they gave you the option," he says.

I shake my head, shamed. "Too many options."

"I bet you go hog wild at buffets."

My eyes widen. How did he know? Wait until I tell him about the fight over King Crab legs at the Caesar's Palace buffet when I was in college. I'm greedy when it comes to 'All-You-Can-Eat' or 'Make your own' combos and I make poor life decisions.

Sighing, I lean my head back to look at the ceiling. A shaft of moonlight streams through the slats of a stripped beam. Wow. Carter was right. This house *is* a money pit. "There's a hole in my ceiling."

Carter opens his mouth, a 'told you so' on the tip of his tongue, then shakes his head. "At least you got your Jacques Pierre."

"Jacques Le Fèvre," I correct. "At least there's that."

He drapes an arm over the maple backing and shifts to get comfortable.

174

"The cushions aren't really doing a damn thing, are they?" I ask, watching him suffer.

"They can use more stuffing." Carter clears his throat and looks the other way. "How's your stomach?"

"Much, much better. Thanks to your nagging. The crackers helped."

"Good, good."

"How do you feel about... No, never mind. Bad idea."

"What?"

He checks his watch, cheeks reddening in the moonlight. "Technically, it's ten till 6 PM. If you're feeling healthier, maybe we can..." He meets my eye and gulps.

"What?" I ask, hanging onto his every word.

He shakes his head. "Forget about it. You're still sick."

"I said I was better! What were you about to suggest?"

Carter rubs the back of his neck. "Maybe we can..." A shrug. "I dunno... test out these cushions?"

I frown. "I thought we established that these cushions are uncomfortable."

Carter wiggles an eyebrow and shoots me an uncertain smile.

"Oh," I say, realization dawning on me. Cushions. 6 P.M. Deadline. *"Ohhhhhhhh!"*

"But only if you're feeling up to it. I wouldn't want to jostle um... jostle anything out of you."

"There's nothing left in me to come out."

A crooked grin spreads across his face. "Then come here and kiss me."

chapter thirty-eight

"Come here and kiss me…"

Okay!

For someone who just lost 50% of her body weight in liquids, I move fast. I'm in Carter's lap in seconds, straddling him and kissing him with shameless abandon. We make-out like it's the end of the world: nibbling, licking, sucking. And let me just point out, a deadline to bone is a *massive* turn on. Everybody should try it, especially long time couples. It'll definitely spice up your love life.

I come up for air. "I have decided I *do* want your dick in my life."

Carter pulls back to look at me. His brows knit in question.

"Is that a weird thing to say?"

His lips twitch. "No, not from you," he says, helping me out of my stained sweatshirt. He hands me a foiled packet and guides my hand between our bodies. To the hard ridge underneath black denim.

Arching an eyebrow, I hold up the condom. "Where were you hiding this?"

"In my pocket," he says, exhaling a harsh breath as I stroke him through his jeans. "God, Theo… that feels so good."

"It would feel better without your pants," I said, trailing kisses along his jaw.

One moment I'm coping a feel, the next moment his jeans are pooled around his ankles and I'm helping him slide the condom on with my hands, then my mouth…

I'm focused. I'm in the zone as I climb back onto his lap.

Branches knock against the roof.

An autumn chill blasts against my bare bottom.

A thump echoes from above.

"Wait," I whisper, glancing overhead. "Did you hear that?"

"No," he says, kissing the swells of my breasts.

"I think it's the ghost."

"What ghost?"

"Eliza Wolcott. The chestnut-ghost-witch."

"I don't believe in ghosts," he says. "But I *do* believe in efficiency. Forget the ghost. Remember the deadline."

I feel his crooked grin against my lips as he reaches down and works me with his *magical* fingers. I forget the racket on the second floor. I forget my name. I forget how to speak and breathe. I toss my head back, greedy for his touch, purring and moaning loud enough to drown out any ghost.

"You're so good at this," I pant against his temple, "why are you so good with your hands?"

"I had a part-time job on a lobster fishing boat in college."

"No…"

"Yes."

"Where?"

"In Saybrook Harbor."

I bite my bottom lip. "Oh my god…"

"I used my hands… all summer long," he whispers in my ear. "Tying knots."

"*Nautical* knots?"

I press my forehead against his. "Tell me about the knots. How many kinds of maritime knots did you… tie?"

"I did them all…"

I shiver. Every muscle in my body tenses. I clutch his wrist, driving my nails into his skin. "Carter, please…"

"Please what?"

"Describe them to me."

"Not yet... Not until you're..." He nudges me with his naked hip and we both exhale as I sink down and begin to ride.

"Describe them to me now!"

"There's the Stevedore Stopper."

"Yes!" I don't know what that is, but it sounds hot and complicated, requiring dexterous fingers. Sailor fingers. "More!"

"Running bowline."

"Yes!"

"That's the knot I tie when I'm on the rigging."

"Yes! Yes! Yes!"

The couch is narrow, not affording us much room to maneuver.

And yes, the cushions are merely for decor. My knees are going to be bruised after this. Totally worth it.

"Form a bight in the end of the rope," Carter whispers in my ear as his fingers dig into my hips. "Pass the tail end across the standing end..."

"Don't stop!"

"Continue around to make two complete turns..."

The yellow couches' claw feet scrape against the floors with my every bounce. By the time we finish, we'll have scooted the couch against the wall.

Something hard, small, and cold bounces off my forehead and clatters to the floor. "Ouch!" I slow my motions and rub my temple.

"What's wrong?"

"Something struck me!" We halt our humping, turn our heads to the left, then gaze down at the ground. The object has landed in a shaft of moonlight. It's solid and brown, not quite a pebble.

"Did you see that?" My eyes widen. "I got hit by a chestnut."

"It's a rock."

"A chestnut."

Carter squints at the missile and nods in acquiescence. "Okay, it's a chestnut."

"I think it's the witch…" I glare up at the ceiling. "She doesn't like us boning in her house."

"She doesn't have to watch. Unless…" He shoots me the filthiest smirk. "You *want* her to watch?"

"Maybe I do…" I see his sultry smirk with a bite to his shoulder.

"Forget the chestnut." He grabs my ass, urging me to go faster, harder. I'm happy to oblige.

"You want this, you sick f—" He wants me to give it to him? I'll give it to him.

Creaks and groans fill my quiet living room. My antique couch is getting one hell of a workout. We're putting my three-hundred-year-old floor through the paces.

Plip-plip-ploop-plip-plip-plip-ploop.

A hail of chestnuts bounces off our heads, shoulders…

Plip-plip-ploop-plip-plip-plip-ploop.

A chestnut pelts me in the ass and it hurts.

Hurts so good…

One thrust.

Two.

Three.

The yellow sofa groans. The claw legs make its last creak before buckling under our weight and splintering like kindling.

We tumble, tangled together on the floor.

I blink down at him. Slowly, we survey the damage. We're lying atop a pitiful pile of dust and rubble, tits out, asses bare… surrounded by chestnuts. A sea of chestnuts. A squirrels' paradise. More chestnuts than the eye can see.

I bite my bottom lip. "I suppose we should clean this up."

His eyes crinkle at the corners and he leans forward, stealing a long kiss from me. It's not a passionate kiss, but a sweet and playful promise that makes my heart twist.

"After," he says, pulling away.

He didn't need to say anymore. I grab what's left of my couch's red maple backing for support and finish us both off.

chapter thirty-nine

I wake up to birdsong outside my window, the nervous creak of a hamster wheel, and an empty bed. I roll over onto my side and contemplate the rumpled sheets, the indent on my second pillow, my sore muscles...

Burying my face in my pillow, I smile in memory as spicy images of last night come pouring back in.

After we smashed my couch to smithereens (totally worth it), Carter and I snuck back into Edith's B&B, threw a blanket over my hamster cage, and had an encore performance. Then a late-night showing. Dawn set in; an early bird special. We missed dinner. Missed the season premiere of *The Crown*. Forgot about checking out Carter's model trains. I won't go into detail, other than to say that we wore out the springs on my mattress and made a huge dent in our condom supply.

Afterward, Carter rolled out of bed and slipped on his boxers.

"You're not staying over?" I had asked, startled by his abrupt departure.

"I can only sleep in my own bed."

"Your bed is a futon on the floor." A futon built for one, which he rolls up and stuffs in his closet.

"What's wrong with this bed?" I had tried to control the creep of annoyance in my voice.

"I like a hard surface. This box spring doesn't agree with my back."

"You can sleep on the good side," I'd said. "I'll take the dip side."

He'd shaken his head. "I need sleep."

"You can sleep here… with me. Do you really *need* to go?"

"Yes."

I couldn't read his expression in the dark. He'd sounded incredibly calm and matter-of-fact for my taste. Then again, I don't know what I was expecting out of him. A grand proclamation of true love? Tears? A love song that he composed on the fly? A poem? A marriage proposal?

None of that now. We're two consenting adults who were just having a bit of fun. Still, the least he could do, the least I *expected* him to do, was stay until morning.

I drew the comforter up to my chin.

I had no reason to be annoyed at him already. Technically, he stayed the night. But what's this nonsense about mattress firmness? He didn't seem to mind this box spring when he was jackhammering me into it. It's *my* back that hurts. And if he was so particular about sleeping in his own miserable futon, why didn't he suggest we go directly to his place?

As he dressed, I had buried my face in my pillow, trying to suppress the overwhelming onslaught of conflicting emotions. When he turned around, I schooled my features in a smile.

"I guess it would be weird if Edith saw us come down for breakfast…"

A man of few words, Carter had leaned down and kissed me goodnight. His lips were soft and tender, promising more kisses to come and erasing my suspicions. My lips had parted, eliciting a deep-throated moan of longing from him. Okay. We're getting somewhere. Maybe he'll forget about his stupid futon after all…

But when I looped my arms around his neck and tried to drag him back into bed, he'd pried himself away with a groan and said, in his matter-of-fact tone, "I'll call you tomorrow. Sweet dreams."

It is now tomorrow.

I stretch my sore arms and legs, blinking as a swath of sunlight bathes me through my open window. The scent of coffee wafts up from downstairs as I detangle my legs from my sheets.

I stretch again, humming along with the bluebirds. The elm tree outside my window is a blazing autumn torch. The sky is the turquoise blue of an anime color palette. Is it me? Or are the clouds especially fluffy this morning?

I know. *I know.* I sicken myself. Picking up my discarded clothes, I edge to my nightstand and casually check my phone. A text from my mom about flight plans for Thanksgiving. Notifications of *Vincent Van Sproot* sticker sales and social media mentions.

My heart squeezes in disappointment. No word from Carter.

Calm down, Theo. Don't be a stalker. He said he'll call tomorrow, not *first thing* tomorrow. Though it *is* noon and—

Stop it.

He's probably still asleep, except…

Carter *is* an early riser. Said so himself. He's also a stickler for routine. Said so himself too.

Stop it.

These are unusual circumstances. Given our road trip to Salem and the couch moving and our sex marathon, chances are he's exhausted. He can afford to break routine.

"The day is still young," I say as I step into a hot shower.

As I towel my hair, I can't help replaying scenes from last night, my emotions seesawing between giddiness and confusion. A few hours in and I'm already plagued by self-doubt, reading into Carter's every word and action. We left things pretty freakin' vague. We both agreed to extend our 6 P.M. 'Deadline to Bone' into the next day, and now we've reached a fork in the road. Do we call it a one-night stand or continue to pursue a (*gulp*) relationship?

Tossing my towel on a floral armchair, I lift the blanket over my hamster cage. Cereal runs in her wheel while Milk gulps water from her spout.

Unlike birds, Hamsters do not fall asleep when you cover their cages. The blanket was for privacy. My fur babies are not used to their mama bringing guys over. Or getting any action for that matter. Naturally, they would want to investigate. Problem is, I can't have sex with their beady little eyes staring at us.

"Good morning, Babies," I say, leaning down to freshen up their food dish. "Have you been having fun with Edith? Do you miss Mama?"

Cereal stuffs two pellets in her cheeks and twitches her whiskers. Milk scurries to the corner and licks her paws.

Edith had agreed to pet sit during my weekend in Salem. Not an easy task since each fur baby comes with a long list of Do's and Don'ts. Milk has a host of food allergies and has a fur loss condition which requires the application of a cream twice a day, which doesn't sound difficult except that she bites.

"Don't worry, Theo. I used to own a chinchilla as a little girl," Edith had said, giving my hamster care list a casual glance and setting it aside. "Enjoy your weekend. Everything will be fine."

The Salem trip was so distracting that I barely had time to worry about my hamsters. I'd check in on Edith via text reminders every few hours.

Did you apply Milk's cream?

Did she bite you?

Please make sure to feed Cereal a handful of pellets every two hours! Don't fill up her entire bowl or she'll binge the whole thing! And make sure she does her wheel exercises at least twice a day.

Edith only responded to me once. On Saturday. *Quit your worrying and enjoy my grandson;) I want a great-granddaughter for Christmas. Eggplant emoji. Hamsters in good hands.*

Radio silence after that.

Because I had my hands full (of Carter —and parts of Carter) last night, I only gave my fur babies a cursory glance to make sure they were alive before covering their cage with a blanket and um… getting down to business. I'm a terrible hamster mom, but even hamster moms need a life.

I pet Cereal, pleased to see that she's getting slimmer. "Great job keeping to your exercise regime! High five!" I grab her tiny paw and tap it to my finger. Her whiskers twitch in triumph.

Moving onto Milk, I squeeze a toothpaste size portion of her fur loss medication on my finger and open her cage. With a frightened squeak, Milk backs herself into a corner and buries her face in a pile of paper shavings.

I frown. "What's the matter, baby?"

Milk usually loves getting her rub down—and she loves biting me afterward. Why is she acting like she's doesn't know me?

I inch toward her, plucking away her paper shred mountain. Her plump little body is shivering with fright. She covers her face with her paws and that's when I notice it:

The fur capping each of her four legs is a chestnut brown. Tiny brown socks.

"What the flip?!"

Milk is an *albino* hamster. I recall picking her up at the pet shop and remarking how every inch of her fur is pure white. Her pink footpads are the only spots of color on her.

I scoop her out of the cage and take a peek at the goods. Milk identifies as a She/Her. This hamster is definitely a He/Him. Either Milk had a sex change while I was away or something fishy is going on.

"EDITH!"

chapter forty

"Another cup of coffee?" Edith shuffles around the kitchen, refilling my mug and piling my plate with eggs, bacon, and toast. She's moving slower than usual, pausing intermittently to rub her back.

"Something the matter, Edith?"

"Just my arthritis acting up," she says, massaging her aching wrists.

"I thought you had osteoporosis."

She makes a face of great suffering. "I'm afflicted with both. I swear, I'm falling apart."

"Uh huh."

She blinks several times. "Do me a favor, Sweetie. Hand me my eyedrops. I'll get them myself, but this arthritis is just *killing* me."

"What are the eyedrops for?" I ask, patiently doing her bidding.

"Glaucoma."

"I thought you had cataracts," I say.

"I have both, dear. I have everything."

"Uh huh."

I have no doubt that Edith has a host of age-related health issues, but she's laying it on a bit thick, don't you think? She's usually a spry senior citizen, despite her age. I took her to the pharmacy. I looked at her prescription. She has a *mild* case of arthritis. Now she's acting like she's on death's door.

I'm on to her…

I cross my arms and eye my hamster cage, which I've set on a window seat in the breakfast nook.

Cereal is burying pellets in her shred bed for later (like she thinks I can't see him) and the hamster pretending to be Milk is finally nibbling at his food.

"Jam?" Edith asks, handing me the jar and spoon with a trembling hand. "You'll have to scoop it out yourself. I can't seem to coordinate what with these damn tremors. I'm really not feeling well today, so I'll leave you to enjoy your breakfast while I take a lie down. If I don't wake up, just know that I love you very much. Don't call an ambulance. I've already made my peace with God and—"

"Cut the crap, Edith, and sit down."

"Let me just — " She gestures to the muffins on the counter.

"Sit down!"

"Well!" Edith tosses her rooster shaped hand warmers on the table and plops down with the energy of a sixty-year-old. "Look who rolled out of the wrong side of the bed."

"Where's Milk, Edith?"

"Why she's right there!" She gestures to the window seat. "Look how darling she is, eating her little treat with her dainty paws."

"That's not Milk."

"What are you talking about?" Edith tips her chin up at a haughty angle. "Of course she's Milk! Look at that snowy white fur!"

"Apparently Milk's paw fur turned brown over the weekend."

Edith nods. "It happens. My chinchilla was brown with white patches, then one day, her patches turned orange."

I arch an eyebrow. Just because Edith is a sweet old lady doesn't rule her out as a pathological liar. I don't even want to know what larks she got into in her youth.

"Did Milk also get a sex change?" I ask.

Edith stops babbling about her chinchilla. "She's not a 'she'?"

"She's a 'he.' I checked."

Biting her bottom lip, Edith glances out the window.

"Damn."

"Edith…" I rub the spot between my eyes. "What happened to Milk? Did she run away? If she ran away, it's fine. She's done that before. We can find her."

The sweet old lady whom I entrusted to babysit my hamsters couldn't look me in the eye. Taking a deep breath, Edith covers my hand with hers. "It's a good thing you're sitting down."

I poke my head up, the hackles rising on the back of my neck. "What's wrong?"

"I don't know how to tell you this, Theo," Edith says. "Milk is dead."

chapter forty-one

"She was alive and frisky one moment," Edith wrings her wrinkled hands, "but when I changed her food dish on Saturday afternoon, she was huddled in the corner, fast asleep. At least I *thought* she was asleep."

With a shake of my head, I bury my face in my hands. My face is grimy and tear-streaked, my eyes red from sobbing. "Poor Milk. She wasn't even that old!"

"Oh dear." Edith plies me with tissues. "You don't need to hear anymore of this. Let's just call it water under the bridge."

I blow my nose. "Continue."

"Theo," she says, wiping a spot of snot from my cheek. "What's the point of reliving a tragedy? Milk is in a better place. She's in the great hamster wheel in the sky."

I narrow my bloodshot eyes. "Continue!"

Edith sighs. "When I came back for her rub down Sunday morning and she hadn't moved from the same spot, I knew something was up."

"So she died of natural causes?"

She nods. "Died peacefully in her sleep."

I sniffle. "She does have a host of health issues. Including a heart problem. I g-g-guess her little hamster heart just gave out!"

Edith throws her fragile arms around me as I descend into a bout of ugly sobbing.

"My chinchilla died too," Edith says. "If it makes you feel better, Fernando's death was grislier than Milk's."

Hiccuping, I peel my forehead from the table. "What happened?"

"Let's just say he snuck out of the Winnebago and my then-boyfriend Karl (massive pothead, by the way) flattened her like a pancake."

I gasp. "That's horrible! Fernando didn't scurry away?"

"He was blind in one eye. Didn't know what hit him."

"My God..."

She squeezes my hand again. "Milk is with Jesus."

"Milk isn't Christian."

"Oh, then..." Edith peers into my almond-shaped eyes. "Buddha?"

I shake my head. I'm not in the mood to ding her on her political correctness, especially after I've blown open her Hamster-Gate cover-up.

"Speaking of Milk," I cocked a thumb at the furry imposter, "who's this?"

"I bought her —"

"Him."

"I bought him," Edith corrects herself without batting an eye, "in a pet store in Mystic. Do you know how difficult it was to find an albino hamster on a Sunday? Rachel and I—"

"Rachel?! There's *two* of you involved in Hamster-Gate?" How did Edith rope Rachel into this? How deep *is* this cover-up?

"You don't expect *me* to drive around the entire state with a dead hamster in my trunk, do you? I have cataracts! We just about raided every pet store in Connecticut. We even dipped our toe in Rhode Island and I swore I'd never set foot in Rhode Island after that swinger party disaster—"

I hold up my hand. Now there's an image I don't need. No wonder Carter steers clear of his grandma. These partner-swapping, reefer smoking, chinchilla-killing boomers are out of control.

I blow out a breath, accepting Edith's efforts with grudging gratitude. "Yeah, well, he's not Milk."

"Do you mean to tell me you don't like this hamster?"

I stare at the imposter. He's squirming around, moving his little arms and doing some kind of intense hamster exercise. His eyes are beady, lacking of Milk's rodent intelligence, and yet his cheeks are chubby and *okay*, his brown paw-fur *is* adorable.

"Socks," I blurt out. "I think I'll call him Socks."

"Then you *will* keep him!" Edith slumps back in her chair.

"I suppose." I take a drink of lukewarm coffee. "I appreciate the trouble you went to, but that doesn't mean I'm not mad about your deception."

A troubling thought occurs to me. I glance around the kitchen. "Where is Milk's," I gulp, "body? Did you at least give her a proper burial? Please don't tell me you flushed her down the toilet."

Edith's eyes shift sideways.

"Edith…"

"Here's the thing," she says. "I wanted to get rid of the evidence."

I scrub a hand over my face.

"But Rachel insisted that you'll want a funeral. We bickered for *ages* and came to a compromise."

"Edith…" I prop my hand on my hip. "Where is Milk?"

"Help me up, dear," Edith says, trying to get up from her chair.

Holding onto my arm, she shuffles to the fridge.

Opens the freezer.

And there she is:

Encased in a Ziplock bag with the date of death scribbled in thick black Sharpie.

Stuffed between a bag of peas and frozen chicken wings.

Her mouth is open, revealing her two buck teeth. Tiny stiff legs. Matted fur.

"Oh dear God!" I say, taking my frozen dead hamster out of the freezer and turning the body bag this way and that.

Not only is this *horrifying*, I'm pretty sure this is a health code violation. Remind me not to eat any more meals here. "Edith?! What the f — "

"It's a morgue," she says sheepishly. "Now we can plan the funeral!"

chapter forty-two

The sun is low in the sky. A bracing wind rattles the haunted chestnut tree in my backyard, pelting us with nuts.

"Ouch," Rachel says, scooting out from under the canopy.

Edith curses and wheels herself away from the shoebox sized hole in the ground, which was quickly filling up with chestnuts.

I shove my phone into my back pocket and exhale a tremulous sigh. I'm shaking with sadness and *fury.* I can't keep checking my phone like this, but would it *kill* Carter to call me back? Or answer my texts?

Screw him. I don't need this aggravation. I have a hamster to bury.

Edith places a sympathetic hand on my shoulder. "Shall we begin? I need to get back to my programs."

"The least you can do after you *murdered* Theo's hamster is mourn with her for however many hours she chooses. Now hold still," Rachel says, fumbling with her gigantic 3rd generation iPad. "How do I take a selfie with this thing?"

As Rachel takes grainy photographs of her own forehead and Edith denies murdering Milk, I can't help peeking at my lock screen again.

They have no idea I've invited Carter. No idea that he went

from my indentured servant to friend to lover in the space of a weekend.

Lover is such an icky word. I prefer friend. If someone nurses you through food poisoning and then sleeps with you the next day... that warrants an invite to a beloved pet's funeral, right?

I'm willing to give him one more shot.

In the last three hours, I've sent Carter approximately ten texts ranging from the casual *'Hey Milk is dead... long story. Will fill you in at the funeral. Meet me beneath the haunted chestnut tree at 4:30'* to *'It's 4:40 where the !@#$% are you?'*

It's now 5 pm and the only notification on my lock screen are emails informing me of more Vincent Van Sproot sticker sales.

He'll 'call tomorrow' my ass.

Now. I'm. Really. Pissed.

Rachel clears her throat and kicks aside a fallen chestnut. "Not to interrupt you in your time of mourning," she says, "but it's getting cold and I've prepared a specialty grazing board for Milk's wake. You'll feel a lot better with some cheese in you."

"And wine," Edith adds. "God knows we can all use more wine in our lives."

"Shall we... um..." Rachel holds up the orthopedic shoebox containing Milk's body, now defrosted and ripe.

With one more hopeful glance at my messages, I text *'Fine. Ignore me. Guess you have more important things to do, so do us both a favor and DON'T CALL/TEXT/SPEAK to me EVER AGAIN."*

I slip my phone in my pocket, wiped my tears away with my sleeves.

"Oh darling." Both Edith and Rachel draw me in for a group hug.

I'm not just mourning Milk. I'm also mourning what could have been a beautiful romance... until my perfect man reveals himself to be an insensitive jerk.

Fuckboi.

I've heard about these lowlifes from Camille, who's had too many experiences with guys hooking up with her and ghosting her the next day.

193

I never thought my path would cross with one.

I'm beginning to see last night with new eyes.

First, he wines and dines me, says he doesn't mind if I diarrhea-destroyed our weekend.

I bet Carter *learned* how to say that from the Fuckboi Playbook just so he could get in my pants. What kind of deviant buys up all the condoms at CVS?

I'm crying loud and hard and ugly. I hate Fuckboi Carter. *Despise* him. *Rue* the day I ever met him. Nat Eaton is *not* a fuckboi. He waited out the winter in *celibacy* before asking Kit to marry him. Nat would never choose a futon over sleeping in her arms, and he'd certainly never ghost her on the day of her hamster's funeral.

"I know you loved that darn hamster," Edith says, "but it's not the end of the world. You mourn your little heart out."

She gestures to Rachel, who clears her throat and begins singing 'Danny Boy,' substituting 'Danny' for 'Milky.' It doesn't quite have the same effect.

chapter forty-three

I'm drowning my sorrows in my second glass of Cabernet Sauvignon when Edith envelops me in another hug. She's very touchy today. Must be the guilt.

"With all the chaos," she says, "I forgot to ask. How was Salem? Did you get the couch?"

I gulp my wine and help myself to another glass. A flush radiates through my body. "We got the couch."

"I can't wait to see it."

"I would love to show it to you," I say, heaving a gigantic sigh. "But we smashed it to smithereens when we got back."

"Oh dear," says Edith, nonplussed. "I thought you said colonial craftsmanship was next to none."

"It's built for sitting and lounging." My eyes shift to the side. Even though I'm getting woozy, I can't help taking another sip of wine. I decimate my second glass, move on to the third. "It was a rough move."

"And you didn't kill Carter by the end of it?"

"Nope," I say, cramming a slice of aged gouda in my mouth.

"Did he…" Edith pokes me in the ribs. "Did you…?"

I glare at her with sleepy eyes. "*Yesssssss?*"

"Have a nice time?"

I shrug. "Eh."

"What did you do?"

I clutch the counter for balance.

"We ate some pizza. Actually, he ate the pizza, and I ate a duck. Then I took a shit. Several shits."

Edith blinked. "Must be the duck fat."

"Went through me like shit through a goose." The wine has taken the edge off of my anger and made my tongue loose. I reach for another glass.

Edith stops me and swaps the wine for a parmesan and herb cracker. Without noticing the swap, I shove the cracker in my mouth. Crumbs skate down my mossy cable-knit sweater.

No stranger to the drink, Edith plies me with cheeses and dried dates and calls for a mug of strong black coffee.

I gaze around the cozy cheese shop and my sorrows lighten. Clusters of autumn leaves decorate every shelf. Rachel has placed a stack of mini pumpkins on the counter. It's warm in here, smelling like an apple cider-scented candle and the ripe tang of one hundred and twenty varieties of cheeses.

A chalkboard sign advertising the 35th annual scarecrow contest catches my attention.

"I'm going to enter," I blurt out. "My scarecrow will be the best this town has ever seen."

"Carter always wins the scarecrow contest," Edith points out.

I arch an eyebrow. "Does he now?"

"He's entered and won every year since he moved back," she says. "Three years in a row."

Just the mention of Carter makes my blood boil. "I thought he hated holidays or anything to do with fun."

"That may be so, but he'll never pass up a chance at winning a contest." Edith helps herself to my crackers. "Especially when first place is a $100 gift certificate to Rachel's cheese shop and three homemade pumpkin pies."

I blink. That's a very specific prize. "What was his scarecrow entry last year?"

Edith pulls up a picture of Carter standing next to a Robo-Cop-esque scarecrow who was also dressed as an old-timey train conductor. Navy coat with golden tassels and brass buttons. A conductor's hat. A whistle. "The judges were very confused about the robot portion, but the mayor's great-great-great-grand-father worked on the Transcontinental Railroad."

I glare at the photo. Look at Carter's smug face. With a grunt of suppressed rage, I snatch a flyer and fold it into squares. "My scarecrow is going to blow his out of the water."

Rachel, who had been chatting with three members of our book club, passes by to refill her plate. "Good! You're entering!"

"I plan to win."

Her eyes glitter with curiosity. "Your entry will be spectacular, you being an illustrator and all. Do you have a design in mind?"

No clue!

I shift my eyes to the side. "I have a few ideas."

We're interrupted by a commotion outside. The bell dings. The door bursts open as Carter barges in, clutching his phone and panting like he's run a marathon.

His wrinkled dress shirt is half tucked into his slacks. He's thrown on a grey scarf. His blond hair sticks up in tufts under an ancient beanie.

His frantic gaze scans the small shop until he settles on me. He holds up his phone, displaying a lock screen packed with missed calls. "I am so sorry about your hamster. I just got your message."

"Uh huh."

"Carter, dear," Edith says. "What are you doing here? You look like you've been run over by a bus."

"I invited him." I fold my arms over my chest and search for another glass of wine. "Five hours ago."

Noting my icy reception, Rachel, Edith, and our fellow erotic book club members turn to Carter for an explanation.

Carter steps forward, still holding his phone up as if showing his missed messages to me will exonerate him. "I forgot to switch my phone off 'Do Not Disturb' or else I would've been at the funeral."

All eyes swivel to me.

"You promised you'll call me today."

"I know! *I know!*" Carter scrubs a hand over his face. His eyes are red and dry, like he hadn't blinked all day. "It completely slipped my mind."

I swallow the lump in my throat. "Uh huh."

"I was going to call as soon as I got home, but I figured you'd sleep in late and I didn't want to wake you up."

Edith cleared her throat. "Get home from where?"

Carter turns to his grandmother, exasperated. "What does it matter, Gran?"

She nods. "Sounds like you didn't spend the night in the Trash Can." Her observation garners 'ahhhs' from Rachel and the book club ladies.

"You're not a detective, Gran," Carter mutters, flushing from the unwanted attention. He steps up to me, lowers his voice. "Let's talk outside."

I turn the other way. "I think you've said enough."

"Theo... look at me."

"No."

He steps in front of me and I twist to the left.

Rachel murmurs, "Look! They're having a lover's spat."

"I told you something happened in Salem!" Edith barks when she should be whispering. "That's fifty bucks. Pay up."

Carter and I glare at our audience, exasperated.

"You're acting childish," Carter says. "Let me just explain."

My eyes widen. "Childish?! Me?"

Our audience groans at Carter's fumble.

"Bad move, you numbskull," Edith says.

"Gran... please."

"I have nothing to say to you," I snap. "I've buried my beloved hamster while you ignored me all day. If you were 'planning' to call me as you say, then what happened? You better have a good explanation for ghosting me!"

Carter steps back, his ears pink with embarrassment. He rubs his palms together and takes a deep breath. "I do have an *excellent* explanation..."

chapter forty-four

C arter rolls over on his futon to where his phone sat on its wireless charger.

7:30 A.M.

Time to call Theo?

Theo was the last thing on his mind when he hopped into bed two hours ago, and the first thing he thought about when he woke up. Even though he was exhausted and achy in every part of his body (not that he was complaining), he's brimming with energy now. He can't wait to see her again.

What would they do today? A paddle boat ride in the Cove? A day trip to New Haven? He'd gone to Yale as an undergrad and even though his architectural tastes veers toward modernism, he'll love to show Theo the ivy-smothered buildings and give her a tour of the charming gothic architecture. She'll love the Rare Books & Manuscript Library, a great glass vault of ancient texts.

7:35 A.M.

He should call her now…

Carter picks up his phone, his thumb hovering over the Call button, when something occurs to him. He'd only just left her bed. Between her food poisoning and their all night sex marathon, Theo was probably passed out with exhaustion.

He sets his phone back down on the charger. He should let

her rest. Flopping over on his stomach, he tosses and turns for a few minutes before chucking in the towel. Sleep is not in the cards today. He's too amped up, his stomach fluttering with, dare he say it? Butterflies?

He glances out the window. What a beautiful morning! The trees in his backyard have turned a shade of burnt cinnamon.

A streak of pink light slashes the cobalt sky. The lark, usually so annoying, chirps a merry tune. Carter whistles along with it as he rolls up his futon and stuffs it in his closet. Is it him or are the clouds especially fluffy this morning?

Still in a chipper mood, he climbs down the ladder and immediately begins working out. Theo seemed to enjoy his abs; that motivates Carter to tone them up for her to touch. He turns on some LoFi music and was finishing up his fiftieth burpee when the doorbell rings.

He's surprised to see the UPS man. That's funny. He didn't remember placing an order…

Imagine his surprise when the UPS man deposits four massive packages on his doorstep.

"Sign here."

As Carter scrawls his signature, his gaze roves over the label. *The Vintage Train Company.* Now he remembers! He'd placed an order of trains, streetcars, bridges, and a ton of miniature scenery models approximately a month ago. The items were from Denmark and he didn't expect them to come until December. It's Christmas in October! This day keeps getting better and better.

Carter grabs a dolly from his garage and hauls the boxes to his hobby shed. He switches on the light, triggering the ON switch for the entire railway system. Three interconnected lines *choo-choos* across mountains and plains, over bridges and into tunnels. Miniature pines and spruces dot the railway, along with replicas of mining towns and city halls.

Carter eyes his new delivery. He should leave them for tomorrow. It's probably time for him to call Theo and get the day started.

He pats his pocket for his phone to confirm the time. *Damn.*

He left his phone in the main house. Poking his head outside, Carter squints at the sky, tracking the sun's position. Then he glances at his packages with longing. It's still early morning, the dew still fresh on the grass.

He could at least open the boxes and check out the Southern Pacific Railroad. That would only take a second. After all, he had to make sure they got his order right.

Yes.

The day was still young.

What's the harm in opening one box?

CARTER FINISHES LAYING the tracks for the Southern Pacific Railroad. He switches on the power and leans on his elbows, beaming with pride as he watches the locomotive run with stealth and precision.

Instinctively, Carter pats his back pocket.

Damn. Damn. Damn.

His phone is still on his kitchen counter. He couldn't exactly glance out the window to track the sun. His hobby shed was designed without windows precisely so he could shut the world away and maintain his focus. But setting up this locomotive didn't take long.

Minutes really, and that's not counting the miniature scenery, which will take *no time* setting up at all.

In fact…

Carter bites on his thumbnail, his eyes swinging toward the door. He shouldn't…

The pile of brand new miniatures on his worktable calls to him. He arches an eyebrow. He could probably set up the covered bridge and the train station before Theo wakes up. He got up at the crack of dawn. An early start, he reminds himself. He got an early start.

The town will need painting. And the pine trees are looking

pretty bare. No worries. He's an experienced miniature painter, fast and clean, with hardly any gunk.

Carter sits down on his stool and flips on his magnifying lamp, mixes his acrylic paints, and searches for his favorite brushes.

Of course, he had the option of ordering his scenery pieces pre-painted, but where would be the fun in that? He would never forgo the opportunity to customize. He's customized his mechanical keyboard, his Tesla, his gaming PC, his house. He likes to get his hands dirty. After all, what's a hobby shed for if not to paint, drill, jigsaw, and solder everything he owns? Would he have swept the Wethersfield Scarecrow contest three straight years in a roll if he didn't like to tinker?

Once the town has been erected, it's all a matter of plopping the passengers with their tiny luggages at the station. He'll have to paint the conductor and the mayor.

Carter rolls up his sleeves, lugging out the bag of pine trees. He's purchased an entire forest.

He slaps his hands together. "Twenty minutes tops."

chapter forty-five

"Seeing as I've already mixed my greens, I figured I might as well paint all the trees," Carter says with his head lowered in shame. "I must have gotten carried away, but I'd already poured out so much paint and I didn't want to waste—"

Edith slides a finger across her neck.

Carter clears his throat, sad puppy dog eyes pleading for understanding. "By the time I left the shed, the sun had already set. And then I checked my phone…"

My legs are crossed, my right foot shaking. Edith, Rachel, and the three members of our bookclub shake their heads in disgust.

His cheeks are flushed and he's gesticulating like a character from an opera. He's one step away from falling on his knees and begging for forgiveness.

Actually… That wouldn't be so bad.

But would I forgive him? Right now, if he got on his knees, I'd probably plant my foot on his face.

"I can't begin to tell you how sorry I am," he begins.

"You should be sorry," Edith says. "You and those goddamn trains."

"They were back-ordered special editions from Denmark…"

One glance at my twitching jaw and shaky leg, and he immediately clams up.

Edith shakes her head and mutters, "Numbskull."

The book club members agree, adding 'idiot' and 'tinkering fool' to the mix. Rachel pinches her brow.

Outwardly, I'm surprisingly calm. Inside, I'm bubbling with liquid hot magma and I'm about to blow all over Carter's pathetic face.

"Theo…" Carter steps forward and attempts to take my hand. "I hope you understand."

I snatch my hand away and hop off my stool. "Oh, I understand all right," I say, poking him in the chest, "I understand that I just took a backseat to your model trains."

"That's not it at all!"

"Actually, it is. You forgot about me."

Carter lowers his head. He can't deny it. His hobbies squeezed me out of his mind.

"Look, I know you like to tinker. It's just unfortunate that you decided to tinker when I needed you the most."

"Theo…" He starts toward me.

I hold up my hand. "You'll have plenty of time now to play with your trains because I release you from your debt. Consider your Saturdays free."

Carter blinks. "You're firing me?"

"That's right."

"But you weren't really paying me."

"Then that makes it easy for you."

"But there are still a ton of renovations on your house," he says. "What happened to your Thanksgiving deadline?"

I tip my chin up at a haughty angle. "I'll do them myself."

He narrows his eyes. "Really? Do you even know how to use a hammer?"

A groan rumbles through our audience. Edith rubs her forehead while Rachel pats her on the back.

"Of course I do! I'm the queen of DIYs. Speaking of which," I arch an eyebrow, "I'm entering the scarecrow contest."

Carter frowns, unsure why I'm giving him this information. "Um… that's great?"

"I hear you win every year."

A confused shrug. "I like scarecrows."

"About as much as you like trains?"

Carter opens his mouth.

"Don't answer that!" Edith barks from the sidelines.

I meet his eyes. "Your winning streak is over, you..." I rack my brain for an insult worthy of his crime. I'm really bad at being mean. "You... tinkering bastard."

"Theo... please." Carter's mouth twitches. Not only is he unfazed by my insult, he's amused! "This isn't a competition."

We both turn to the stack of contest flyers on the counter. Competition is printed in big bold Papyrus letters (I've got to talk to Rachel about her font choice).

"So says this year's loser," I say.

Rachel and the book club members *ooooh* on the sidelines.

Edith shakes her fist in the air. "That's better than 'tinkering bastard,' dear!"

"Thanks, Edith," I say. "Now if you'll excuse me, I have potato and cheese wedge stickers to pack and a new hamster to get to know."

Holding my head up high, I squeeze past a baffled Carter on my way to the door.

"Theo!" Rachel calls me back. "You forgot your care package." She holds up a basket stuffed with cheeses, blackberry preserves, cured meat, and a bottle of white wine.

"Right. Thanks." I march back with as much dignity as I can muster, sidestepping around Carter as I take the monstrous basket from Rachel and lug it to the door.

"Did she just dump you?" I overhear Edith shout at Carter— her version of whispering.

"I think she did," he says.

"Huh," Edith says, "I didn't know you two were together."

chapter forty-six

The deadline for the scarecrow contest ends on Halloween. This gives me a week to conjure up an entry that will blow Carter's out of the water.

I have no plan. No concept. No design. Just an indomitable will to wipe the floor with Carter. Should be easy, right?

Some people nurse their broken hearts at the bottom of a bottle. Or with chocolate binges and spending sprees. I craft.

That night, after three hours of intense sticker cutting and charm packing for *Vincent Van Sproot*, I huddle in bed with my comforter wrapped around my head (full potato mode) and pull up photos of past contest winners in the town archives.

"Let's see what we're dealing with here," I say, waiting for the website to load.

I scroll through three years' worth of blurry snapshots. Rachel is the official town photographer, and it looks like she took all her pictures with her ancient iPad. Her thumb makes a cameo in several photos and 80% of the entries were way off center.

I start with the contest runners up:

A *Beetlejuice* scarecrow. (Easy stuff). A pumpkin-head construction worker (Child's play). A scarecrow couple on a bicycle built for two (Please! My sticker kingdom for a worthy competitor!).

I scroll and scroll, scoffing and eye-rolling, my arrogance growing... I have this contest in the bag. I'm a big *craft* fish in a small pond.

I land on Carter's entries...

And then a sour gummy worm falls from my mouth and plops on my keyboard.

"What the f—"

Oh, he's good. He's very freaking good.

'RoboCop Conductor.'

Last year's grand prize entry, winner of a $100 cheese gift certificate and three mini pumpkin pies. The entry sounds stupid, but damn damn damn. It's visually impressive. The scarecrow must be 7 feet tall if it was a foot. I squint at the details. A laser gun? How did Carter acquire 19th century train conductor clothes big enough to dress a gigantic scarecrow?

Moving onto the previous year's entry: a werewolf in Buffalo check flannel, overalls, hiking boots, and a faux ax.

His first scarecrow entry: a sea captain dressed in a navy peacoat coat with spyglass in hand. The sea captain mans the wheel of a miniature wooden sailing ship, complete with masts, nets, and the figurehead of a mermaid. There are even fake barnacles on the hull.

"You've got a lot of spare time, Carter."

Of course he does. He's a retired thirty-four-year-old bachelor with nothing but time and money to devote to his tinkering.

He thinks he's hot shit with his tiny trains and his ultra modern trash can home. Well, he's not the only one who tinkers. I'll tinker him into last place!

I grab a sketchbook and begin to brainstorm. In order to beat Carter, my scarecrow entry has to be big and grand and take up *a lot* of sidewalk real estate.

chapter forty-seven

The pumpkin patch is fenced in by a forest of fiery maple and bustling with locals and tourists alike.

On a twenty-five acre farm, there's a trim red barn where families gather for apple bobbing, face painting, and carnival games. The line for the tractor hayride is thirty people deep. A group of toddlers crowd around the petting zoo, which consists of exactly three goats, two sheep, and one donkey.

The air is crisp and sparkling with festive cheer. The sky is big, vast, and turquoise blue. Perfect sweater weather. I'm dressed in ankle boots and a red flannel jacket. I feel like I've stepped over the garden wall and into a vintage New England postcard.

Under normal circumstances, I can spend all day soaking in this beautiful autumn day. I *want* to try my hand at the pumpkin cannon and beat the corn maze, but I'm strapped for time. It's T-Minus twenty-three hours until Halloween and I'm *stressed*.

Between renovating my house (see watching YouTube videos on how to renovate a historical home on a budget), keeping up with *Vincent Van Sproot* orders and commissions, and committing myself to winning this scarecrow contest, I haven't had time to stop and bob for apples. I'm busier than a Wall Street stockbroker (except with crafts) and it's sucking the fun out of the holidays.

Disgruntled from lack of sleep, I tromp through a row of warty pumpkins on a mission to select the biggest, ugliest one for Papa Scarecrow. I'm making a family of scarecrows: Mama, Papa, two kids, and a dog. I plan to keep my entry simple and *organic*, sourcing all my materials from local growers. Let Carter import his robotic gizmos and plastic parts. The judges will be much more impressed by my locally sourced and environmentally responsible scarecrow family.

I'm pushing a wheelbarrow filled with pumpkins to the register when I stop dead. The blood drains from my face. *No.* Of all the pumpkin patches in all the world...

Well, technically, this is the only pumpkin patch in town, so chances are high that I would run into Carter at this one. What's he doing out and about, anyway? He has everything he needs inside his high-tech trash can.

Crouched at the end of the lane, Carter picks up two massive pumpkins and takes an extraordinarily long time weighing them.

He's blocking my path and looking good in camel corduroy pants and a hunter green button down, sleeves rolled up to reveal those firm forearms that I know and love. How do I 'know' his forearms? I had to bite down on something to keep from making too much noise and waking up B&B guests.

Shivering at the memory, I turn my wheelbarrow around and try to make a quick getaway. I'm no longer furious at Carter for ghosting me. It's been three weeks since we hooked up and broke up. I've had time to cool my head, but that doesn't mean I'm ready to face him today. I need to be *gone*, fast...

I make a good head-start at retreating when the front wheel jams in a rut. My wheelbarrow, weighed down with pumpkins, lists to the side. I attempt to right it when the heel of my ankle boot sinks in the soft dirt. My giant pumpkins bite the dust, followed by a trickle of mini pumpkins. *Plop. Plop. Plop.*

"Theo?"

Shit.

Taking a deep breath, I glance over my shoulder.

Carter stands up and brushes the dirt from his pants.

We make eye contact.

I whirl around so fast I almost give myself whiplash.

Think he'll buy it if I pretend I didn't see or hear him? I busy myself with picking up my spilled pumpkins. I can hear his shoes squishing the mud.

Oh my God. He's coming this way!

Carter sidesteps my wheelbarrow and kneels down, picking up a warty green pumpkin from the fallen lot. His blond hair spills out from under his rust-colored beanie. I've seen him in a beanie only once, when he pathetically tried to talk himself out of hot water at the cheese shop. I was too mad to admire how *good* he looks in hats. Deliciously good.

"Were you trying to ignore me?" he asks, helping me lug the last of the fallen (a twenty pounder) into my wheelbarrow.

"Absolutely not! I um... I didn't see you there."

His blue eyes flashed with amusement. "Yes, you did. You looked right at me. We made eye contact."

I drop my eyes to my shoes. "No, we didn't."

Okay. Stupid thing to say. We obviously did. Trust me to make things more awkward than they have to be.

I clear my throat. "I have to go," I say, grabbing the handles of my wheelbarrow and pushing onward. In my attempt to get away, I didn't realize that my front wheel was still stuck in the rut. *Red alert! Red alert!* Pumpkin spillage 2.0.

"Steady there!" Carter dives toward the front of the wheelbarrow and makes a shield with his body before the first pumpkin can fall. "You're still stuck in the mud."

"I figured that."

Together, we right the wheelbarrow.

"It just rained the night before," he says.

"I know."

Carter tips his head up at the sky. "Nice day, isn't it?"

Oh God. He's trying to make chit chat about the weather.

"Yeah." I grit my teeth and try to dislodge my wheel.

"Let me help you," he says, grabbing hold of the metal sides.

"I've got it, thanks."

"Just hold still…" *Pop* goes my wheel. He slaps his hands together. "There. That wasn't so hard, was it?"

"Thanks for your help," I mutter.

With my head held high, I wheel away. Carter keeps pace beside me, oblivious to my cold shoulder. At the end of the row, he stoops down and picks up two massive pumpkins, tucking them easily under his arms without losing pace. Interesting… What is he using them for? Front door decor? He doesn't have a porch, and he hates unnecessary holiday decorations, unless he can win a prize. Food? Possible. Two big pumpkins can feed him for weeks and he'll save money on Healthy Choice Steamers.

"Why so many pumpkins?" he asks, reading my mind.

"Wouldn't you like to know."

"I would like to know, actually," he says. "Are they for the scarecrow contest?"

My eyes shift sideways. "Maybe."

He jostles his massive pumpkins. "Can I set them in your wheelbarrow?"

I stiffen. And chance having to spend more time with him tiptoeing around the elephant in the room? "No room to spare," I blurt out, sounding snipper than I intended.

"It's okay," he says, taking a hint. "They aren't that heavy." He clears his throat. "So what's your theme?"

I mash my lips together, chin high, eyes steely. He's not getting any information from me.

"I get it," he says, after a long bout of silence. "Top secret, but I can take a wild guess."

I glare at him. The checkout line is ten people deep. Carter files in behind me. I sense his longing gaze on the nape of my neck. No way am I turning around.

"I'm incorporating pumpkins in my entry too," he says.

Noooo! There goes my leg up on the competition. Granted, using pumpkins in a scarecrow contest isn't the most original idea, but what am I supposed to do? I'm strapped for time!

I stare straight ahead, maintaining a stoic facade. "I don't care."

"I probably deserve that."

"*Probably?*"

"You're still mad at me."

I whirl around on him. "No, I'm not. I forgive you."

"Really? Because I sense..." He juggles his pumpkins. "Hostility."

I turn back around, schooling my face into a mask.

"I heard about how Gran swapped the hamsters," Carter says, "that must have been traumatic."

I stand on my tiptoes. How many gourds is that lady buying? "It was."

He sighs. "Look, I'm really sorry about... about everything. The trains, my poor timing—"

"And poor priorities," I can't help adding, "you forgot about your terrible priorities."

"That too. I know I screwed up, but I *do* have self-control," Carter says, shamed. "If you give me a second chance, I will never, *ever* enter my shed without my phone again. Believe me, my phone will be strapped to my body like a pager. No call or text will go unanswered."

I narrow my eyes. That's not the promise I was expecting, and yet, it sounds strangely familiar. "I've heard that one before."

Carter blinks in surprise. "You have?"

"This last guy I dated promised he'll get rid of his collection of polo shirts and yet," I shrug, "not."

He frowns, confused. "You have something against polo shirts?"

"No, just the type he wore."

"What type was that?"

"Ralph Lauren," I say, "but the kind with the *gigantic* polo player logo." I gesture to my flannel chest, miming the sheer surface area this logo took up. "You know what I'm talking about?"

If Carter didn't have his hands full of pumpkins, he would've pinched his brow. "The Big Pony line?"

"Bingo."

"You hate the Big Pony line?"

"Can't stand it!"

"Let me understand something," he says, "you dumped this poor sap... because of a *polo shirt*?"

Well, when he puts it that way, I sound super hard to please and shallow. "You don't understand. His *entire* wardrobe consisted of these shirts. He doesn't wear anything *but* Big Pony polos."

"If it helps my case, I only own one polo from Ralph Lauren. Tiny polo player. Christmas gift from my mom. I never wear it— too scratchy. Now I'll make sure never to wear it around you. Don't want to offend you."

I open my mouth to defend myself, but Carter cuts me off.

"It's interesting that something as small as logo size would cause you to go off the deep end." Carter rocks back on his heels and scrutinizes me over the tip of his nose. "Very interesting indeed."

"What?" I ask, feeling suddenly self-conscious.

"So you don't like logos that take up too much shirt real estate and you don't like men with hobbies—"

"I never said that. I don't mind if you— if men have hobbies. What I don't like is being *ignored* because of these hobbies."

Carter continues to scrutinize me. Now that my 'Big Pony Polo breakup' is out of the bag, he seems determined to turn the tables on me. Now it's *my* problem we can't be in a relationship. I'm overreacting over his model train mistake.

We march forward in line. He sets his pumpkins on the checkout counter and stretches his sore arms. "How many other hearts did you break over a pet peeve?" he asks. "Speaking of which, how many other pet peeves do you have?"

"I don't know what you're talking about," I say, shifting my eyes to the side. Now would not be the time to mention Long Pinky Nail guy.

213

"Is a foot fetish one of them?"

"No!"

"I think it is." Carter strokes his chin like he's cracked the mystery of the century. "That's why you enlisted Gran to spill tea on my socks. Everything's starting to fall into place…"

My face turns crimson. We're two people away from the cashier. "Is everyone buying up all the pumpkins in the farm?"

Carter studies me like I'm a newly discovered specimen. "When you were breaking the poor Big Pony logo guy's heart, were you, by chance, comparing him to Nat Eaton?"

Red alert! Red alert!

My eyes widen. I step back, bumping into the man in front of me. I mutter a quick apology. "That's a silly theory."

"Is it?"

He sees my panicked face and nods, proud of himself for figuring me out. "Right before you broke Big Pony Polo guy's heart, I bet you were thinking, 'If Nat Eaton were *real* and living today, he would never own a Big Pony Polo?' No, he would only wear classic Armani suits or whatever. Nat Eaton is *perfect* and no real life man will ever live up to him."

The line shuffles forward. We stand in place, staring at each other until the lady behind Carter clears her throat.

I whirl around, face flaming, ears pink.

"Interesting," he says. "I bet Nat Eaton doesn't like model trains either."

"Of course not. Trains weren't invented when he was alive."

"But he was *never* alive. He's not real." He leans forward and speaks in my ear. "But I'm real…"

Sweat breaks out on my brow. "I don't want to talk about this anymore."

"I'm real, Theo," he repeats. "I'm *real* and I'm *flawed* and I'm *here*. I'll wait as long as it takes for you to get *your* priorities in order, but I won't wait forever."

It's my turn to pay at the register. With Carter's final words ringing in my ears, I dig for my wallet and swipe my VISA in the credit card machine.

Beep. Declined.

I swipe again.

Declined.

"Do you have another card?" the cashier asks.

I slip out my MasterCard.

Beep. Declined.

This is so strange. Did I max out both my credit cards? I knew all those renovation/craft supplies I bought at the hardware store were expensive. I just didn't know they would take me to the end of my credit limit.

The line grows impatient as I dig for my debit card. I just paid my bills yesterday and I have twelve dollars in my checking account. The rest is in stocks and savings.

As I dig for my Nordstrom store card, Carter slips his American Express into the card reader.

Ding. Transaction completed.

"No!" I snatch the card out of the slot and hand it back to him, mortified. Knowing Carter, he's probably thinking, "this will never happen to a true FIRE follower."

"I insist," he says.

Eyeing the cashier and the people in line behind me, I grit my teeth and lower my voice. "I don't want your charity."

"You'll spot me later."

"Return it," I tell the cashier. I pluck each pumpkin from the counter and return them to the wheelbarrow. "Actually, I don't need these pumpkins after all."

The line behind me groans. "I'm sorry to take up your time," I apologize to everyone. "Sorry for the wait."

Carter's eyebrows shoot up to his hairline. "Are you serious?"

I lug a giant pumpkin into the wheelbarrow. With my head held high, I wheel my pumpkins back to the patch. The wheelbarrow jams in another rut and my pumpkins go tumbling down.

chapter forty-eight

S o I don't have pumpkins for my scarecrow family…
There's no set rule that says their heads *need* to be made out of pumpkins. When life gives you lemons, make lemonade…

I have a pile of junk in my backyard. Stacks of scrap wood pulled from the Witch House. And chestnuts. Let's not forget the chestnuts. I can definitely make something with nuts.

Am I an artist or am I an artist?

My backyard is covered with yellow leaves and a literal sea of gleaming brown chestnuts. I perch upon a stump and assume the thinking man's position. A wrinkle creases my brow. The sun is high in the sky when I began my brainstorm and edges behind the roof of the rotted eaves when inspiration finally strikes.

I bolt up and snap my fingers. Eureka!

I'll sculpt my scarecrows out of cornhusks, wood scraps, and chestnuts. BAM. Perfect. Inspired!

I'm using locally sourced ingredients (what's more locally sourced than junk pulled from a three-hundred-year-old house?). And best of all: all my building materials are *free*.

I spend the afternoon sawing, hammering, and nailing together pieces of reclaimed wood. The next morning, I gather up all the fallen chestnuts in a basket and set about painting and gluing them to my scarecrow in an alternating mosaic pattern.

My scarecrow family contains Mama, Papa, Big Sister, and

Little Brother in a Woody station wagon. Both car and family are fashioned entirely out of reclaimed wood. Red ear corn and chestnuts accessorize the family's painted wardrobe. Their faces are made entirely out of chestnuts, each nut painted a different hue of burnt amber so when you step back, the individual nuts merge into a face that took…

How long did this project take?

Time escapes me.

I put on the finishing touches on Halloween morning. It's noon by the time I haul my scarecrow family over to Main Street, where all the entries are on display. Moving my scarecrows takes three separate trips by car (the kids are small enough that I can take two at a time) and loads of grunt work. I'm sweating by the time I arrange them in the shadow of an impressive Headless Horseman scarecrow.

I thought my entry was impressive, but this one takes the cake.

"Wow." My stomach bottoms out as I circle the Headless Horseman. The rider is dressed in a maroon leather coat and black cape, tan breeches, and knee-high riding boots—a wardrobe of exceptional quality and detail. He's mounted on a rearing black stallion and is about to launch his head (a gigantic Knucklehead jack-o'-lantern) at his unsuspecting victim.

Someone taps me on the elbow. Rachel, dressed in slacks and a floral scarf, peers at the chestnut faces of my scarecrow family.

"Theo, this is very impressive! How long did this take you?"

"Too long," I say, still frowning at the horseman. "Who did this?"

Rachel is silent for a beat.

I sigh. "Of course."

Carter. Wethersfield's Master Tinkerer.

"What's the horse made out of?" I ask.

"Chicken wire and monster mud," an all too familiar voice says behind us.

Carter joins us on the sidewalk, his hands jammed in the pockets of his jeans. "A wooden support structure. Chicken wire

217

molding. Monster mud," he tells me, "works like spackle and dries in minutes."

"How long did this take you?" Rachel asks.

"Two weeks."

"Impressive," she nods, slipping on her glasses to get a better look.

I roll my eyes. "Show off."

"Well, I have to join the other judges," Rachel says. "We're making the rounds." She lowers her voice. "You didn't hear it from me, but I've selected my two favorites."

"But what's your #1 favorite?" I ask.

Rachel taps her nose, poker face on. "Wait and see…"

After Rachel leaves, Carter gives me a curt nod. "What were you doing? Slipping her a twenty?"

I glare at him. "Maybe you need to resort to bribery to win. I rely on skill."

"Pretty convenient that your best friend Rachel is one of the judges and the other three judges are part of your book club," he says.

I prop a hand on my hip. "What are you saying?"

"Sounds like a rigged game to me."

"If it's so rigged, how come you won three years in a row? Wouldn't have anything to do with Edith being on the panel?"

"I won entirely on merit."

"Uh huh."

Carter steps toward my station wagon. "This your entry?" He scrutinizes the woodwork and studies the chestnut mosaic.

I fold my arms over my chest. I can tell he's impressed, but after our last fight, he'll never admit it.

"It's good," he says after a long time, "I grant you that."

"Merely 'good'?"

"Fishing for compliments?" he asks with a crooked smile.

I scowl.

He points to Papa Scarecrow's face. "How long did it take you to do this?"

"I used to volunteer making Rose Parade floats in high school, except we had a team."

"So a long time?" He tips his head to the side. "Only thing missing on the Dad is a..." he turns to smile at me, "Big Pony polo."

"Har Har."

I walk away before he can make fun of me some more.

Carter falls into step beside me. "I'm surprised you didn't recreate a scene from *The Witch of Blackbird Pond*. Nat Eaton swinging on the rigging, perhaps? What's the matter? Couldn't find a puffy white shirt perfect enough for your dream man? Do you have a pet peeve when it comes to puffy shirts? Too much puff not to your liking?"

I whirl on him. "Can we *not* talk about that book?"

"Has the world ended?" His hands pretend-flutters to his chest. "*You?* Not want to talk about the book?"

Furling my hands into fists, I pick up my pace. Carter follows, determined to taunt me into punching him. "I've really hit a nerve yesterday, haven't I?"

"Quiet," I shush him, "I want to check out our competition."

We pass 'Rock Star' scarecrow with big '80's metal hair, a 'Raggedy Ann' scarecrow, and a 'Suffragette' scarecrow with a blue 'Votes for Women' sash.

At the end of Main Street, the judges have gathered around a scarecrow carefully propped on a lamppost in a perfect imitation of Gene Kelly in 'Singin' in the Rain.'

"They look smitten by that entry," Carter observes.

"That entry? *Seriously?*" I snort. "Child's play."

"So you think your entry is a shoe in?"

"Your words, not mine." I chew my inner cheek. "Your head-less horseman is not bad. It will either come down to one of us."

"Thank you." His jaw twitches, all trace of mockery gone from his face.

"That's not a compliment. Just a logical observation."

"So it is." He hides a smile, and then: "How's your solo renovations? I can still come by Saturday if you need me."

"I *don't* need you," I say.

He arches a brow, says nothing.

I can feel the doubt radiating off of him. Smug. He's *so* smug! "Renovations resume after I set up Halloween decorations."

He blinks. "Today is Halloween."

"Your point?"

"Four hours until sunset."

"I work best under pressure. Besides, I live in an *actual* haunted house. My cobwebs are real. All the heavy lifting is already done for me," I say. "I assume you're all decorated for Halloween."

"I don't decorate for Halloween. The scarecrow is it."

"So what do you do? Hide in your trash can with the lights off and the blinds up?"

"I help Gran pass out candy."

My turn to radiate doubt. "Do you even like children?"

"I love children." He shoots me a meaningful look that turns my face red and my knees liquid.

I hope he's not implying what I think he's implying.

"Only the nice ones," he backtracks. His expression turns solemn. "Just so you're not disappointed, the Witch House doesn't get many trick-or-treaters."

Now *this* is a surprise. "Why not?"

"Too scary. All the children avoid it."

"That's because it's been abandoned and left to rot," I say. "Of course it's scary with the lights off, but I have a secret weapon in store."

"What's that?"

I turn from side to side to make sure no one's eavesdropping on us. "Jack-o'-lantern lights."

Carter nods. "Ah."

"And I plan to line my walkway with spooky paper lanterns. It's going to be so cozy and inviting."

"Luring kids like the witch in Hansel & Gretel, I see."

"That's the general idea, except I don't plan to eat them. I have care packages with gluten-free candy corn and stickers. I will become a Halloween legend."

"This is the first time I've heard of someone trying to dehaunt their haunted house for Halloween," he says. "Are you still aiming to renovate before Thanksgiving?"

I blow out a big breath. "Oh yeah."

"Sounds like you've got a lot to do."

"I can handle it."

His dimples deepen. "I'm still available this weekend."

"Noted."

By now we've scoped out every scarecrow and made a loop of Main Street, returning to our own entries.

The judges gather outside Rachel's gourmet cheese shop, drawing a small crowd of senior citizens, teenagers taking a half-day from school, and families with small children. Carter and I are the only single contestants who are not over seventy or attached to a family. We have time, energy, and advance-level craft skills at our disposal. I feel bad about robbing the prize from old people and kids, but all's fair in holiday craft wars.

"They're announcing the winner." I bounce at my heels, suddenly seized by excitement.

"Good luck," he whispers.

"You too." I clasp my hands together, waiting for the judges to consult their clipboards. "Looks like they're debating. It's all theater. The winner is obvious."

Carter chews on his inner cheek. "Meaning the winner is… *you*?"

"My scarecrow family contains over a thousand hand-painted chestnuts. I built an entire station wagon out of reclaimed wood from my house, which is like the equivalent of donating the Witch House's kidney to this entry. I mean, *come on*. But don't worry, I'm sure you'll win second place."

He scoffs. "Glad to see you're humble."

"Shhhh." I suck in my breath. "It's happening!"

Rachel steps forward and clears her throat. She does the usual song and dance about how spectacular all our entries are and how we're all winners. I nod along with a smile plastered to my face. We all know who the clear winner is, so let's get this show on the road. I've got an entire front lawn to decorate for Halloween. I'm a busy woman.

"… after a long, difficult debate," Rachel says, "the first prize winner of our 35th annual scarecrow contest is…"

I step forward.

"Susie Hodge for 'Singin' in the Rain.'"

"What the flip!" I clasp a hand over my mouth. "I mean, congratulations!"

I narrow my eyes as five-year-old Susie and her dad collect their blue ribbon, $100 gift card, three mini pumpkin pies, and a 5 lb wheel of parmesan (a bonus gift!).

That's *my* ribbon. That's *my* cheese!

The Raggedy Ann Scarecrow wins second place, '80's Rocker Scarecrow third.

"Thanks Grandma," the little boy responsible for the rockstar scarecrow says, kissing one of the judges on the cheek.

I glare at Rachel, who refuses to meet my eye. Then I turn to Carter and mouth, "What the — "

He shakes his head in disbelief. "Man, this contest is rigged. No wonder Gran left the panel. Too corrupt for her."

"This takes Hamster Gate to a whole new level."

"Scarecrow Gate."

I sigh as the five-year-old winner and her dad truck their prizes to the family mini van. "I was crushed under that cheese." I shrug. "Well, I'm taking my scarecrow fam to my front yard, where they'll be appreciated by trick-or-treaters."

I snatch up Papa Scarecrow. A chestnut pops off his cheek. See? He's so mad he busted a nut. I shove him in the backseat of my car and reach for Little Brother.

"Need help?" Carter reaches for Mama Scarecrow.

I beat him to it. "I've got this."

Carter lingers on the sidewalk. "Well, it was nice not talking to you."

"You too," I say curtly.

"Maybe we can not talk to each other again this evening when no one shows up to your house for candy."

I narrow my eyes. "I plan to empty out my stash."

He rocks back on his heels and laughs. "How?"

"If I build it, they will come."

chapter forty-nine

My Halloween decorations are the cutest on the block. Anyone can stack pumpkins on the front steps.

I've shipped my stash of Halloween decor from home, and now I have skeletons hanging from my windows and tombstones on my front lawn. There's a giant cobweb with an equally giant spider dangling from the trees and vintage paper lanterns leading to my front door.

As for the Witch House, well, there's not much I can do to make it creepier than it already is. It's tumbledown and ominous — the perfect haunted house. I expect all the trick-or-treaters to flock to me.

Dressed in my flapper witch costume with a bowl of wax paper care packages tucked under my arm, I peek out the window. A bracing wind whips through the street, shaking trees and fluttering cloaks. The branches of my haunted chestnut tree raps against the back siding, hailing chestnuts all over my rooftop.

A group of elementary school ghouls accompanied by two adults hits up my neighbors' homes. They scurry past my house like frightened rabbits.

Damn.

What *is* going on here? That's the *second* group that's avoided the Witch House.

"Maybe they're too young..."

A screechy draft whistles through my hallway.

I nearly jump out of my skin as another gale shakes the house. Right now I'd rather be out there with the trick-or-treaters than alone in my haunted house.

I perk up as another band of monsters come within sight. I race to the door, ready to fling it open when they knock.

No knock.

Peeking through the broken window slats, my hope plummets as I spy the trick-or-treaters race past my house and spill onto my adjoining neighbor's front lawn.

"Trick-or-treat!"

Sighing, I open up one of my goodie bags and bite into a Snicker's bar. Save for a table lamp with weak light, my house is suffused in inky shadows.

I take another bite of my chocolate bar and side-eye the drafty hallway and the pitch dark stairwell.

And then...

The ceiling rumbles.

CREAK.

STOMP.

CREAK.

BOO!

I nearly choke on a chunky bite of peanut-studded nougat. *Boo?* Okay. This really is too much. I grab my coat, my candy bowl and skedaddle, running three blocks to Edith's B&B.

The porch light is on and the front door is so crowded with trick-or-treaters that I have to wait my turn to get inside.

"What happened?" Edith asks as I run up her porch steps.

I hug her and eye her near-empty candy bowl with envy.

She's dressed as Ingrid Bergman from *Casablanca*, trench coat, fedora, nylons, orthopedic shoes in place of sturdy '40's pumps.

"Eliza Wolcott is up to her old tricks," I say with a grim expression.

"The chestnut-ghost-witch?"

"She's out of control!"

225

Carter pops up behind Edith with a fresh bag of candy. "Hello. Aren't you a little too old to be trick-or-treating?"

I look him up and down. He's wearing his normal clothes (blue sweater over black jeans), but has slipped on a cheap vampire cape and slicked his blond hair back. "That's the saddest Dracula costume I've ever seen."

He nods to my Halloween care packages. "No one brave enough to knock on your front door?"

I shake my head, my disappointment plain on my face. "Even though I worked my fingers to the bone trying to cozy up the place, the chestnut-ghost-witch is putting out bad juju."

"You're the first person who's ever tried to de-haunt the haunted house," Edith says. "Want to help us pass out candy?"

I nod and then steal a glance at Carter.

"Up for another session of not talking to each other?" he asks.

"I can ignore you all night."

Edith rolls her eyes. "You two take over. I'm going to sit down."

"What's the matter?" Carter asks, staring at my profile. "You look like you've seen a ghost."

"Eliza Wolcott is *boo-ing* up a storm upstairs and being a bloody nuisance."

His reaction is the picture of 'huh?'. "Does she really '*Boo*'?"

"Indeed she does."

He narrows his eyes. "I don't believe it."

"Believe it or not, I got an earful of 'boo-ing' and it's driving me up the wall." I hold out my bowl. "Do you want a goodie bag? It has stickers."

"I hate stickers," he says, but takes a wax parcel and opens it up. "What's this?" He holds up one of my premium water proof stickers: a potato with useless arms and legs in a black hat and cloak made of stars.

"It's a sproot."

"It's dressed like a witch."

"It's a Halloween sproot," I say. "I'm sure you'll throw it away. I know how you feel about clutter."

"You're probably right." He studies the sticker for a beat too long, a secret smile ghosting his lips. "Though this sproot is not without her charms," he says, and tucks it securely in his pocket.

chapter fifty

Two weeks before Thanksgiving...
I replay the renovation video again.

This YouTube couple had spent two years and all their life savings renovating a 1760s farm house in Upstate New York. Their house was in worse shape and had more icky black mold than my house. The buyer had to painstakingly take the structure down to the studs.

I watch them knock down a wall, then glance back at my own rotted walls and peeling wallpaper. Originally, I wanted a complete home makeover. Now I'd settle with patching up the holes in the walls, floor, and roof.

Then there's the minor issue of Eliza Wolcott, the resident chestnut-ghost-witch. After two nights alone with her, I've concluded that she's not out to harm anyone, but she *is* loud and obnoxious and would probably freak out my guests. The chestnut tree is her weapon of choice. Her creep factor increases after dark.

I'll have to do something about her.

First things first.

I watch another renovation video of a woman grunting as she yanks apart an entire section of funky wood panels with a crowbar. I glance behind me. My dining room wall is in a similar state of disrepair. All it takes is a little elbow grease and a whole lotta of gumption. I strap on my respirator, roll up my sleeves, and grab my crowbar. "Looks easy enough."

"Oh no…"

I'm standing in a pile of dusty rubble, sweat dribbling down my temples. The divider between the living room and the dining room is history.

I strip off my foggy goggles and sidestep the mountain of discarded wood in my living room. I'd taken down the wall to the studs.

So the thing is…

I had only planned to remove the 'bad' parts, *except* the more I got down to the nitty gritty, the more I discovered that the rot went deeper and deeper. It's like peeling the moldy layers off of an onion. You'd assume the bad parts were only surface level and the next thing you knew, you've reached the moldy core and realized you should have tossed the whole thing in the trash.

Carter's warning echoes in my mind. *Money pit.*

The last thing I want is to admit he's right. Two weeks until my friends and parents arrive and I have no wall. Worse, I have no money (or professional know-how) to build a wall and I would rather take a bath in boiling hot oil than ask for Carter's help. My pride may kill me.

"Okay, calm down." I circle the rubble. "Think. Think."

Stepping outside, I pull out my phone and Google: *How to DIY a wall on a budget.*

Three days later…

Pile of rubble: gone.

Total spent at the Home Depot Garden Center: $500.75.

Okay. Sounds like a lot of money, but hear me out…

There was a sale on indoor plants, hooks, and macrame wall

hangers. I went wild collecting pothos, donkey tails, string of hearts, English Ivy, and ferns. There's a Pinterest DIY Tutorial on making macrame plant hangers out of cotton twine, which is cheaper than buying them pre-made, but I have a roof to fix and floors to rip up, a ghost to exorcise, and a turkey to roast. In other words, there's no time to fiddle with macrame!

I hang up the final plant on its hook, climb off my stepladder, and take a step back to admire my new botanical wall. It's modern, green, and airy. I can see the dining room through a curtain of dangling vines, which is far better than closing off each room with an old-fashioned wall, anyway. Lemons into lemonade.

I sit down on my decimated yellow couch (it's more like a sofa/futon now with the claw legs removed) and stroke my chin.

A thin shaft of sunlight streams through the front and back windows, hitting my botany wall *just so*, providing the plants with a much needed dose of photosynthesis.

I quite like it. And I know Lena, a self-proclaimed plant mom, will *love* it. My mom enjoys gardening, so I'm pretty sure she'll approve while my dad will make a beeline for the Thanksgiving spread and barely notice it.

"I think it opens up the room," I say to the empty house. "What do you think, Eliza?"

I glance up at the ceiling.

CREAK.

THUMP.

HOP. BANG.

It sounds like someone is jumping up a storm right over the botany wall. A piece of plaster rains down on the English Ivy, widening the already conspicuous hole in the ceiling. Sunlight pours in. Ironically, if I keep the stacked holes in both roof and floor, I'll have a self-watering system for my plant babies.

"Good idea, Eliza! My thoughts exactly."

The *thumping* ceases for the space of a second before starting up again—louder and more obnoxious than before.

"Eliza! Stop it! It's not even night time."

BANG. THUMP. ZONK. BOO!

"Please stop saying 'Boo!' It's super annoying and not at all scary."

"BOOOOOOOO!"

"Eliza!"

CREAK. GROAN. THWACK. BOING.

It sounds like she's jumping on an old box spring. Talk about an obstinate ghost. Reminds me of Edith.

If she makes this much noise now, imagine the ruckus she'll make during Thanksgiving.

"Okay, Eliza..." I roll up my sleeves and yank out my phone. "I really hoped we'd be able to coexist together, but you forced me to do this."

Google search: *How to exorcise a ghost.*

One of the suggestions involves contacting a priest to perform an old fashioned exorcism.

Sounds perfect. Let's find a priest...

Oh, *hell* no.

You have to *pay* one? I thought Fathers exorcised for free? Isn't it part of their job description to fight ghosts/demons/Satan pro bono?

I look up how much it would cost and nearly faint when I saw the price.

Google search: *How to exorcise a ghost on a budget.*

"Sage, eh?" All right. I can afford herbs.

"*Pee-ew!*"

With a cough, I wave away the sage-infused smoke. My eyes burn and water. I don't know how much more of this I can take. But the instructions say I have to burn bundles of dried sage in every room of my haunted house to clear out the spirits like an insect fumigation. Or aroma therapy session.

As much as I want to throw in the towel, I've only fumigated the first floor. I know Eliza is haunting somewhere upstairs, possibly in the attic, a likely chestnut-ghost-witch hangout.

I hold two smoking bundle of sage in front of me and creep up the stairs.

I smoke the hallway.

The master bedroom.

The bathroom.

The linen closet.

The online exorcism instructions say it would help if I chant something as a priest would do so I alter between '*in nomine patri et espiritu santo*' which I learned from the movie *Boondock Saints* and '*the power of Christ compels you.*'

In case the traditional chants don't work (they *do* sound mean), I sing a few lines from *Let It Go* because letting my house go is essentially what I want Eliza Wolcott to do.

I climb up to the attic (empty) and wave the sage. "Eliza! Wherever you are… Let it go. Let it go. Move on already!"

A pin drop silence.

The only light in the attic comes from a window slat. It's a quarter past noon (I sure as hell am not exorcising in the dark). I circle the dusty floors, waving the sage and switching back to my Latin chants when, out of nowhere, a gust of wind blows the sage bundle from my hand. The sage lands on the floor and it's like an invisible foot comes out of nowhere and stomps them out.

Damn it. I guess sage doesn't work after all. Maybe I should have tried something stronger? Weed?

"Eliza?" My voice bounces off the bare attic walls.

Silence

"Eliza? I'm having people over for Thanksgiving. I would very much appreciate it if you moved on into the afterlife and not ruin my party with your noises."

I wait for her reply. Another bout of judgmental silence.

Something hard and cold strikes me on the forehead and bounces on the floor.

"Ouch!" I rub my forehead and bend down to pick up the missile: a chestnut.

"Stop it, Eliza! You're three-hundred-years old. Act your age!"

A second chestnut nicks my temple. "Ow!"

Where are these nuts coming from? I jump from side to side, expecting to find Eliza crouched like a snipper with a BB gun.

"Eliza, I'm telling you one last time."

A third nut pings off my shoulder. I fumble backward and run down the stairs, chased by the sound of mischievous giggling.

"Okay! Eliza. You asked for this! Now I mean business."

I burst onto the porch and yank out my phone.

My mom picks up on the third ring.

"Have you found a decent job yet?" she asks without a proper hello.

"Mom, can you overnight me some more durian?"

1.5 DAYS LATER...

I'm in the kitchen, slicing open my overnighted durian. Mom has done well, sending me a gigantic one that is especially pungent. It's the sweetest onion x armpit smell imaginable and I take a big bite, loving the flavor because I grew up on it and my taste buds are attuned to it. But I know some people, *most* people — including 18th century ghosts who grew up on bland 18th century food—would think otherwise.

I dish out a slice onto a plate.

One plate for every room.

A double serving for the attic.

To cover all my bases, I place a stinking serving at the base of the old chestnut tree in the same way my mom would offer food to our dead ancestors.

Slapping my hands together, I return to my durian perfumed house, water my plants, and watch the ceiling for movement.

233

"Eliza? Are you there?"

Silence.

"Eliza! I got you something to eat."

CREAK. GROAN. BOOO. AWK.

Doors slam. Chestnuts scatter.

I smile to myself. Have you ever heard a ghost-witch spill her chestnuts? Every time she AWKS, chestnuts pelt the floor like pebbled vomit. It sounds revolting, but it's music to my ears. "There's more where that came from…"

AWK. BOO. AWK. *NOOO.*

The shutters rattle. It sounds like the wind is saying 'No' but we all know it's Eliza losing her battle to durian.

I smile to myself and bite into another slice. Something tells me Eliza won't be a pest during Thanksgiving.

chapter fifty-one

O*ne day before Thanksgiving…*
There's a knock on my door.

My three friends are huddled on my Welcome Mat like penguins against the cold. The moment our eyes lock, we jump and scream and hug and okay, one of us (me) cries.

Once inside, they ply me with housewarming gifts. A massive bag of Flaming Hot Cheetos from Camille. An air plant from Lena. A bath sponge from Sadie.

"Wow." Camille circles my living room as she strips off her puffer jacket. "This place is *so* old."

I'll take that as a compliment.

"I can't believe you're a homeowner! The first one of us." Sadie unravels her scarf and shakes her curly auburn hair. She makes herself at home, zooming from one corner of the living room to the kitchen. "An actual historical home! It's so… so…"

"Rustic," Camille says, checking out the boarded up hole beneath the stairs and running her hand over the cherry wood banister. She knocks on the newel post. "Quality wood, this. I see what drew you to this house."

Cleaning her thick tortoise-shell glasses on the hem of her shirt, Lena makes a beeline toward my botany wall. "I'm in love! Where'd you get this idea?"

"Pinterest." I beam. See? I didn't need a wall there after all.

"I knocked out the wall, then realized I couldn't afford the materials to put one up. Maybe I'll get one up before Christmas."

"No!" Lena says, practically shielding the hanging plants with her body. "Never get rid of this."

Sadie strokes her chin. "It opens up the room."

My eyes widen. "That's what I said!"

Camille tilts her head up to the double-stacked hole in the ceiling. "Love the skylight," she says without a hint of sarcasm. Like me, my cousin thinks out of the box.

"It's a self-watering indoor gardening system." I sigh, relieved that we're all on the same wavelength. No judgements. No passive aggression. Basically the opposite of my parents, who are scheduled to land (*gulp*) tomorrow.

Sadie stands before my yellow couch, peering down at it with her hand on her hip and a perplexed knot to her brow. "So this is the Jack le Farb sofa from Salem?"

"Jacques Le Fèvre," I correct. While I usually tell my friends *everything*, I've 'left out' certain details of my Salem weekend. By 'detail,' I mean my entire ill-fated romantic entanglement with Carter. As far as they're concerned, Carter is still my sexy indentured servant/contractor and I'm still crushing after him because of his uncanny resemblance to my version of Nat Eaton, which happens to include eight-pack abs. In short, I've looked, but I never touched.

"What happened to the legs?" Sadie asks, kneeling down to inspect the splintered claw feet. "It's busted. Did you buy it like *this*?"

Sweat beads at my temples. "Yeah. I got a stellar deal."

"You were ripped off!"

"I was not! Antique couches are supposed to be low to the ground."

Sadie narrows her eyes. "But this low?"

"People of yore were very short."

She touches the broken feet. "And splintery?"

"Jacques Le Fèvre was a master of… rustic woodworking."

Camille and Lena kneel beside Sadie and now all three of them are scrutinizing my couch.

"I thought you said the couch was recently re-upholstered," Camille says.

"It was."

Lena points to a spot on the cushions. "Then why is there a giant stain? Ewwwwww. It looks fresh."

Oh shit! I forgot to spot clean that out. "What stain?"

Lena screws up her face in disgust. "You need to get a refund. It looks like the former owner left you something to remember him by!"

Camille tips her head to the side. "It looks like a cu—"

I slap my hands together. "Who wants a house tour?"

All three of my friend jump at the opportunity. "I do!"

Relieved to distract them from the couch, I lead them up to the second floor. I point out the crown molding (what's left of it anyway) and the various quirks and features of the Witch House.

I point to the carvings threaded through the banister like a museum docent. "The humble chestnut is a symbolic design decor for Captain Wolcott, as his nickname on shipboard was 'Old Chestnut.'"

"Why?" Camille asks. "Was he voted most likely to roast on an open fire?"

Lena and Sadie snickers behind her.

"He ran a tight ship. If you didn't swab the deck and keep your quarters spick and span, he was likely to bust a nut."

"That's..." Camille blinks. "Horrifying."

Upstairs, I point to a weak spot on the floor. "Mind that area," I say, which amounts to three King's Wood planks spread across a narrow hallway. "Do as I do." I plaster my back against the wall and creep around the weak spot like a burglar.

Camille, Sadie, and Lena mimic my moves. I'm pretty sure I won't be taking my mom on a house tour if I can help it.

Camille sniffs the air. "Why does it smell like durian?"

Sadie pinches her nose. "Yes, *why* does it smell like durian?"

"It's part of the exorcism." I open a squeaky door. "To your right, the master bedroom. As you can see by the lack of furnishings, I don't sleep here yet but I have an entire Pinterest board on paint colors and—"

"Exorcism?!!"

I twist a finger in my ear. Do they all have to shout at once?

"You have a ghost?" Camille's eyes are wild with excitement. She turns in a circle like a puppy dog after her own tail. "Where is he?"

"She," I say.

"Where is she?"

"She's not here."

"Will she be back?" Camille asks. "What does she want? Does she come in peace? Friend or foe, Theo? *Friend or foe?*"

"By ghost," Lena gulps, "how demonic are we talking here?"

"Not demonic at all. Eliza is harmless."

"Eliza?!!!" says the trio.

"She has a name?" Sadie's hands rake through her hair.

"Guys, she has a whole backstory." I fill them in on Eliza Wolcott's life and death.

"I knew it!" Camille pumps her fist in the air. "I knew something was up the moment I came in. This house has bad juju."

"It doesn't have bad juju!" I say, suddenly defensive over the Witch House's aura.

"Explains why there's a stain on your new couch," Sadie says. "Ghosts are known to leave ectoplasm. Remember *Ghostbusters?*"

I tip my head to the side, warming to my new cover. *Ectoplasm, eh?*

"She *tripped* on a chestnut?" Lena's owlish eyes widen behind her Coke-bottle lenses. "Everything comes back to the chestnut..."

As if on cue, the chestnut tree bashes the back of the house, chucking nuts through the open windows.

"*Ahhhh!*" My friends scramble into a three corner huddle with their backs pressed against each other.

"*It's Eliza!*"

"Where is she?"

"She wants us gone!"

"She wants us dead!"

"She'll nut us straight to hell!"

Yikes! My friends are overdramatic. Sadie presses a hand to her chest. She looks like she's having a heart attack. Lena's glasses are steamed up and Camille is waiving her gold Crucifix neckless against a moldy spot in the corner.

"Guys! Calm down! Eliza's gone. She won't be a problem anymore." I toe the dish of week old durian, ripe and stinking to high heaven. "She's been humbled by durian."

chapter fifty-two

"So this is where the magic happens," I say, gesturing to the pebbled shores and serene waters of Wethersfield Cove.

The four of us suck in great lungfuls of crisp autumn air. Water breaks against a thicket of trees, blazing bright orange leaves yet patched with bare branches, signifying that winter is just around the corner. Save for an old man walking his Golden Retriever, we have the Cove to ourselves.

This is our last stop after a whirlwind day of playing tour guide to my friends.

After I calmed them down and got them away from the ghost and, most importantly, the couch, we trekked back to Edith's B&B where all my holiday guests are staying as there's no way I can make my house habitable.

A quick lunch and chat with Edith (my friends adore her!), it was off to the cheese shop where I introduced them to Rachel, who stuffed a complimentary picnic basket with brie, crackers, jam and a thermos of warm apple cider.

"Everyone is so friendly!" Lena, who lives in Seattle and is intimately familiar with the 'Seattle Freeze,' gazes around Wethersfield in wonder. "Like a Hallmark movie."

Camille's lips twitches. "Do eighty-year-old ladies talk about their Rhode Island swinger parties in Hallmark movies?"

I rub my brow. "Edith certainly knows how to break the ice with strangers."

"That lady has lived a *life*," Sadie says.

Lena chokes down a giggle. "Does Rachel's husband really have a penis piercing?" We met him at the cheese shop where he was helping his wife restock the jam shelves. "He looks like a retired accountant."

I chew on my inner cheek. "I'm sure Rachel appreciates Edith blabbing about Harry's Prince Albert."

Camille frowns. "How would Edith know about Rachel's husband's…"

We freeze for a moment, recalling Edith's accounts of the Rhode Island party scene in the '70s and shiver.

"Let's change topics!" I say, leading the group away from the cheese shop.

"Is that the first prize winner of the scarecrow contest?" Sadie asks, pointing to 'Singin' in the Rain.' All the entries have been cleaned up from Main Street, and yet, Scarecrow Gene Kelly persists. "It's pretty good."

I roll my eyes. "It sucks."

"Who's the winner?"

"Don't let me get started about Scarecrow Gate…"

Armed with food and good cheer, we took a short walking tour of town, *oohing* and *awing* at the stately colonial and Victorian homes, halting to read the historical plaques in front of each house. We take our picnic basket to the Ancient Burying Grounds, where graveyard girl Camille almost busted a vein at the sight of so many old and mossy graves. She jumps up and flits between one crooked tombstone to the next.

"Hand me my grave-rubbing equipment! STAT!"

Near sunset, we route back to Wethersfield Cove where, I kid you not, a blackbird swoops down from a branch and skids across the surface of the water before disappearing into tall marsh grass.

"This is it," Camille says, wrapping her arms around my shoulders, "your Blackbird Pond dream come true."

"The *real* Blackbird Pond has been turned into a highway," I point out, "but we can still pretend."

The four of us sigh. We have a moment of silence in respect for our '90s camp bookclub and the stories we bonded over during those misty Tahoe summers in Cabin 13. I'm obviously the ultimate *Witch of Blackbird Pond* champion, but my girls love and understand this glorious book. Who'd have thought that twenty years later, all four of us would be standing in the shadow of a four-hundred-year-old shipping warehouse where the Dolphin (Nat Eaton's ship) would have docked, the water gently lapping against our shoes, staring off into the middle distance as blackbirds caw in the trees beyond yonder highway?

"Hey Lena," Camille says, toeing a waterweed, "what's this plant called?"

Lena's owlish eyes grew so wide we all thought she was about to faint. "Why?"

"You're the plant expert, right?"

Lena straights up. "Of course I am."

"So what is this?"

"It's a weed," Lena says, straightening her glasses.

"Well, what's the scientific name?"

"Why do you need to know the scientific name?" Lena's nostrils flared. "Are you *testing* me, Camille?"

"I'm just curious. It's okay if you don't know."

"Of course I know!"

"Then what is it?"

"It's called..." Lena gathers her peacoat closer to her body, muffling her words with her sleeve *"mumble mumble... aqua-ish Weedpllyus."*

Camille and I exchange a frown.

"Uh, Lena?" I venture. "Did you make that up?"

Lena tips her chin up. "N-no. Why would you ask that?"

"It doesn't sound like a real scientific name."

"Well, it is. And you can... p-p-put that in your pipe and smoke it," Lena says, walking rapidly away from us toward the other end of shore where Sadie is yanking off her boots and wading into the cold water. "Hey Sadie! What do you see?"

"Sponges!" Sadie looks like she's won the marine invertebrate jackpot. "So many sponges. Oh man, this one's purple with yellow edges. I think it's *Callyspongia,* but I can't tell for sure if it's *Callyspongia elegans* or *Callyspongia fadwae.*"

Camille and I exchange another meaningful look. "Now that sounds like a *real* scientific name," I say.

"It's almost like Sadie is a *real* marine biologist," Camille whispers in my ear and we both sneak another look at Lena. "There's something fishy going on with this one."

"Lena! Camille! Theo!" Sadie hollers at us. "Bring the picnic basket. I've got a big one."

We check out Lena's French braids and fold our arms across our chests like we're private detectives. "An investigation for another time."

chapter fifty-three

I t would have been a perfect day had we not taken the east route from the Cove back to the Witch House. That route passes by Carter's ultramodern home and, of course, as I try to hustle my friends along, they stop to gawk at the cube-shaped 'trash can.'

Whereas his neighbors' houses have jumpstarted their Christmas decorating early, his prefab home is sleek and cold, holiday neutral.

"Is that where—?" Lena turns to me for confirmation. During our Zoom dinners, I've described to them — in detail—about my tour of Carter's minimalist home.

"Yeah," I say, not meeting their eye.

"I can't wait to meet him." Sadie's cheeks are apple red with excitement. "Is he home?"

If Carter is home, he's probably locked up in his hobby shed playing with his model trains. It's the important things, ya know.

I shoo them along. "He's busy."

Camille refuses to budge. "Oh no."

"What?" I whirl around.

"I see what's happening here. Another one bites the dust. You seemed really into him. His feet checks out. His fingernails are maintained. He doesn't own any Big Pony Ralph Lauren Polos.

You said he was datable. Now you're acting funny again." She props a hand on her hip. "What's wrong with this one?"

"He's cheap, remember?"

"Frugal isn't the same as cheap. You said you could work with frugal."

I draw my scarf up to my mouth and feign a shiver. "I'm ready to get inside."

Camille narrows her eyes. "We should knock and say hello. I want to see this real life Nat Eaton for myself."

"Yeah!" Lena and Sadie seconds.

"No, no." I shake my head. "We can't do that."

"Why not?" Sadie asks.

"W-w-we can't just knock on people's doors and say 'Hello.' It simply isn't done."

Lena frowns. "But I thought that's what small towns are all about."

"It isn't true. Besides," I gestured to the drawn windows. "He isn't home."

Camille peers at the corrugated steel facade and tips her head up to check out the solar panels on the rooftops. "I thought you said he was retired. Where else would he be?"

I let out a massive sigh. "He's got more hobbies than sense."

If I'm going to lose this battle, I might as well control the narrative. I tell them a sanitized version of our Salem weekend. The pizzeria date. My food poisoning. I leave out the juicy bits. One day I'll give them the X-rated version once I've come to terms with the embarrassment of it all.

That day is not today.

The driveway is empty, but his car could be charging in the garage. The awkwardness has worn off our run-ins, and if I'm being honest with myself, I rather enjoy 'not talking' to Carter. But that doesn't mean I want to see him with my friends in tow.

I begin to walk home, hoping they'll follow.

The trio lingers on the sidewalk in front of his house.

"Guys, let's…" I freeze as Carter's Tesla pulls into the drive-way. Damn these electric cars! You can't hear them coming.

"It's freezing out there!" I say, rubbing my bare hands together. "Let's get a move on. Move. Move. Move!"

Too late. They've caught sight of Carter climbing out of the driver's side door. He's dressed in the same pair of camel corduroy pants he wore at the pumpkin patch, but is wearing a hunter green parka and a maroon stripped scarf (points for *major* Harry Potter vibes).

Carter is midway to his trunk when he freezes at the sight of three women gawking at him like he's a movie star.

My shoulders hunch inward. There's a crack on the sidewalk. Can I sink into it?

He frowns and catches sight of me in his peripheral vision. Unlike my friends, I'm on the move, creeping like a burglar away from the action. I jump behind the shrubbery dividing his property from his neighbor's and crouch down.

"Um, hello." I hear him greet my wide-eyed friends. And then: "Theo? Everything okay over there?"

Oh. My. God. I squeeze my eyes shut. If I can't see him, maybe he can't see me?

"Come out, Theo!" Camille calls. "Everybody sees you."

Dang it.

Taking a deep breath, I pop out from behind the shrub. "Thought I dropped my keys."

"Did you find them?" Carter asks, lips twitching.

I take one more glance at the grass. "Looks like everything checks out." I square my shoulders and casually stroll toward the group. "Oh Hi, Carter," I say, picking a piece of lint off the hem of my cable-knit sweater, "didn't see you there."

Carter gnaws on his inner cheek. "Must be the bush obstructing your view."

Camille shakes her head. "You're so weird," she mutters, then whirls on Carter with a brilliant smile and a sultry bat of her lashes. "Hi! I'm Camille, Theo's cousin. This is Lena — " Lena pushes up her glasses and gives him a shy wave. "And Sadie." Sadie beams at him with a swoony expression that makes Carter take a step back.

246

My friends are officially too embarrassing to take out in public.

"These are my best friends, though the verdict is out now about the 'best' part," I grumble, avoiding Carter's eyes. "They're visiting for Thanksgiving."

"Ah yes. Thanksgiving." Carter lifts an eyebrow. "Staying over at the Witch House?"

"No," Camille speaks before I can answer. "We're all at the Bromley B&B, but Theo's hosting the party at her new house."

"At the *Witch House*? Wow. You're really going to do this?" Carter arches an eyebrow at me. "There's going to be a storm on Thanksgiving. How's the roof?"

"The roof is fine," I say. "The weather reports say there's a 'chance' of a storm."

"The weatherman says it's a nor'easter."

"The 'weatherman.'" I scoff. "Do you believe everything the 'weatherman' says?"

Carter blinks. "Yes. I do."

"Well... shows what you know."

My friends follow our bickering like a tennis match.

Sadie clears her throat. "What are you doing for Thanksgiving?" she asks Carter.

"Spending it with my grandma."

My friends hold back an *Awww*.

"But isn't Edith coming to your Thanksgiving, Theo?" Lena asks me. "Don't tell us you're stealing away Carter's company!"

"She's just popping in for cocktails." I see where this is going and I don't like it!

"Cocktails?" Carter switches to chewing on his opposite cheek. "Since when do you drink cocktails?"

"I've always offered cocktails when I host a soirée."

"But you've never hosted a dinner," Lena says.

I glare at her. "Yes, I have. And we all had the time of our lives."

"Buffy marathons in middle school and pizza bagel bites don't count."

Traitor!

"So what kind of cocktails will you be serving," Carter presses, "at this 'soirée'?"

All heads turn to me. Propping a hand on my hip, I lift my chin. "V-vodka martinis." I nod. Good save. "Shaken not stirred."

"Perfect," Carter's blue eyes twinkle, "that's Gran's favorite drink."

"It is?" I clear my throat. "I mean, of course! That's why I'm serving it at my wet bar."

My friends whirl on me. "You have a wet bar?"

"Indeed I do."

Sadie nudges me with her elbow. "So Edith's coming all by herself?"

I lock eyes with Carter. "Uh huh."

"That's not very convenient for an old lady," Camille jumps in. "Carter! Why don't you and your grandma stay the entire evening?"

I shake my head. "We'll be short on food."

"We'll have plenty of food to spare," Camille says.

"Not enough room."

Camille slaps her hands together. "Did you see the size of Theo's house? Of course you have! You're her contractor. Plenty of room. Everyone will be there. Even Theo's hamsters will be there. The more the merrier, right?"

"I'm sure Edith has her traditions," I say.

"She hates traditions," Camille says. "She told me so over breakfast."

I level Camille with a death stare.

"Carter likes to be alone."

"Actually, even a loner like me likes companionship during the holidays."

His comment earns an *Awwww* of sympathy and puppy dog eyes from my friends.

"But I wouldn't want to impose on your 'soirée,'" he back-tracks. "I know you're busy with your turkey and shaking your vodka martinis. I have some Healthy Choice steamers to tie me over."

All eyes turn to me. Sadie actually looks like she's on the brink of tears. "You're not going to let him eat *frozen dinners* for *Thanksgiving,* are you?"

Damn.

I've been ambushed. Bamboozled. "Fine. Carter," I say between clenched teeth. "Would you like to come over for Thanksgiving?"

His dimples deepen and his eyes laugh down at me. "I thought you'd never ask."

chapter fifty-four

W hy did I think it was a good idea to host Thanksgiving? I'm in *way* over my head. It seemed doable at the time, something to check off my adult bucket-list, an accomplishment to show my parents that I'm thriving on my own.

In my expectations, I'll have a spic and span house with a fire blazing in the hearth, festive holiday music, porcelain plates, silverware, chestnuts roasting on an open fire.

Ideally, my parents would enter a gleaming house with pies baking in the oven.

But this is reality:

"Oh my god." My mom eyes the plant wall. She doesn't see my innovative thinking, my ability to flip a bad situation on its head and repurpose an unsalvageable wall. She doesn't know how plants purifies the air, opens up the room, and adds rustic charm to an otherwise dilapidated structure. My mom is very narrow-minded. She only sees a torn-down wall, a hole in the ceiling, water damage, and oldness.

Feeling like this day is going to be an uphill battle, I gesture toward my newly acquired Ikea LACK table. *Okay.* It's not authentic Colonial furniture. Give me a break! Between chasing after my romantic ideals and trying to please my parents, I'm broke.

"Have you seen my wet bar?" I have martini glasses, ice, tiny pickled onions, gin and vodka, and a cheat sheet about how to make a vodka martini.

My mom takes a look at the bar. "Huh, no Hennessy?"

Hennessy is the special occasion drink in our family and I hate it. Also, I can't afford it. "James Bond drinks martinis," I say, rocking back on my heels.

"James Bond has a job with health insurance." The boarded up hole beneath the main staircase catches her eye. "Oh my god..."

Mom looks like she's about to toss her cookies. *Sigh.* She doesn't understand what it means to be bohemian.

"There's a hole in your ceiling," my dad points out.

"It's a skylight."

He studies my skylight for a minute and shrugs. "Is the turkey roasted or deep fried?"

"We're not having turkey." Because of my tight timeline, I ended up last minute grocery shopping after all. Good luck getting a turkey on Thanksgiving day. "But we do have five Costco rotisserie chickens and beer, Ba, beer..."

My dad brightens up and joins Sadie, Camille, and Lena at the dining table, which isn't a table in the traditional sense of the word. I've repurposed two slabs of wood (Connecticut Oak, very fancy) and covered it with a red flannel table cloth.

The chairs are an eclectic mix of camp chairs, metal fold-aways, and a cushy armchair I found in a dumpster. And of course, pushed discreetly into the shadowy corner of the living room, my low-riding Jacques Le Fèvre with the 'ectoplasm' stain on the cushion. My friends avoid the couch.

My mom passes by it, muttering something about my strange taste in furniture. "That stain could have been avoided if you cover your couch in plastic like I told you..."

"Ma!" I roll my eyes. "I'm not covering everything in plastic."

"Then you will not have nice things."

I have no television yet, but I have something better. My friends pooled their money together and gave me the *perfect* housewarming present: a travel-sized bio-dome for my hamster babies. Instead of a cage which is cruel and unimaginative, Cereal and Socks can now graze on a bed of self-watering grass. It comes with a pipe system and a cute little bamboo handle. Now Cereal and Socks can thrive in a low maintenance ecosystem with little effort from me, though I do have to scoop their poop from time to time.

Mom doesn't notice the hamster bio-dome. If she did, she'll comment that my hamsters are in a better living situation than I am. She gives my friends a scant nod of acknowledgement and ignores the yummy smorgasbord I've prepared. Granted, most of the food is from Costco and Trader Joe's, but she could have at least compliment me on how nicely I've arranged five rotisserie chickens.

I even got those Costco cream puffs she loves, but Mom looks like she's sleepwalking through a nightmare. She shuffles into the kitchen, her lips tucked into a perpetual frown.

"She's displeased," Lena whispers.

Sadie says, "She looks mad."

"That's just how Auntie Hua looks," Camille swats me on the back, "Sorry, Theo."

I eye my friends and reluctantly follow my mom before something bad happens.

She's scoping out the avocado green fridge and the dated appliances. "Oh my god... I need to sit down."

I run to her side. "Are you going to faint?" Oh shit. Is it the residual mold spores?

Waving me away, she returns to the dining room, her face drained of blood. Camille immediately offers her a fold-away chair. Mom plops down and mutters something in Vietnamese, which sounds suspiciously like 'The horror. The horror.'

Geez, I know my new home isn't on par with Spanish-style houses of our California relatives, but *come on!* I don't think she appreciates the artistry of this place. The craftsmanship. The historical significance. The lack of an HOA.

Mom is laying her distaste on thick. I'm offended she doesn't appreciate all the work I've sunk into this place.

Camille pours her a glass of water.

Mom asks for Hennessy. "I suspected things were bad with you," she begins. "I just didn't know things were *this* bad."

"You don't like this place?"

"You have a hole in your ceiling and '70's appliances," says my mom, who recently renovated her kitchen with the finest Tuscan granite Lowe's had to offer.

"It's a skylight and I happen to love my '70's appliances."

"The only people who say they like '70's appliances are poor people." She heaves a long-suffering sigh. "What have I done to deserve this? I give up everything I own and immigrate to this country so my daughter can have a better life and live in a two-story house."

The entire table turns to my staircase.

Mom ignores this gesture. "Instead she chooses to move three-thousand-miles away and live in a crack house."

"Don't be melodramatic, Auntie Hua," Camille says. "There are no drugs here."

I wish there were.

"It's a colonial house, Mom." I rub my aching temple and force myself to breathe. "And it's still under renovation."

"I love it, Mrs. Dy," Sadie jumps in. "It's got loads of rustic charm and you can't beat the $6,000 price tag."

"She would say that," my mom mutters in Vietnamese, "she's a barefoot hippie."

"She's a marine biologist, Mom!" I say, also in Vietnamese.

"She wears those hippie sandals."

We glance down at Sadie's Birkenstocks. I don't know what my mom is on about. Sadie's wearing her best woolen socks in preparation for the New England weather.

"Auntie Hua," Camille shakes her head, "no one's a hippie anymore."

Sadie notices the language swap. "Are you talking about me?" she whispers.

"Theo!" My mom switches back into no-nonsense English. "Enough is enough. You've had your vacation. It's time for you to forget this silliness and come home."

My mom whacks my dad between the shoulder blades, causing him to choke on his mouthful of Trader Joe's stuffed mushroom. "Say something to your daughter."

He gulps and gazes wildly around as if he's just remembered where he was. "I like the house?"

My mom sucks in air through her teeth. She's building up destructive momentum like a hurricane about to blow. Dad sinks down in his seat. I wish I had a turkey to check on, but all I had were five Costco rotisserie chickens, a Margarita pizza, and a cheese board.

The door bell rings.

Thank God.

"I'll get it!" I race to the door.

Carter and Edith are bundled in coats and huddled against the brace of early winter wind.

Carter smiles when he sees me.

I quickly turn my attention to Edith.

"Come in, come in," I hustle them inside. "Whatever you brought smells delicious."

"I didn't know what kind of pie you liked," Edith unravels her scarf, "I made pumpkin, pecan, and strawberry rhubarb."

Carter follows his grandma inside, his hands piled with pies in Tupperware. He's looking deliciously academic in ear warmers, grey mittens, and camel corduroy trousers. I take his bundle and, as he peels off his navy peacoat, I catch a whiff of smokey autumn leaves in the wool fibers.

I scan the pies, my attention caught by an extra dish. "What's this?"

"Green bean casserole," he says.

"Carter made it himself," Edith points out.

I peek up at his wind reddened cheeks. "I didn't know you cooked."

He clears his throat.

"He made it for you," Edith says.

"Gran!"

"Well, if you're not going to tell her, I will."

Unsure of how to respond, I move them into the dining room. "Hey everyone, pies!"

Carter helps Edith to a chair.

Lena and Sadie giggle when Carter takes a seat beside them and rolls up the sleeves of his flannel shirt. Camille leans against a chair, admiring his forearms.

Even my mom can't help checking him out.

"You know Camille, Lena, and Sadie. My parents. Ma, Ba…" I gesture to the new arrivals. "This is Edith and Carter Bromley. Edith owns the bed-and-breakfast you're staying at and Carter—"

"How do you know my daughter?" My mom's eyebrows perk up in interest.

"He's — "

"Her new boyfriend!" Edith blurts out.

chapter fifty-five

"*Boyfriend?*" Mom's eyes light up.

My stoic mother, who disapproves of public displays of emotions, is on the verge of dancing a jig. "Theo! You didn't tell me you had a *boyfriend*."

A giggle escapes from Sadie. Then Lena. Camille leans back in her chair, waiting for the drama to unfold. My dad helps himself to a chicken thigh and shovels more than his allotted portion of green bean casserole onto his plate.

"Gran!" Carter turns red.

I slap a hand over my forehead. Never have I ever been more embarrassed than I am right this moment—*and* that's coming from someone who has managed to get herself stuck in a wall, crushed by cheese, and had violent diarrhea during foreplay. I'm also contemplating the murder of an eighty-year-old woman.

"Edith," I clench my teeth, "please tell my mom you're mistaken."

"*What?*" Edith fiddles with her hearing aid. "I call it like I see it."

Not-so-gently shoving Dad out of his seat, Mom takes a baffled Carter by the hand. "Why don't you sit next to me?"

I narrow my eyes at Edith. "I'm on to you, *troublemaker*."

She feigns wide-eyed innocence. "I don't know what you're

talking about. Oh look! Artichoke dip! How fancy. Don't mind if I do."

For the next hour, I sit between Lena and Sadie and quietly pick at my cold Costco chicken. My dad is shoveling food in his face like a wombat while Edith questions him about his childhood in Vietnam.

"You might have met my first husband, Chuck," Edith says. "He was in 'Nam in '71. He manned the gunship."

Dad shakes his head. "I really don't think so."

Edith nods. "You're probably right. Let's just say Chuck was a little trigger happy. Smoked a lot of weed."

Dad is silent for a moment. "Ah yes, I remember 'Chuck.'"

"You do?"

"Was he missing in action?"

Edith's eyes widen. "How do you know?"

In reply, Dad chomps down on his chicken leg and that's the end of that.

My mom corners Carter, dragging him through a gauntlet of hard-hitting questions.

"… Retired? At thirty-four?" Mom throws a suggestive glance at me. "What do you do for money?"

"Mom! You can't ask him that."

"It's an honest question. I want to know how he plans to support you," she says, then smacks Dad on the shoulder. "Pay attention."

I blanch. "Support me?"

"And your children."

I bury my face in my hands. "I'm so sorry, Carter. My mom is crazy."

"It's okay, Mrs. Dy." Carter's cheeks flush crimson. "I founded a prefab construction company, then sold it and live off the…" he clears his throat, "profits from the sale."

I can see my mom's pupils morph into dollar signs. "Theo! You never told me your handsome boyfriend was rich."

"Um…" Carter rubs the back of his neck. "I'm not rich!"

"He's not rich," I second. It's not that my mom is a gold

digger. She's just very practical. I mean, you have to be when you grow up outrunning napalm drops and trigger happy Americans named Chuck. I just don't want Carter thinking I'm a gold digger.

"Of course he's rich," Edith says. "He's got a great investment portfolio. He bought Tesla stock before it went to the moon."

I slam my utensils on the table. I can't sit idly by while my mom and Edith plan my future and marry me off to Carter. "I'm dishing out pie. Anyone want to help? Camille?"

My cousin waves me off. "I want to know about this investment portfolio."

"Lena? Sadie?"

"Yeah, no…" Sadie says. "I'm comfortable here."

Lena leans forward and gawks at Carter. "Not when things are just getting juicy!"

Traitors! All of them. I give my dad puppy dog eyes. "Ba?"

"Can you bring me a slice of everything?" he says.

I throw my hands in the air and stomp into the kitchen, slamming the door behind me.

I clutch the countertop and count to three. Lord, give me strength not to throttle my mom. And Edith. I have it out for her, too.

With blood buzzing in my ears, I grab a kitchen knife and began hacking away at the pecan pie. The white noise obscures the creak of the door. "Camille, help me carry out the pies."

"Not Camille," Carter says, "but I'll help you."

I check over my shoulder and almost drop my knife.

He presses his back against the door and we blink at each other over several excruciatingly awkward seconds. Laughter rings out from the dining room as my mom's voice drifts through the wall. Oh God. She's telling the story about how I got lost in Target when I was seven and they found me huddled behind the tomato plants in the garden department.

My mom has worked me into a foul temper. I'm in no mood for teasing.

I whirl around and concentrate on dishing out the pies. My knife work is sloppy, my scooping a disgrace. More pie lands on the counter than the tray.

Carter appears beside me and holds out his hand for my knife. "Shall I?"

I scoot away. "I can handle it."

"You're kind of um... massacring the crust."

That does it. After listening to my mom's criticism all evening, I don't need Carter's two cents on how I can't slice the pie. "Listen," I snap, brandishing my kitchen knife. "If you want to help, hand me that dish... in silence. Don't heckle me."

Holding his hands up, Carter takes a step back. "Easy. Just set the knife down."

I blow a strand of hair away from my face. "Sorry. I'm a little stressed."

"I can see that."

"If I'm snippy, it's because of my mother. I don't mean to take it out on you."

He smiles. "Understood."

I gently place a slice of strawberry rhubarb on a new plate. We work as a team on an assembly line. Pie-plate-whipped cream-fork. "And I accept your apology," I say, waiting for the next plate.

Carter halts the production, causing me to turn to him in question.

"Apology?" he asks. "What am I apologizing for?"

"Inviting yourself to my Thanksgiving."

He steps back with a frown. "That's a new one."

"What do you mean?"

"I seem to recall you inviting me. The words came right out of your mouth."

"I was put in an awkward situation."

"You put *yourself* in that awkward situation," he counters. "I wasn't the one hiding behind a bush." His eyes flash with anger. "Is it really so bad? To have me over for dinner?"

259

I grumble and feign an intense concentration in slicing the pumpkin pie.

"I haven't done anything to embarrass you," he says.

True. That prize goes to my mom and Edith. I take a deep breath and glance at the abundance of plated pies—more than enough to feed eight people.

"Shall we?" I gesture to door.

Carter makes no move to take the plates.

Fine help he is. Guess I'll just have to do everything myself. I begin balancing plates on both arms like a super server. "Help me get the door?"

"Are we going to talk about it?"

"Talk about what?"

"About us," he says, taking the plates off my hands and setting them back on the counter. "Our... relationship status."

"Really? We're doing this now?"

"No time like the present."

"My guests. The pie…"

Boisterous laughter echoes from the dining room.

Crossing his legs at the ankles, Carter leans against the kitchen counter. "Sounds like they're getting along fine without us."

I utter a long-suffering sigh. "Okay, I'll give you five minutes. What do you want me to say?"

"Where do we go from here?" He tilts his head to the side, studying my reaction.

"Is it up to me?"

"No bushes to hide behind, Theo. You know my answer is always yes." A hopeful smile ghosts his lips. "I see you've kept the couch."

My cheeks flame at the implication.

He takes one step forward. I take two steps back. Hurt ripples across his face as he notes my reaction.

"I know what I want," he says softly, "*do you?*"

I lower my head, scrambling for words. The truth is, I have thought about our relationship status and I was hoping to avoid doing anything about 'us' until a later time. An *ideal* time when I've had more sleep and can get my thoughts together.

I didn't want to do this on Thanksgiving, but he pressed my hand.

How do you break up with someone you were never with? How do you end something that never existed in the first place?

I take a deep breath. "I think it's pointless to begin anything."

Carter blinks. "Pointless?"

"You and I are just two different people—"

"We're not all that different."

"You're a leopard who has found your spots and you're not going to change. You like energy efficient tiny houses and I like big rambling historical houses. You're a miser. I enjoy life."

"I enjoy life!"

"You enjoy model trains."

"What's wrong with model trains?"

"Nothing. You've loved modeled trains longer than you've known me and you'll always lose hours to your hobbies. I'm all for hobbies, but I don't want to take a backseat to them."

"You won't!"

"I already have."

"For *one day*. It was a mistake, and I apologized. Do you want me to throw all my trains away?"

"No." I shake my head. "Of course I don't want that."

"Then what *do* you want? I just want to date you, but you're treating this like it's an audition for marriage." He narrows his eyes. "Is it?"

"No! Yes. I don't know!" I rake my hands through my hair. "Look, the point of the matter is we have different expectations of how we want to live our lives and we both think we know what's best. Our future relationship will be a long list of battles. How much should we spend on coffee, furniture, entertainment... I'm always going to nag you to go out. You're always going to want to stay in. I want a bunch of stickers and magnets on the fridge. You can't stand clutter. I want a bed. A real bed with a box spring and a headboard, maybe even a canopy. I

261

don't want to sleep on a goddamn futon. Neither of us will want to compromise."

"I'll get rid of the futon," he says. "There. That's compromise."

"I don't want you to get rid of your futon."

"But you—"

"We can only end in heartbreak. And people," I give a defeated shrug, "people I know… Sadie's parents, for example, got a divorce over as something as trivial as her dad leaving the kitchen cabinets open and her mom chewing too loudly. Fifteen years of marriage and this is what they split over! What if that happens to us?"

Carter pinches his nose bridge. "It won't happen to us. You're already thinking about divorce and I haven't asked you to marry me."

My indignation flares. "Well, why haven't you?"

"Because I've only known you for two months!" He narrows his eyes. "Wait… what? You want to get married now?"

"Yes." I blink. "No! I mean, I would like for you to want to marry me sometime in the future."

"But you don't even want to date me."

I fold my arms over my chest. "But it's just nice to want to be wanted."

Carter looks like he's on the brink of seizing me by the shoulders and shaking me until my teeth chatters. He props both hands behind his neck instead and glances up at the ceiling. "What are we even talking about now?"

"You not wanting to marry me," I say. "And that's another thing: I can't be with someone who doesn't want to settle down. I'm thirty-two, not twenty-two, and my biological clock is…" I stomp on the floor. "Ticking."

"This is so stupid," Carter mutters.

I prop my hand on my hips. "What's stupid?"

"This…" he gestures at the space between us. "You."

"How *dare* you call me stupid!"

"I don't mean that you're stupid, but the way you handle

things is stupid. Your logic is the problem and quite frankly, you're the problem."

"Me?! I'm not the problem."

"Yes, you are," he says matter-of-factly. "You're the cause of your own unhappiness—and mine. You're still mad at me long after you should have stopped being mad at me. Your anger is inefficient."

Is there such a thing as *efficient* anger?

"Are you *kidding*? You ghosted me for an entire day... during my hamster's funeral."

Carter raises a finger. "Not ghosted. To ghost implies I intended to ignore you. It was an accident and I've already apologized. Several times, in fact... but it seems you want me to get down on my hands and knees and do it all over again until you're satisfied. Well, I won't."

I scoff. "You're laying it on a bit thick, don't you think?"

"You tell me," Carter says. "How else do I explain the cold shoulder?"

"What — "

"Don't you dare say 'what cold shoulder.' You know exactly what I'm talking about."

I bite my tongue.

"I've been working hard to get out of the doghouse, but you won't even give me the time of day." He slumps against the counter. "It takes two people to make a relationship work. Hell, what am I talking about? It takes two to make a relationship begin and..." he shakes his head. "I can't seem to figure it out. You seem to want to torpedo 'us' before we can begin."

A lump forms in my throat. Can it be that he's hit the nail on the head? I yank open my avocado green fridge and stick my head inside so he won't see me cry.

"Well?" Carter asks from behind me.

I spot a dish of butter and focus all my attention on it. The butter is my life raft. It will keep me from falling into pieces.

Seeing that he's not going to get anything meaningful out of me, Carter sighs. "Look, I like trains. Love 'em. I can and *will* lose track of time when I'm setting up my models. Did I screw up that day? Big time. Will I screw up again? Maybe. But all I need is a tap on the shoulder or a swat upside the head. It's as simple as that. Just don't expect me to read your mind. Most of the time I can't even read my own mind."

I turn around and arch an eyebrow. "I'm not mad about the trains."

"Oh really? You certainly gave a brilliant imitation of it."

I lower my eyes to the ground.

"I'm not giving up my model trains," he says.

"I'm not asking you to! And can we stop talking about trains? I'm sick of these trains and I haven't even seen them!"

"We're fighting about trains because you don't want to talk about the real problem here." Carter sucks in his breath. "This isn't about trains, is it? It's about you."

I poke my head up. "Me?"

"Yes, you. You're the problem."

I open my mouth to counter. He holds up a hand to stop me. "One word: Nat Eaton."

"That's two words."

Carter rolls his eyes.

"What about him?" I ask.

"My theory still stands," he says, "I said it before, I'll say it again: You believe Nat Eaton would never choose model trains over you."

AHHHHHHHHHHHHHHHHHHHHHHHHHHHH! If we were married, I'll want a divorce. No, an annulment. Okay. We can *never* get married. He's driving me crazy.

"Of course he won't. Trains weren't invented in his time."

"Ships, then."

I cock my head to the side. "No, I'm pretty sure he chose his ship over Kit plenty of times."

He tosses his hands up in exasperation. "You know what I'm saying."

"Actually, I'm super confused."

He falls into silence. We've been bickering in circles about those goddamn model trains that I haven't stopped to notice the lines of hurt on his face.

"You want Nat Eaton," he says at last. "He's your perfect guy and you're not going to settle for less. For me…"

"Carter — " I try to reach out for him.

"No!" He shields me away. "Try to deny it. You can't."

"Carter — "

He steps back. "You're chasing after a dream man that doesn't exist. I'm a real man who likes you and you won't even give me a chance. I'm not perfect. I'm not Nat Eaton." He swallows, his voice shaky with the sting of rejection. "And I have too much self-respect to try to be something I'm not. You want a beautiful romance? I'm offering it to you and you're too dumb to take it."

I take a step toward him.

He steps away, holding up his hands to keep me back. "I'm not offering anymore. You're not worth the effort."

There's no holding it back now.

I bury my head in my hands and burst into tears. He reaches out, instinctively wanting to comfort me then realizing that *No*, he shouldn't. I don't deserve his sympathy. I've treated him like shit and he has too much self-respect for take backs.

"I'm sorry I crashed your Thanksgiving," he says and presses a bundle of napkins in my hands. "I'll leave right away. Good-bye, Theo."

With a regretful squeeze of my shoulder, he pushes through the kitchen door, leaving me to sob over the sink and deal with my pies, as I requested, alone.

chapter fifty-six

I'm ugly crying on the floor when the door swings open again. I poke my head up, expecting Carter, got my dad instead. He sees my tear-streaked face and snotty nose and gulps.

"I was just," he looks with longing at the pies and then at me, the disheveled obstacle in front of his dessert, "I'll come back later."

He slowly backs away. Seconds later, I hear the laughter stop. My dad, sounding more angry than I've ever heard him, lays into my mother in Vietnamese about making me cry.

My mom is furious. "What did I do?"

"You nagged her too far!"

"Me?! What did I say?" Mom roars. "You are always blaming me for everything!"

I can't help smiling through my tears. My dad is a man of few words, but he sticks up for me when it counts.

There's a loud crash in the dining room and I imagine my mom pounding her fists on the table. "*I* didn't ruin this trip," Mom shouts, "*you* ruined this trip. We wouldn't even have to be on this stupid trip if you hadn't spoiled her. You let her do everything she wants. Now your daughter is unemployed and living in a crack house and you only have yourself to blame."

"No, dear," Edith shouts, "we don't do crack in this town. Weed, perhaps. No crack."

A fourth voice joins the argument. "Whoa! Whoa," Camille says, "Auntie Hua! Put the plate down!"

I can imagine Sadie and Lena huddling in fright.

And Carter... Would he have time to sneak away in all the sudden ruckus? Knowing him, he would want to say a proper goodbye and take Edith home.

The thought of Carter wrings a fresh wave of tears from me. The raw hurt on his face will forever be imprinted in my memory. I hunch forward, trying to blot out his last words to me.

I'm not offering anymore. You're not worth the effort.

Was he right?

Am *I* the problem here?

Was I too blind to appreciate the fragile thing we had?

Am I so picky and afraid of commitment that I would subconsciously torpedo our romance before it even began?

Would I be happier nursing a literary crush over a *real* relationship with a *real* man?

There's a lot to unpack here. With every bit of insight, I'm starting to think Carter was right. I'm all those things and more. Makes you wonder what he sees in me to want to deal with *all of that*...

But he *doesn't* want to deal with my emotional baggage and unrealistic expectations anymore. It's too late.

Too late.

Too... CRACK.

Lightning.

BOOM.

Thunder.

I wipe my tears on my sleeves. Lightning *and* thunder. There will be a storm after all. Guess the 'weatherman' was right. Funny how that happens...

Hiccuping, I stand up and run to the window.

It's still a dry night. The old chestnut tree is silhouetted against an amethyst sky, its branches rapping against the house.

All of a sudden, an earth-shattering crack of lightning streaks across the sky. It's close. Very close. A few feet away from my backyard.

I press a hand to my hammering heart.

CRACK. A symphony of concerted lightning strikes. The wind howls. The chestnut tree rattles, hailing chestnuts against the windows and wooden siding.

CRACK. This is the big one. It shakes the house. Lights up the dark corners like a flashbang. I hear a CRASH from above. Glass shattering. Wood splintering. Smoke.

Smoke?

I sniff the air.

It smells like a fireplace and chestnuts...

Chestnuts roasting on an open fire.

Holy shit. I burst into the dining room to find my guests in an uproar.

"Did you feel that?" Sadie grabs my hands. "The entire house shook."

Carter, dressed in his coat, drops his ear warmers and races to the back of the house.

An orange glow illuminates the entire back window. He shields his eyes with his arms. "The tree's on fire!"

"My chestnut tree?"

Carter races back to the dining room. "The entire thing's lit up like a torch."

"Holy shit!"

Whereas it's been chilly during dinner, the first floor warms up. All of us tilt our heads up. The ceiling plaster shrivels. Paint drips. Smoke rolls down the stairs and pours through my 'sky-light,' engulfing my botany wall in acrid fumes.

Carter and I exchange a terrified glance.

"Everybody out!" I scream. "The house is on fire!"

268

chapter fifty-seven

"Go! Go! Go!" I hustle my parents and friends away from the flames. Carter scoops Edith off her feet and hauls her toward the exit.

Everybody squeezes through the door at the same time, creating a bottleneck of bodies.

"One at a time," my mom hollers. "Get in line. Elders first!"

"I'm first!" Edith says.

"Toan!" Mom barks at my dad. "Get over here. Stop piling your plate. This is not a time for leftovers."

Mom organizes us like an elementary school fire drill. After a count of heads, we march single file out the door and pour onto the street.

I jog to the opposite sidewalk, coughing and hacking up smoke. My friends collapsed on my neighbor's front lawn. My mom fans herself. My dad swats her on the back while clutching a plate of leftovers and a six-pack of beer. Carter sets Edith down on the sidewalk beside me.

"I'll take one of those beers," Edith says to my dad.

The entire neighborhood spills onto the street, watching in open-mouth shock as the Witch House burns.

Someone shouts: "Call the fire department!"

Camille has her phone pressed to her ear, barking orders. "Done and done!"

Lena tugs on my sweater, pointing at the baby pothos and string of hearts tucked under her arms. "These are all I can save, Theo! I can go back for more."

She starts back toward the house. Sadie yanks her back by the elbow. "Leave it! It's not worth it."

Flames reflect off Lena's thick lenses. "But the plants—"

"The plants are dead, Lena. Dead…"

On that tragic note, a drizzle settles over us like a light mist. It's not enough to douse out the fire.

I glance over my shoulder.

The chestnut tree is a flaming torch. The entire roof of my house is ablaze. Flames flicker in the attic window. Carter's roof repair, my botany wall, the fresh coat of paint… Two months of hard work down the drain. And all my stuff: the couch, my Ikea wet bar, my avocado fridge, my waterproof Vincent Van Sproot stickers, my hamster bio-dome…

My stomach bottoms out. My blood turns to ice. I kneel over, about to blow my Thanksgiving dinner all over my neighbor's lawns.

Lena saved two plants.

My dad saved beer.

I forgot my fur babies.

I FORGOT MY HAMSTERS.

With a cry of horror, I jump to my feet and race toward my burning house. My action produces as uproar.

"What is she doing?" Camille says.

"Stop her!"

Shoes pound the pavement behind me. A strong pair of arms loop around my waist, lifts me off my feet, and turns me around.

"Get off of me!"

"Are you crazy?" Carter barks in my ear. "The house will collapse with you in it!"

I scratch up his forearms and kick my legs, trying to break free from his vise-like grip.

"Cereal and Socks! I left them inside!" A horrifying image of my hamsters bursting into tiny balls of flame grips me with panic. I slam my foot into his shin.

"*Oof!*"

He drops me.

"Don't try to stop me!" I take off and sprint all the way to my front lawn before Carter yanks me back.

"Theo! The house is on *fire*."

"I don't care what happens to me. I have to save them!"

How many more hamsters must die because of me? If Cereal and Socks came out of this alive, hamster social services should just come and take them. Look what happened to Milk! I'm negligent. I'm officially the worst pet owner ever.

My sobs are wretched and desperate. The fight goes out of me and I slump in his arms. "Please let me go. I need to get them out!"

Carter's expression flickers with compassion. He turns to the burning house, then peers into my pleading face and his resolve breaks.

He releases me. "Wait here," he says, squeezing my hands.

I hiccup. "Carter?"

With one final glance back at me, he bolts toward the porch and kicks open the door. A blast of smoke and embers greets him. He shields his face with his jacket and plunges into the inferno.

chapter fifty-eight

Seconds tick by.

I keep my eyes peeled to the front door for signs of movement.

Flames lick the roof. The house makes a crackling noise as the old skeleton buckles under the heat. Plumes of smoke pour from the windows.

Sirens blare in the distance. Too slow. Too far away. Will they reach us in time? A drizzle covers the street, but it's not the downpour I need to put out this fire.

It's all my fault if something happens to him. *Especially* after how we ended it. If Carter dies in this fire, he's going to die angry at me and I fully deserve it.

At my wits' end, I pace the sidewalk, overwhelmed by guilt, kicking myself over my negligence and outright stupidity.

I took him for granted. I made a big freaking deal over model trains when trains weren't even the issue. It's me. I'm the problem.

He was the perfect guy all along, and I was too blind to see it. I'm the one who's afraid to take a leap of faith, and despite all my nonsense, he still risks life and limb to save my hamsters.

Now, because of me, Carter's probably going to die a fiery death…

My mom wraps a blanket around me and squeezes my shoulders. "Nothing is going to happen to him. It's a quick in-out."

I'm slowly going mad from waiting. "He should be out by now. The hamsters are not that far from the entrance."

Edith appears by my side. She's in ship shape, if a bit winded. "Don't worry. He'll get them out." She sounds certain, but her anxious gaze searches the front door.

"It's all my fault. If I wasn't such a lousy hamster mom…"

"Hush now," Edith squeezes my hand. "Even you can't cause a freak lightning strike on Thanksgiving."

Thunder rumbles in the distance. Harder rain washes over us. It's still not enough. We need a downpour to put out the fire.

A crash jars us. The northwest portion of the roof caves in. Mom stifles her screams. Edith flinches and tightens her grip on my hands. Our eyes lock in fear.

Blind panic jolts me into action.

I run toward the house, ignoring the frantic calls from my mom and friends.

"Carter!"

I halt just short of the front porch, my eyes burning from the smoke. I strip off my cable-knit sweater, hoping the rain has drenched it enough to wrap it around my nose and mouth as a makeshift filter against smoke inhalation. I'm just about to plunge into my fiery living room when a shape materializes in the doorway.

Carter lurches out, hacking up smoke. My hamster bio-dome is tucked under his arm. I'm about to wrap my arms around him, but he bats me off, turning to the flying embers behind us. No dallying next to a house that's about to collapse on us at any moment.

I seize him by the wrist and lead him across the street. As Carter catches his breath, I check on Cereal and Socks. They're huddled on their grass bed, flustered and disgruntled, but in good shape—saved from smoke inhalation by the bio-dome's closed air system.

Carter rests his hands on his knees, his eyes bloodshot and

watery, his cheeks soot smeared. His blond hair is disheveled and covered with ash, and there's a giant tear down the front of his shirt. A shiver zips through him as he guzzles down a water bottle. He pours a second bottle over his head.

He refuses a blanket from my mom and thwarts Edith's fussing. But he doesn't push me off when I throw my arms around him and chant 'thank you' and 'I'm sorry' in his ear.

"Sorry?" Carter has a dazed look in his eyes from the moment he exited the house. That look has not left him now that's he's safely outside in the pouring rain. "What for?"

"For almost getting you killed."

"Oh that," he says. "I've already forgiven you."

"And being an asshole about your trains."

Carter pulls back to look at me, his lips twitching in a pained smile. "That's a whole other kettle of fish altogether."

"I like trains, too." I sob into his shoulder, shivering as his arm wraps around me. "That's what so ironic about the whole thing. I'm not opposed to trains. Please show me your trains."

"Theo…" He tightens his hold on me.

Sirens blare in my ears. I peek over his shoulder. My friends, parents, and Edith are huddled in a group, watching us, eavesdropping no doubt. Well, in Edith's case, trying to eavesdrop.

"What's she saying?" Edith shouts. "She like *planes*?"

"Trains, Mrs. Bromley," Sadie says.

Edith adjusts her hearing aid. "What's that?"

"Trains!"

"What's this about trains?"

Carter clears his throat and leads us around my neighbor's shrubbery and away from the spectators.

I break down into another crying fit. By now, there's more water coming out of my eyes than the sky. "When the roof collapsed and you still hadn't come out… I thought you were done for."

"I thought I was done for too." Carter shakes his head. He tells me about how he dove into the living room and located my hamsters (running frantically in their wheels) when he heard a *creak* and *snap* from the ceiling.

A shower of embers. He glanced up just in time to shield himself from being crushed by a falling wooden beam.

"My life flashed before my eyes. There was no time or space to move. I was surrounded by a circle of fire and the couch was in my way."

"My Jacques Le Fèvre couch?"

"The very one. I tried to move it, but it was too heavy."

I toe the wet grass sheepishly. "Must be the American maple...a high density wood."

"I waited for the beam to hit me," he continues, "and when it didn't, I looked up and — "

A shiver zips through him. Carter shakes his body like a wet dog.

"What happened? What did you see?" My heart skips a beat. "You look like you saw a ghost."

"I *did* see a ghost!"

My eyes widen. "You saw Eliza?! What did she look like?"

"A giant blue light," he says.

"Like God light?"

"No. Just a big blue blob."

"With God rays?"

"I don't know." He scrubs a hand over his face.

I grab his wrist. "Don't touch your eyes."

"It—she was holding up the beam and she... smelled like chestnuts... *roasting* chestnuts."

"*Holy shit.*" I let out a big exhale. "What was she wearing? Was she wearing a fancy colonial gown?"

"I didn't pay attention to her clothes," Carter says.

Typical guy.

"I don't think she had on any clothes," he continues.

"Like she was naked?"

He shrugs. "She was a blob. But she did say—"

I gasp. "She *speaks*? What did she say?"

"I couldn't hear her clearly, what with the fire roaring in my ears and the house crumbling around me. It sounded like 'Get thee out of my house.'"

"Whoa! What did *you* say?"

"'Okay. Thank you. Goodbye.'"

The fire truck pulls up to the curb. The firemen scramble out and get to work with their hoses. Not that there's anything left to save. The Witch House is history.

"It looks like I'm homeless," I say, watching them try to salvage the wreckage.

"You've never really lived there in the first place," he says, smiling down at me.

"At the very least, I, like William Ashby in *The Witch of Blackbird Pond*, am now the proud owner of a growing pile of wood."

The paramedics arrive. My mom heckles them about taking their sweet time and points at Carter. The team starts for us.

"I think they want to check you for smoke inhalation," I say.

Carter takes my hand and our fingers interlock. Real. This hand is real. And so is the man before me. For the first time in my life, I take a leap of blind faith. I loop my arms around his neck and kiss him until he pulls back and coughs in my face.

"Sorry," he says.

"It's okay. You've had a rough time tonight. I can back off and —"

He swoops in, covering my mouth with his. He kisses me with an intensity that knocks the wind out of *him*.

The entire neighborhood claps behind us.

"Yay!" My friends cheer.

My mom whoops.

"Ha! I knew it!" says Edith. "Bring on the great-grandbabies."

Suddenly Carter breaks the kiss and falls into a coughing fit.

"Oh. Okay." I swat him between the shoulder blades and ease him to the curb. "Maybe you should sit down."

"Your kisses were too much for me," he says, dragging in a painful-sounding breath.

One of the paramedics jams an oxygen mask over his face

and after a few hard hits, Carter tips his head in my direction. "So what happens now?"

"We take you to the hospital and I try to figure out if my homeowner's insurance covers fire damage by act of God."

His eyes crinkle. "That sounds surprisingly practical."

"Oh, you know," I gesture to the smoldering wreckage that used to be my glorious Witch House, "look where being a hopeless romantic got me."

"I don't mind romantic Theo. In fact, I was thinking that I could be a little more like you. A little more free-spirited and romantic."

I arch an eyebrow. "Oh yeah?"

"A little more like Nat Eaton."

"I don't want Nat Eaton..." I kiss his bruised knuckles. "I want you."

He takes off his oxygen mask and leans in to kiss me, but a hitch in his throat causes him to descend into another coughing-choking-hacking fit. "Hold that thought," he says and spits in the grass.

I wrinkle my nose. *That didn't look good.* Actually, it looks like a — "Is that a chestnut?"

I don't know how or why he'd managed to swallow a chestnut inside a burning house, and I don't want to know.

"Sorry," he wipes his mouth, "it was either spit it out or swallow it. Where were we again?"

His face is reddish purple and his neck still veiny from choking. I don't think we should kiss anymore. Kissing is robbing him of much needed oxygen.

"Carter," I say, smoothing down the tufts of his disheveled hair, "let's get you on that gurney."

He relents as the paramedics help him onto the gurney. I hold his hand as they hoist him up into the ambulance and stick by his side as they shut the door.

"What's your health insurance deductible?" I ask him. "I'll make sure the ER doctor checks all the right codes so you don't get screwed over in billing."

"I don't have health insurance." His head lolls to the side. "Premiums." *Cough.* "Too expensive." *Cough.* "Not getting my money's worth."

"*Oof.*" That's not something I want to hear. I chew on my bottom lip. "Please don't hate me, Carter…"

An amused smile ghosts his lips. "Why would I ever hate you?"

"Because saving my hamsters has just cost you a lot of money…"

He squeezes his eyes shut. "What's the point in having money if you can't spend it?"

"Now I *know* you're delirious."

As the paramedics check his blood pressure, I manage to squeeze between them and peck Carter on the forehead.

"This isn't very romantic," he apologizes for the last time before the oxygen mask comes down over his mouth and he's ordered not to remove it.

"No," I learn in and whisper in his ear, "but it is the beginning of a beautiful romance."

chapter fifty-nine

5 *months later…*
    The spot of land where the Witch House had once stood
for three-hundred-years is once again a hive of activity.

According to my homeowner's insurance investigation
report, lightning struck my backyard chestnut tree, knocking a
flaming branch into my attic window, and the whole thing went
up like a tinderbox. Between the dry wood, ancient layers of
pitch, and God knows what faulty electrical wiring had been
installed in the 1950's, the Witch House didn't stand a chance
against a fire.

Good thing I was insured against random acts of God,
though the investigator tried his darnedest to nail me for 'suspicions of arson.' Apparently, owners setting their bad real estate
investments ablaze happens more often than you think. Offen-
sive, isn't it?

In the end, I walked away with a settlement that allowed me
to rebuild. According to the property assessor, my land is worth
three times more than the house. I guess Carter's idea of bull-
dozing the Witch House and starting over would have saved me
time and money, but I'll never admit he was right. He's smug
enough as it is.

Clearing the sooty remains of the Witch House had to wait

the winter. Now it's early spring. With the frost melting, Carter and his former construction company got down to business clearing the foundation.

Did I tell you that Carter is working as a consultant for the very company he founded and later sold? He never told me why he went back to work. My guess is that he's either bored to death with retiring in his thirties and needed something to do with his time or his ambulance ride/overnight hospital stay took a chunk out of his savings. Despite incurring a *massive* medical bill for rescuing my hamsters, Carter refused to sell his Tesla stocks. He buys to hold.

In any event, he seems happier now that he has a project, his job offers him great health insurance, *and* he gets to help me rebuild my new house.

I didn't believe him when he told me putting together my prefab house would be a piece of cake. Once the sections arrived from Germany, I was blown away by how quickly all the pieces came together. Like a perfect jigsaw puzzle, just as Carter promised. After all, everything he touches runs like clockwork. Efficiency is part and parcel of keeping his model trains running on time.

The prefab is small and sustainable—like Carter's ultra modern Trash Can home—but with a few whimsical touches. I've selected a simple cottage design that comes with a book nook and plenty of big, open windows to read by. The temperature controls are voice activated. I can open and close the blinds with my phone.

I climb the ladder.

Carter is hard at work laying out the finishing touches. He's literally 'thatching' the roof (just like Nat Eaton did in *The Witch of Blackbird Pond*!) with pallets of grass. It's an environmentally friendly design trick he picked up in Europe and I'm all for it.

I can plant a variety of things like toadstool mushrooms and herbs. I can even have a fairy garden with teeny tiny gnomes. And while I'm sure a lawn on my roof will set traditional tongues a-waggin', like the chestnut-ghost-witch Eliza Wolcott, I'm a bit of a maverick.

As I crawl up the roof, Carter drops his grass pallet and smiles at the sight of me. I love the way his eyes crinkle at the corners and how the sun-kissed strands of his hair stick up like tufts of summer wheat. I have an urge to drag my fingers through his hair and tug him to me for some late afternoon nookie, but not now. Later…

"I brought water," I say, side shuffling until I reach him. Carter nails down his last pallet and meets me in the middle where the rooftop lawn is already complete. We settle down on the lush carpet of grass.

I hand him a water bottle and he drinks it in three gulps. Before he could wipe his mouth on his sleeve, I greet him with a slow, luxurious kiss that leaves us both tipsy.

"You're going to make me fall off the roof," he says, peering down at me over his nose bridge.

I lavish his face with tender kisses, quick pecks around the bracket of his mouth, a bite to the chin, an Eskimo kiss that is so cute it would literally make a bunny hurl. I can't help myself. I am head-over-heels in love with my new boyfriend.

Yes. You heard that right. I, Theodora Dy, have a new boyfriend. He's handsome, intelligent, fiscally responsible, and between you and me, pretty good in bed. He's also the kindest person I know, a friend to both old ladies and hamsters, which definitely makes him worthy of being the father of our future children. I would like to have a baby by next year, preferably before I turn thirty-three, but I won't spring that one on him yet. It might freak him out.

It should come as no surprise that I haven't moved into my new prefab house yet. I divide my time between Edith's B&B, where I have established an artist residency (my *Vincent Van Sproot* Sticker Company has been doing exceptionally well amongst Edith's senior friends) and Carter's tiny home. The Trash Can is hard for us to move around in, though his loft gets significant use and I'm not talking about sleeping.

To accommodate another person, Carter has succumbed to lifestyle inflation. He got rid of his futon and bought a full-sized roll-up mattress. I think it's a Casper. At first I was wary about sleeping on the floor, but Carter keeps his house critter free and the mattress provides great lumbar support. No complaints here.

The sun is warm on my face. From my rooftop, I see a sparkling slice of Wethersfield Cove and the first green buds on the branches of my neighborhood's trees. The chestnut tree is a blackened stump covered in melting frost, but green shoots are starting to peep out from the slush.

I draw my knees to my chest, basking in the sunshine like a happy tortoise.

Carter nudges me with his shoulder. "Heard anything from our resident witch?"

"Eliza?" I glance at the burnt chestnut stump. "Something tells me she's moved on. She definitely doesn't approve of this modern European design."

"Little did you know I've given this new house a new name."

"I don't suppose it can be called The Witch House. No witch has ever or will ever live here." I press my palms against the rooftop lawn and smile. "What is it?"

"The Sproot House."

My smile widens. "You don't even know what a sproot is."

His blue eyes dance with merriment. "On the contrary, I've become an expert on the mythical sproot."

"And what have you found?"

"It acts on flights of fancy, scorns logic and any forms of practicality," he says. "The sproot is an impulsive creature. A hopeless romantic. It has more dreams than sense."

"Hrumph!"

"Wait! Hear me out. The sproot is clumsy and is likely to get crushed by giant wheels of cheese. You can find it reading erotic novels at senior citizen book clubs or tagging a fridge with clutter, er… I mean, 'stickers.' Stickers of potatoes with tiny legs and disgruntled faces, which I find absolutely adorable."

I narrow my eyes. "You better."

"You can find the sproot 'potato-ing' on the couch, watching an extremely loud and obnoxious movie called *Hocus Pocus*."

"Hey!" I whack his arm.

"The sproot has a foot fetish."

"She does not!"

"It hates Big Pony Ralph Lauren Polos."

"Gah!" I stick out my tongue. "Hate 'em."

"It loves durian and unnecessarily expensive furniture and would rather fight one hundred duck-sized horses than face one horse-sized duck."

I nod. "All true."

He laughs. "But listen up, I'm not finished."

"I'm listening."

"You can't reason with a sproot."

"I think you can."

He tilts his head to the side, his eyes roving over my face. "It's a challenge... doable, but no picnic. She's a moonbeam that's hard to pin down."

"Oh, a sproot is a 'she', is it?"

Carter gathers me in his arms and plants a kiss on my temple. "But once you catch her, keep her close and love her well," he whispers in my ear, "this one is for keeps."

THANK you so much for reading my quirky little book. I hope it provided you with an escape and a few chuckles. If you had as much fun reading it as I had writing it, **please leave a review** on Amazon or your preferred book retailer.

Reviews help readers discover my books, motivating me to write *more* books. I read and learn from every review. Not only do your words help me improve, but I save screenshots from some of them to refer back to when I'm in my creative low. So you see, Dear Reader, your thoughts mean more than you know. Please leave a review:)

Sign up for my newsletter to stay up to date on new releases and get a **free book** delivered to your inbox. An email from me is like a letter from a pen pal minus the postage. I aim to entertain you... infrequently but with a lot of passion.

about the author

Teresa Yea is an awkward bean with a fondness for British period dramas and minimalism. In the grand scheme of romance novels, she likes dukes and viscounts, adorkable rom coms and spicy ebooks that blazes up her Kindle (you know the kind). She is obsessed with The Witch of Blackbird Pond, a book she has read over 15+ times and wrote about (lustfully) at her website teresayea.com

She seriously wants you to SIGN UP for her NEWSLETTER (https://teresayea.com/newsletter/) where she aims to entertain you… infrequently but with a lot of passion.

Follow her on Instagram @teresayea. She has never influenced anyone, unless you count book recs.

Follow her on Facebook @teresayeawriter for romance novel swooning and Benedict Cumberbatch ogling.

She also penned some broody fantasies about Victorian monster hunters and that gothic one about a cursed ruby. All have sexy times, spice level: Sriracha.

facebook.com/teresayeawriter

instagram.com/teresayea